*Big Prisons, Big Dreams*

CRITICAL ISSUES IN CRIME AND SOCIETY

*Raymond J. Michalowski, Series Editor*

Critical Issues in Crime and Society is oriented toward critical analysis of contemporary problems in crime and justice. The series is open to a broad range of topics including specific types of crime, wrongful behavior by economically or politically powerful actors, controversies over justice system practices, and issues related to the intersection of identity, crime, and justice. It is committed to offering thoughtful works that will be accessible to scholars and professional criminologists, general readers, and students.

Mary Bosworth and Jeanne Flavin, eds., *Race, Gender, and Punishment: From Colonialism to the War on Terror*

Michael J. Lynch, *Big Prisons, Big Dreams: Crime and the Failure of America's Penal System*

Raymond J. Michalowski and Ronald C. Kramer, eds., *State-Corporate Crime: Wrongdoing at the Intersection of Business and Government*

Susan L. Miller, *Victims as Offenders: The Paradox of Women's Violence in Relationships*

Susan F. Sharp, *Hidden Victims: The Effects of the Death Penalty on Families of the Accused*

Robert H. Tillman and Michael L. Indergaard, *Pump and Dump: The Rancid Rules of the New Economy*

Mariana Valverde, *Law and Order: Images, Meanings, Myths*

Michael Welch, *Scapegoats of September 11th: Hate Crimes and State Crimes in the War on Terror*

# Big Prisons, Big Dreams

## CRIME AND THE FAILURE OF AMERICA'S PENAL SYSTEM

MICHAEL J. LYNCH

RUTGERS UNIVERSITY PRESS
*New Brunswick, New Jersey, and London*

LIBRARY OF CONGRESS CATAOLOGING-IN-PUBLICATION DATA

Lynch, Michael J.
  Big prisions, big dreams : crime and the failure of America's penal system /
Michael J. Lynch.
      p. cm. — (Critical issues in crime and society)
  Includes bibliographical references and index.
  ISBN 978-0-8135-4185-3 (hardcover : alk. paper) — ISBN 978-0-8135-4186-0
(pbk. : alk. paper)
  1. Criminals—Rehabilitation—United States.   2.  Imprisonment—United States.
3.  Criminal justice, Administration of—United States.   I. Title.
  HV9304.L96 2007
  365'.973—dc22                                                    2007000037

A British Cataloging-in-Publication record for this book is available
from the British Library

Visit our Web site: http://rutgerspress.rutgers.edu

Manufactured in the United States of America

*To Graeme R. Newman, mentor, friend, and guru*

# Contents

# Preface

THIS BOOK WAS WRITTEN in response to troubling trends in American society. Since 9/11, America has been edging closer and closer to a limited democracy that accepts the curtailment of freedom and the enhancement of governmental power and control as the price for safety. This movement, however, has been underway for decades in the way America responds to crime, especially street crimes, or those offenses most likely to be engaged in by the lower classes and Americans of color. It is no accident that these crimes, more so than the more harmful behaviors of corporate and government officials, are the prime subject of crime control, and that the prime suspects are those unlike "us"—they represent economic decay and difference.

It is also no accident that America's use of imprisonment has grown so dramatically in recent decades, and that the prison targets the poor and minorities. This is true despite the fact that they also do not represent the greatest threat to our health and well-being. Rather, it is the corporate criminal who pollutes the environment, uses his economic and political power to alter the course of American politics and law, who poses the greatest threat to the average American. But this book is not about them; it is about the runaway train that has become America's penal system.

Today the average citizen regards the prison as an appropriate response to crime; and so too do America's politicians. As a result, the rate of imprisonment in the United States has expanded exponentially since 1973. Since then, the number of inmates imprisoned in the United States has grown each and every year. More than thirty years later, our prison system is the biggest in the world, in terms of both raw numbers and rates. And, contrary to popular opinion, the United States has the longest average prison sentences of any nation in the world. And still, we have a substantial level of crime.

These few facts, which are examined in detail in the pages that follow, make it clear that the U.S. penal system is the harshest in the world. Add to these facts the observation that the United States, unlike any other Western democracy, also employs the death penalty for criminals, and the picture of an extensively repressive penal system is nearly complete. These drastic measures, however, have not lowered our rate of crime.

To round out this picture, we must add that the people subject to this form of repressive control are the poor and the minorities in our nation, the least well-off, those who have the fewest quality choices to make during their life courses. In contrast, the well-off get away with their crimes, or, if punished, are treated rather kindly in comparison.

Not only is this system of punishment repressive, but it fails at its mission of reducing crime. The balance of evidence—and we should make it clear here that we mean the balance of scientific evidence produced by independent social scientists who are not supported by grants, stipends, or salaries from conservative think tanks, and who have not produced pro-prison research as part of their governmental duties—illustrates that prisons are not an effective crime control response. Much of this book is dedicated to demonstrating this point.

At this stage in history, it is also time to recognize that there looms on the horizon important environmental and energy problems that must be addressed now, which also have important implications for the future of imprisonment in America. In contrast to the position taken by the Bush White House, scientists around the world and leaders of the majority of other nations have come to recognize that the most important issues facing the world today with respect to long-term survival are global warming and the end of oil. How will America's big prison system fare in, or respond to, a world where oil is becoming more and more scarce, and where burning oil produces global warming? When will U.S. criminal justice policy experts recognize the end of oil and global warming as significant issues that should affect criminal justice policy? When will these issues become so important that they will alter the practice of imprisonment in America? These issues are examined in this book. To my knowledge, outside of the few mentions I have made of these themes elsewhere, this is the first book on criminal justice issues and policy to make environmental issues a major theme.

I expect that this work will be controversial. Without such controversy, there is little hope of progress on the issues examined here.

I OWE THANKS to several people who contributed to the writing of this book. More than anyone else, I must thank Graeme R. Newman, Distinguished Teaching Professor at the School of Criminal Justice, State University of New York at Albany. Newman recruited me to be his graduate student at a time when the radical ideas I was expressing in class were not so popular among the school's student body or faculty. Without his encouragement, my graduate career would not have lasted long. I have known Newman for two decades now, and during that period his role in my life has been transformed from mentor to friend. Anyone familiar with Newman's work will see the many contrasting views we hold on issues, and that I am certainly not repeating the words or views of my mentor in writing this book. Yet, despite the differences in our views, Newman has always been supportive of my work—and the work of all of his students—which has made him an invaluable mentor to numerous students with divergent points of view. In addition, it would be impossible for me to write a book that deals with the topic of punishment without thinking constantly of Newman's widely respected book, *The Punishment Response*, which analyzes the history and philosophy of punishment. In order to fully recognize the importance of Newman's scholarship—and friendship—to my own work, I have chosen to dedicate this book to him as teacher, scholar, and friend.

I also owe thanks to Raymond Michalowski, the series editor, who, despite having worked with me on other projects, read my manuscript and encouraged me to submit it to Rutgers University Press for review. Ray was also available for comment as I wrote this manuscript. Despite my inability to publish any of my previous work on the topic of global warming, the end of oil, and criminal justice, thanks are due to Todd Clear for encouraging me in this endeavor, and being among the only criminologists I know to see the relevance of this issue. Thanks are also due to Adi Hovav, social science and religion editor for Rutgers University Press. Adi's comments have been most useful in preparing this book for press. I would also like to thank the manuscript reviewers for Rutgers University Press, Jeffrey Ian Ross and a second, anonymous reviewer. Special thanks are owed to several of my colleagues who provided useful comments and criticisms on ideas I bounced off them from time to time: John Cochran, Thomas Mieczkowski, Wilson Palacios, Herman Schwendinger, Shayne Jones, and Thomas Kovandzic. Thanks are also due to Elizabeth S. Cass (Ph.D.), my wife, who manages to take the more conservative view against which I can test my ideas, and who can still put up with me after twenty years together. Finally, I owe thanks to the University of South Florida, which granted me a sabbatical during which I wrote the main portion of this book.

*Big Prisons, Big Dreams*

CHAPTER 1

# Introduction

## BIG, DARK SECRETS AND AMERICA'S PRISON SYSTEM

*The prison, the darkest region in the apparatus of justice, it is the place where the power to punish, which no longer dares to manifest itself openly, silently . . . function[s].* —Michel Foucault, *Discipline and Punish*

THIS BOOK EXAMINES whether a bigger prison system, such as the one we have built in America to control crime, necessarily makes for a better prison system. Many things make a prison system better. Being bigger is not necessarily one of them.

Over the past three decades, the United States has built the world's largest prison system. This system is ten times larger today than it was in the mid-1970s. This book examines why America's prison system has grown so large and what the consequences are of having such a big system. From a philosophical and policy perspective, we want to discern the reason(s) for placing offenders in prison, and what goals we hope to accomplished by this practice. Various data can be used to determine if these goals are indeed being met. In the chapters that follow, these data will be employed to assess whether imprisonment reduces crime, one of its widely stated goals.

Outside of philosophy, policy, and politics, what other factors have helped shape the emergence of America's big prison system? Specifically, this book examines whether economic factors influence the volume of imprisonment in American society. Undertaking such an examination requires discussing how broad economic processes such as the decline of the industrial and rise of the service economy, or smaller trends such as the privatization of prisons, have affected the U.S.

I

prison industry's growth. Outside of economic forces, one of the least often discussed factors affecting the trend in imprisonment over the past three decades relates to race control and conflict. While the prison population has grown dramatically over this period, growth in the minority incarceration rate has well outpaced the growth of the white imprisonment rate. The differences in the level of imprisonment across racial groups is not the result of vast differences in the criminality of these groups, especially if one considers that the most serious crimes in our society—corporate and governmental crimes—are nearly devoid of minority offenders.

After examining these issues, I will examine a topic not often found in criminal justice literature, let alone penological literature. Framed as a question, that issue can be stated as follows: Can we afford to continue building and using a big prison system in light of the ecological and energy costs and crises that have appeared on the world horizon? Will prisons become too costly to run in a world where energy prices continually increase? Will energy shortages pose security threats in a nation that depends on a large prison system to control its criminals? More importantly, since the data indicates that the big prison system the United States has built fails to control crime adequately, can the economic and environmental costs of big prisons be justified? Finally, the emerging energy crisis linked to the decline of oil resources and its association with global warming highlight the need for criminal justice policy makers and researchers to address these problems when planning crime control strategies. In other words, the costs of a big prison system extend beyond its failure as a crime control mechanism and its tremendous financial costs. The future of criminal justice policy lies in the ability of today's policy makers to take environmental concerns seriously.

Finally, these issues will be summarized and drawn together within the context of American cultural values. This discussion employs a classic argument made by Thorsten Veblen at the end of the nineteenth century, which examined patterns of conspicuous consumption in the United States. Is the vast system of imprisonment in the United States one such form of conspicuous consumption?

These are the issues that unfold throughout this book. Before each of these issues can be addressed, there is much background that needs to be covered.

## HIDING BEHIND BIGNESS

Behind America's big prison system lurk dark secrets hidden by assumptions about the nature of punishment and the ability of imprisonment to reduce crime. These dark secrets are known to scholars, though many other scholars have played a part in keeping those secrets hidden and in supporting America's massive prison expansion. Nor have policy makers shared these secrets with the general public, which, for its part, continues to believe that crime will be controlled if the system of punishment becomes more severe and the prison system gets bigger. The secrets about the failures of imprisonment as an effective crime control strategy are also obscured by common American cultural themes, including the belief that "bigger is better." Americans lust after big cars, such as four-wheel drive SUVs, even though the majority of these vehicles never leave suburban or urban terrains, negating the need for an SUV's special capabilities. They crave the security of the SUV, even though these vehicles have proven to be more unsafe than cars in real-world conditions. Americans continue to drive SUVs, even though the majority of these vehicles produce more pollution and consume greater quantities of gas, edging us closer to catastrophic greenhouse effects and the depletion of the world's oil reserve. The American tendency to consume too much isn't limited to cars. Americans desire big-screen TVs so they can watch the big game. They crave big bucks and big houses on a big lot as evidence of the status they hold. They supersize their meals at chain food restaurants and shop at superstores, while watching their weight and cholesterol rise, standing by as superstores crush small shop owners. Americans have big dreams and the big debts that go along with the big American dream of consumption. They consume oil at a rate that is five times the size of the population—one-quarter of the oil produced in the world each year is consumed in America. Americans also have a big crime rate. More than that, they also have the world's biggest correctional system.

This desire for bigness has created a big problem in America. This big problem is what Austin and Irwin (2003) call "America's imprisonment binge," which we can define as the tendency for America's prison population to continue to expand. This expansion has been underway since 1973, through Republican and Democratic administrations, through good and bad economic times, unabated through the dawning of a new century. The imprisonment binge is a big problem to the extent that imprisonment fails to accomplish its mission of reducing crime; to the extent that it has had large negative effects on American minorities and the poor; to the extent that it negatively affects not only those upon whom it is imposed, but their families and communities as well; and to the extent that its costs (financial, social, and environmental) far exceed its worth. And, rather than own up to this problem, America's political and policy leaders have declared that the real problem is that prisons haven't yet gotten big enough to serve as an effective crime control mechanism.

The chapters that follow examine the growth of the American prison system over the past three decades, how much Americans spend on imprisonment, whether imprisonment is an effective crime control strategy, and whether America can continue to operate its big prison system in an oil-strapped world. In examining these questions, this book challenges many widely held beliefs about imprisonment, though this is not the first book to do so. In writing this book, I am adding my voice to the list of scholars who have discovered that our big prison system doesn't accomplish the big goal it set for itself. Before beginning this journey, let us turn to a review of the literature on imprisonment.

## PRIOR RESEARCH

There is a significant scholarly literature on prisons. Surprisingly, only a small portion of that literature actually examines the question of prison effectiveness. With respect to crime control, existing studies examine a variety of questions such as: Do prisons deter other criminals? Does a rise in the rate of imprisonment lead to a reduction in crime? When the rate of imprisonment increases, are the crime reduction effects seen across all crimes? Are the incapacitative effects of imprisonment large enough to reduce crime? When current criminal populations are incarcerated, are they replaced by new offenders?

There is no consistent answer to the question of whether prisons reduce crime. From a scientific and statistical perspective, this uncertainty alone suggests that prisons probably are an ineffective mechanism for reducing crime.

*Literature Supporting Prison Effectiveness*

The most widely known publications supporting prison expansion as an effective crime control strategy *are not* found in the scholarly literature. This is a significant observation because scholarly literature is reviewed for accuracy of methods and analysis by other scholars who are experts in a field before it can be published. The same cannot be said for non-scholarly publications. For example, in 1994, one of the leading proponents of prison expansion, John DiIulio, published an article in the *Wall Street Journal* titled, "Let 'Em Rot." The article reviewed President Clinton's crime control comments made in the State of the Union Address. The article, incorrectly it should be noted, laments as the source of rising crime rates the decline of imprisonment in the 1980s, reductions in sentence length, and a general liberalization of crime control policy. Citing a handful of supportive studies, DiIulio argued that "the best available evidence ... suggests that prison pays for most prisoners"; he used his highly visible publication to make his case in favor of prison expansion. Ignoring counterevidence and appealing to public fear of crime as he had done previously when he invented the idea of the "super predictor," DiIulio ends his discussion by noting that "if the president breaks faith with the public on crime, he will be a three-time loser—morally, intellectually and politically."

In their 1995 report, *Crime and Punishment in America,* the National Center for Policy Analysis (NCPA) makes the case that a liberalization in the response to crime caused the rise in crime that occurred during the 1960s and 1970s. The report claims that punishment remained low until the 1980s, when it rose significantly, which in turn led to a significant decline in crime. Unfortunately, the NCPA fails to recognize that the escalation of crime in the 1970s could not be due to the liberalization of punishment. Indeed, as NCPA's own data showed, court commitments for crime remained at "38,000 admissions while the number of serious crimes reported to police tripled." What these data indicate is that crime rose while the level of punishment remained the same—hardly a "liberal" approach to crime, and surely not data supporting the contention that more severe penal practices reduce crime. Despite the obvious contradictions, NCPA staff, such as Morgan Reynolds, continue to support the "obvious" connection between punishment and deterrence of crime. For example, in a report written for the Heartland Institute titled, "Does Punishment Work to Reduce Crime?" (2000), Reynolds wrote that the rising rate of imprisonment clearly suppressed crime during the 1990s. This association is not at all "clear," and many factors may be behind that crime drop.

In his 1997 pamphlet *Does Prison Work?* published by the Institute of Economic Affairs, well-known conservative Charles Murray uses 1990s data from the United States in an effort to persuade European communities that expanding the use of imprisonment is an appropriate mechanism for controlling crime. Murray, who has been a fellow at the American Enterprise Institute and the Manhattan Institute, is also the coauthor of the controversial book *The Bell Curve,* which argued that African-Americans are biologically inferior to whites.

Popular discourse on crime and punishment in the media has been dominated by the ideas contained in these and other position papers produced by conservative think tanks (see also Hayward and Izumi, 1996). In addition, the widely publicized and long-term crime drop in New York City, though it began before the institution of zero-tolerance crime policies by New York Mayor Rudolph Giuliani (see Jacobson, 2005; and chapter 3), has also done much to fuel conservative crime control policies such as prison expansion.

In a series of studies of legislators' attitudes toward crime control policies (Flanagan and McGarrell, 1986; McGarrell and Flanagan, 1987; Flanagan, Cohen, and Brennan, 1993; Flanagan, Gasdow, and Cohen, 1991; Flanagan, McGarrell, and Lizotte, 1989), Flanagan and his colleagues have demonstrated that legislators are more likely to adopt a conservative approach toward crime control. Moreover, this research indicates that legislators' attitudes toward crime persist over time. Drawing on public opinion research, Flanagan, Cohen, and Brennan (1993) also note that legislators tend to misperceive public opinion on crime control and interpret it as more conservative than opinion polls indicate. The political dimension of crime policy may help explain why conservative crime policy positions are more likely to be adopted by lawmakers, and why prison expansion programs have been favored.

Despite the conservative bias favoring harsher punishments and expansion of imprisonment found in research sponsored by partisan groups, there is some support in academic literature for the idea that prisons reduce crime. Historically this idea has been promoted by the research of economists, most notably Nobel Prize–winner Gary Becker (1968). In the economic view, human beings are viewed as rational actors (this assumption is also found in numerous criminological studies). As such, their behavior is seen as responsive to external conditions such as punishment. Rational actors, in other words, respond to punishment by avoiding criminal behavior.

Using attitudinal surveys, some criminologists have found that sentence severity marginally increases deterrence (Grasmick and Bryjack, 1980; Kleeper and Nagin, 1989). The problem such research fails to acknowledge is the fit between attitudes and behavior or the attitude-behavior consistency problem (Bandura, 1977, 1986). As an example, health researchers have discovered that attitude-behavior consistency or the state of rational thinking can be disrupted by, among other things, incomplete knowledge (Sapp, 2001). As Sapp notes, a lack of knowledge may make it impossible for an individual to act rationally with respect to their beliefs. Regardless of this caveat, others have found that perceived severity is not related to deterrence (Paternoster and Iovanni, 1986). Thus, the evidence on this issue has been mixed.

Support for the deterrent effects of imprisonment have also been found for specific crime types. For instance, Weinrath and Gartell (2001) found specific deterrence effects for increased sentence lengths among a sample of offenders sentenced for drunk driving in Alberta, Canada. Prison sentence length was associated with the tendency toward diminished recidivism. It should be noted, however, that sentences for drunk driving in this Canadian study were rather short, especially compared to U.S. standards. Indeed, drunk drivers were deterred by sentences that were significantly shorter than those handed out for other offenses. Weinrath and Gratell argued that longer prison sentences—which in this case amounted to six months or more in length—produced a greater deterrent effect than shorter sentences. Thus, compared to U.S. sentencing practices, "longer" Canadian sentences are still quite lenient.

The crime suppression effect of imprisonment has also been studied with respect to homicide offenders. In a recent study, Kovandzic et al. (2004) discovered that "prison population growth greatly reduced homicide rates." The authors report that the reduction was on the order of 1 less homicide for every 200 additional people incarcerated. The authors, like others who have performed similar research, failed to explore the policy implications of this empirical result. The problem is that reducing homicides through incarceration would require an extensive expansion of the prison population. Consider, for example, that there were approximately 14,200 homicides in the United States in 2004, the year of the Kovandzic study. Using the Kovandzic study's estimate of 1 less homicide for every 200 additional offenders incarcerated, the elimination of homicide through incarceration alone—and assuming there are no other causes of homicide beside the level of punishment—would require locking up an additional 2.8 million people. Doing so would more than double the already exaggerated level of imprisonment in the United States.

Similar evidence of a deterrent effect of imprisonment rates on homicide rates has been found in several other studies. Using data for the entire United States for the period 1930–1994, Marvel and Moody (1997) reported that a 10 percent increase in the imprisonment rate corresponded with a 13 percent reduction in homicides. While this seems like a significant trade-off because crime is lowered by more than the increase in punishment, currently a 10 percent increase in incarceration amounts to an additional 220,000 new inmates. This would lower the number of homicides (14,200 * .13) by 1,846. Assuming that the number of homicide offenders deterred or incapacitated by an expansion in the use of imprisonment remains constant, and assuming no other factors cause homicides, eliminating the homicide problem through incarceration would require incarcerating nearly 1.7 million more inmates, a somewhat lower estimate than derived from the Kovndzic study, but still significantly large. In an earlier study, Devine, Shelley, and Smith (1988) used U.S. imprisonment and homicide rate data for 1948–1985 and found that a 10 percent increase in the incarceration rate would lower the homicides rate by 15 to 19 percent (the variation is due to the specific variables included in the models specified in this study).

The deterrence and incapacitation effects of imprisonment on homicide reported in the above research are questionable, however. For example, consider that in 1973, at the beginning of the imprisonment binge, there were 19,640 homicides in the United States (Fox and Zawitz, 2006). In 2004, the number of homicides had fallen by 3,503 to 16,137. During that same period, the number of incarcerated offenders rose from 204,211 to 1,433,793, or by 1,229,582 inmates. As a rough estimate of the deterrent effect of imprisonment on homicide, we can calculate that eliminating 1 homicide required adding 351 inmates (1,229,582 / 3,503). Assuming that the rise in incarceration caused the decline in homicides, the actual increase in imprisonment required to cause the decline in homicide from 1973 through 2004 would be 75 percent greater than estimated by the Kovandzic study. Clearly, we can see that for the 1973–2004 period, a 602 percent increase in the use of imprisonment corresponded with an 18 percent reduction in homicide, which is inconsistent with the estimates noted by Devine et al., and Marvel and Moody.

In a 1998 study, Marvel and Moody examined the effects of "displacement" and "free riding" to assess the impact of changes in incarceration rates on homicide rates. Displacement occurs when offenders move from states with high incarceration rates, or are deterred from crime in a specific state, because of that state's elevated use of imprisonment. In contrast, a free riding effect is a deterrent effect that occurs in other states. That is to say, a free riding effect is assumed to exist when crime declines in state A when state B raises its rate of imprisonment, even if state A's rate of incarceration remains constant or declines. The authors report that their findings support a substantial free riding effect and a smaller displacement effect. Outside the theoretical issues that could be raised, one can question Marvel and Moody's interpretation of their results. Their analysis revealed significant in-state effects for twelve of fifty states, and significant out-of-state effects for only five states. Thus, for 76 percent of states there was no displacement effect, while for 90 percent of states there was no free riding effect during this time period. Considered in this light, and contrary to the conclusion Marvel and Moody reached, there was little benefit from an increased rate of incarceration.

In a more general study of the impact of incarceration rates on crime rates, Marvel and Moody (1994) employed pooled cross-section data for the United States covering the years 1971–1989. The results indicated that for every additional inmate incarcerated, seventeen crimes were suppressed. As the authors note, the majority of the impact emerged as a decline in property crimes. This may not be unexpected, since the cost of incarceration is extensive in comparison to the benefits that result from the average property crime. Yet, these results could also be questioned. In 1971 there were 198,061 inmates in U.S. prisons, and by 1989, this figure had increased by 482,846 to 680,907. If Marvel and Moody are correct, and assuming that no other factors caused crime to rise or fall, the number of offenses suppressed by the increase in incarceration by 1989 should be more than 8.2 million (if each incarcerated offender suppressed the number of crimes by 17, then 17 * 482, 846 should yield the number of suppressed crimes). In 1971, there were slightly less than 5.4 million crimes known to police; by 1989 that figure had increased to slightly more than 12 million. This trend, although it only measures known crimes, seem inconsistent with the claim that an increased rate of imprisonment during this period led to a substantial reduction in crime.

Summarizing a number of studies produced prior to the mid-1980s, Visher (1987) noted that assessments of enhanced sentencing practices enacted during the 1970s and early 1980s produced crime reduction estimates that varied from 10 to 30 percent. The variations related not only to differences in the type of sentencing practice examined, but also to the selection of the research method and variables employed in each study. In reviewing these studies, Visher astutely noted that while sentencing reforms seemed to reduce crime, they did so only by substantially increasing the size of the incarcerated population. In light of this observation, and in an effort to avoid the problem of extensive prison growth, Visher recommended the use of selective incapacitation strategies that carefully targeted specific kinds of offenders.

### Literature That Fails to Support Prison Effectiveness

The literature reviewed above supports the idea that prisons are an effective means for controlling crime. Indeed, if one accepts the validity of these studies, then the number of crimes reduced by expanded imprisonment appears significantly large. The results reported above are, however, challenged by the results from a number of other studies.

In 1998, one of the leading criminal justice policy experts in the United States, Alfred Blumstein, argued that "even though incarceration rates increased steadily and are now almost quadruple what they were 20 years ago, most crime rates have remained confined within a fairly narrow range, with no strong trend. Perhaps most strikingly, we have not seen the anticipated downward trend in crime rates that might have been expected as a result of the growth in incarceration" (127). Using data from 1972 through 1995, Blumstein argued that crime was constant overall, with both upward and downward fluctuations. Examining crime and imprisonment data from 1980 through 1994, Blumstein shows a long-term increase in crime at the same time that imprisonment rates were rising.

Blumstein's conclusions are supported by several other studies. DeFina and Arvanites employed state level data covering 1971–1998 to study the impact of incarceration rates on the seven major crime types. While some crimes showed evidence of a deterrent effect from rising rates of incarceration, most did not, leading the researchers to conclude that it was "inappropriate" to assume that imprisonment affected crime at the national level.

Johnston (1999) examined data on offender recidivism rates after their release from prison. He concluded that "unless researchers determine and society changes the causes of what makes some individuals offend, the reactive approaches currently used will continue and the crime rate will not improve" (1). A similar conclusion was reached by Smith (1997), who studied the impact of various crime control policies on homicide rates in the United States between 1976 and 1990. Moreover, Smith found that the effect of prison population size on the homicide rate was the opposite of that predicted by deterrence theory.

In contrast to several of their other studies, Marvel and Moody's (1995) study of the impact of enhanced sentencing for gun-related crimes found limited evidence of deterrence in a few states. The effects were so sporadic that the policy of expanded prison terms as a deterrent for gun crime could not be supported from the results.

In their review of recent literature on sentence severity and crime, Doob and Webster (2003) concluded that sentence length had no appreciable effect on crime. Moreover, the significant disagreement in this literature was sufficient to lead them to argue that the null hypothesis—that sentence severity has no impact on crime—should now be accepted. This conclusion is supported by Lippke's (2002) review of the impact of prison sentence length on crime.

Several studies of more specific issues also refute the idea that imprisonment reduces crime. In a study of three-strike legislation in twenty-four states, Austin et al. (1999) concluded that, with the exception of California, tougher sentencing practices have had little impact on crime. Weisberg, Waring, and Chayet (1995) examined the impact of specific deterrence on white-collar offenders. The significance of this research is the assumption that white-collar offenses serve as an excellent example of behaviors that are rational, thus fitting the expectations of deterrence theory. In other words, among a variety of offenders, white-collar offenders would be assumed to be more amenable to the effects of deterrence. Their study compared reoffending among a matched sample of white-collar offenders sentenced to prison versus those who received other sanctions. No difference was found between these two groups with respect to recidivism.

Perhaps one of the most important recent studies of the relationship between imprisonment and crime was published by Clear, Rose, and Waring in 2003. This study provides a partial test of Rose and Clear's (1998) earlier theory that high incarceration rates have negative effects on local communities by undermining informal social control and other community networks that prevent offending. Thus, contrary to deterrence or incapacitation arguments, these researchers suggest that incarceration destabilizes communities and enhances local social disorganization, which in turns expands the problem of crime. Their study confirmed these assumptions. They discovered that prison admissions had a small impact on crime in communities with a low level of crime. In communities where a larger proportion of residents are removed via incarceration, they found that crime increased.

It is also useful to consider the comparison made by Ouimet (2002) of crime and penal trends in the United States and Canada during the 1990s. Ouimet notes that both nations experienced a significant decline in crime during this period. In contrast to the United States, however, in Canada there was no enhanced policing and no expansion of sentence lengths or in the use of imprisonment. As a result, Ouimet concludes that increased punitive responses cannot be the cause of the crime reduction in the United States.

In sum, the empirical literature examining the impact of imprisonment on crime leads to no clear conclusion concerning the relationship between these two social events. From a scientific vantage point, the evidence is not compelling and the degree of uncertainty is sufficient at this point to lead to the conclusion that the impact of incarceration on crime is not uniform, and, because of these uncertainties, certainly should not become the basis for crime policy.

## Other Relevant Literature

At the present time, no book on America's prison system can be written without reference to James Austin and John Irwin's *Its About Time: America's Imprisonment Binge.* In that book, Austin and Irwin examine numerous issues that have contributed to what can only be described as an obsession with locking up criminal offenders. Austin and Irwin examine a variety of factors that contribute to the level of crime and punishment in society, from economic conditions that affect participation in crime (e.g., unemployment, poverty, loss of high-wage manufacturing jobs), to policies (e.g., mandatory sentencing, three strikes, third-felon sentencing, legislation affecting sentence lengths and time served), the focus on drug crimes, and the privatization movement. Building on the themes in that book, the present book specifically employs a materialist economic perspective, and delves further into the question of whether prisons accomplish crime reduction goals. More so than any other piece of research, Austin and Irwin's book has greatly influenced my views on the problems presented by America's big prison system.

In *Harm in American Penology,* Todd Clear sets out the argument that we must consider the human costs of imprisonment, especially in an era where imprisonment has grown so rapidly. In brief, Clear's argument is that the American system of imprisonment imposes an extensive array of human costs that not only affect offenders, but which also have important consequences on communities with high concentrations of ex-offenders. The community effects, which include disruption of social and family structures and informal systems of social control, should not be overlooked nor downplayed simply because imprisonment removes offenders from the community. Extrapolating from what Clear wrote nearly a decade ago, we can assume that the continued expansion of the American prison system has exacerbated and magnified the human costs he identified. Clear has done such an excellent job of describing and analyzing these issues that I will not comment directly on them here. To be sure, not only would my description pale in comparison to Clear's eloquent argument, but any effort I made in this regard would appear to be squeezing this issue into the present work, and, in my view, would appear to minimize the importance of Clear's argument.

No full-blown effort to describe the trends in imprisonment in America from an historical perspective would be adequate if it failed to address the goal or purpose behind the use of prisons. Over the past two decades, the public conversation that has been carried out on the topic of prison and punishment in America (and by public conversation I mean the messages the news media reports, and those of the spokespersons it has allowed to occupy broadcast time and craft the content of news) has been captured by a conservative position that supports our big prison system as necessary to crime reduction. Theoretically, these positions are consistent with incapacitation and deterrence strategies. The public conversation has omitted a useful discussion of the rehabilitative goal and potential of the prison. We seem to have forgotten that the idea behind the founding of prisons in the United States was the rehabilitation and reform of inmates. Indeed, the portion of utilitarian philosophy devoted to the idea of reform and rehabilitation informed the development of America's prison system for more than a century after its founding. In the 1960s and 1970s, rehabilitation made a short-lived return, though it failed largely because of inadequate implementation and faulty fiscal investment strategies. In hindsight, the required financial investment needed to operate a rehabilitative prison system is rather insignificant in comparison to the investment we have made in our current prison system infrastructure based on the "bigger is better" approach. A number of scholars, however, have continued to promote rehabilitation as an appropriate prison goal. In addition to scholars such as Todd Clear, one of the most prominent scholars in this area in the contemporary period is Francis Cullen. To some extent, it is impossible to understand the growth of America's prison system over the past thirty years without having some knowledge of rehabilitative strategies, how they have been used, and why they failed. It was this "failure" that helped stimulate the growth of our present prison system, fueling its focus on deterrence, incapacitation, and an exaggerated form of retribution. Thus, the work of scholars including Cullen is a necessary supplement to the present book, especially if the goal of such a work is to suggest some alternative to the current "lock 'em up" approach. It is not my intention, however, to offer an alternative to the current system, and I leave that task to those who are better informed about such issues (Austin, Irwin, Clear, and Cullen, to name but a few).

The view of the prison as industry developed in the present book was influenced by Nils Christie's *Crime Control as Industry: Towards Gulags, Western Style* (1994). Though Christie's view is summarized later, one point that he made in his book which merits discussion here is captured in the following quotation: "The major dangers of crime in modern societies is not the crimes, but that the fight against them may lead society towards totalitarian developments" (16). The problem, from my perspective, is that the issue Christie raises—that American society's punishment response is moving us toward a totalitarian regime—is sufficiently significant and real enough to require an independent analysis. Doing so would require subjecting various philosophies of punishment to in-depth analysis and critique. But the analysis could not stop there, and would need to explore the fit between political preferences for democracy and the implementation of various penal strategies. The question such an analysis would be required to address would be, How does each penal strategy fit with democratic principles? More importantly, we must ask questions that policy makers have not asked when selecting penal responses: How would the implementation of a specific penal philosophy be modified by the assumptions of a democratic form of governance? How do we balance our emphasis on freedom and democracy with the goals and outcomes of our penal process? To make a long story short, this balancing effort presents a real problem in a democracy. How do we determine which principles—penal or democratic—are to be privileged? From a purely philosophic position, the short answer in the United States is—or rather should be—that principles of democracy ought to outweigh penal philosophies. That is to say, democratic principles should be employed to temper penal reactions whenever penal approaches become overly oppressive. Clearly, such a dialogue has not occupied much time or space in the American prison debate. And, as a result, as Christie suggests, we are coming very close to establishing the grounds for totalitarian rather than democratic penal responses. This tendency presents a greater threat to America than terrorism, though few Americans would be willing to make or support such an argument.

In my view, it is also impossible to think about our current state of punishment without reflecting on the importance of punishment and penal trends as described by philosopher Michel Foucault in *Discipline and Punish*. Foucault's complex analysis picks apart the prison regime to expose its connection to reinforcing and building social structure in ways that are consistent with scientifically recognized assumptions about order, and how the order reinforced by prisons is modified to fit the requirements of a society's economic organization. Unfortunately, it is not easy to understand Foucault's position in *Discipline and Punish* without also being familiar with the numerous books he had written previously that relate to the problem and origins of order. In a nutshell, we could say that the way we punish has been and is influenced by social, governmental, and economic structures, which in turn are affected by assumptions about the order of the world described in scientific writings, which are also likely to reflect assumptions about order that stem from economic origins. Our tendency to conserve order makes the problem of crime—which we take as an indicator of disorder, disorganization, and disruption—appear to be particularly important. Because the nature of order, especially natural order, is taken to be a scientific problem, our approach to solving the crime problem is presented in scientific ways. The point in providing this brief and insufficient summary of Foucault is to examine how this view might apply to the contemporary American prison situation. In short, we would discover that policy makers have pushed policies that include big prisons as a solution to the problem of crime in our time, and they have bathed their arguments in scientific sounding justifications. They have offered to the public, press, and other policy makers statements that appear and sound scientific because they seem to be supported by "scientifically" produced evidence. Often, however, there is little real "science" that stands behind the claim that big prisons reduce crime. Hidden behind this veneer of science is the impact that social order has on punishment and crime. The scientific-sounding call—and the appealing logic it entails—to expand prisons as the appropriate approach to controlling crime hides the fact that crime and punishment are not connected in the way we assume; it also hides the fact that our social response to crime may be strongly influenced by the nature of our economic and social order rather than being simply a scientifically crafted crime control policy. Once this is recognized as a possibility, we can come to grips with the idea that the direction in which penal policies are pushed by social and economic order may lead us down the wrong path as far as crime control is concerned. To see this dilemma, we must first understand the nature of the order upon which society is built. This is no simple task, and to do so requires a great deal of reflection. In short, when we reflect on the issue of crime and punishment, we are again led to the conclusion that the relationship between the two is not clear-cut or straightforward, and that no policy that takes the relationship to be simple can offer an appropriate solution. Elements of this argument will become more apparent as the evidence in this book is presented and examined.

Finally, we must consider Graeme R. Newman's (1985) history of punishment, from which we can extract the idea that it is the orienting penal philosophy of "society" (or those charged with directing a society) that affects the direction of its system of punishment or its response to crime. The "choice" a society makes with respect to how it will employ its penal system is, as Newman illustrates, connected to historical forces that affect how different philosophies of punishment are interpreted and put into action.

### Summary of What Follows

The goal of this book is to review the rapid growth of the U.S. prison system that has been underway and unimpeded since 1973. Later in this book, data for the U.S. prison system complied from the fifty state systems will analyzed to examine whether that system suppresses crime. These data will be be analyzed over time and across regions to make specific points about the growth of prisons. The growth of imprisonment will also be assessed by comparing growth rates of the prison system to the growth rate of crime. It will also be relevant to this discussion to look at the predicted costs of our nation's continued push to expand the use of imprisonment as a response to crime. In addition, this book will examine who is sent to prison. The common assumption is that our growing prison system has and is being used to lock up the most dangerous of society's offenders. As the data in this book reveal, this assumption is not very accurate. An unfortunate dimension of the American prison system has always been its use as part of the war on the lower classes, which in the modern era has taken the guise of a war on primarily lower-class drug users and their drugs of preference. Prisons, in other words, are most likely to hold the poor, and as Ronald Goldfarb argued in the late 1960s, prisons are America's poor houses. Since the civil rights era, imprisonment has also come to be part of the race war, and the number of minorities held in prisons has escalated at a much faster rate than the incarceration of the non-Hispanic, white population.

I will endeavor to keep these arguments simple, avoiding complex mathematical models that are difficult for the ordinary person to comprehend. Fancy mathematics won't make the argument any more persuasive; simple models, where needed, will be persuasive enough in my opinion. This is not to suggest that there won't be any data or models to examine; to be sure, the story I am about to tell is one found in largely in numbers.

The effort to comprehend what is happening with the modern-day system of imprisonment is, in my view, one that needs to be told. It needs to be told so that American people can make informed decisions about the direction their society is or should be taking; so that Americans can have the kind of information they need to participate in our democratic form of government.

The story of the modern prison that will be told here cannot be told with numbers alone. In order to interpret data, the person doing the interpreting must employ some frame of reference or theoretical background in order to make sense of what the numbers say. These assumptions appear throughout this book, but are reviewed more extensively in chapter 5. The view I present in chapter 5 is not the only one that leads to the conclusions that I draw from the data. And, for those who really don't care about the perspective I employed to reach these conclusions, this material could be easily skipped without compromising the rest of my argument. As an academic, however, I feel compelled to provide readers with these background theoretical issues.

The theoretical perspective that informs my work is grounded in materialism. In simple terms, materialism is the idea that the social world around us must be interpreted relative to the way in which a society is designed. That means connecting social events, such as imprisonment or the growth of the prison system (or any other topic), to material conditions of society, such as its economic and political systems, its class structure, and other important hierarchies that tell us about a society, such as its race relationships. Thus, to understand why the U.S. prison system has grown so dramatically over the past three decades, we need to understand something about the structure of that society's material conditions and how imprisonment connects with those conditions.

The various chapters in this book point toward the conclusion that the big prison system the United States has built in not an effective mechanism for controlling crime. Further, this system has detrimental consequences for large segments of society. In part, these negative impacts are more often felt by the poor and minorities. But the bulk of society is affected by the costly tax bill that accompanies a big prison system.

If a big prison system is ineffective, what should we so with the criminal population? This book does not provide a complete answer to this problem. What it points toward, however, is how a smaller prison system can become more efficient at reducing crime by using innovative interventions that have worked to reduce crime (Cullen, 2005). Beyond this, I argue that the expansive U.S. prison system is a waste of resources in a world facing an energy crisis and problems related to massive energy consumption, such as global warming. These issues are reviewed in chapter 8, which makes the first extensive argument that criminal justice policy makers pay attention to energy issues when crafting crime control legislation.

The final chapter sums up the data and issues examined here by referring to Thorsten Veblen's theory of conspicuous consumption. This chapter continues the theme introduced at the beginning of this book— a theme which is also tied to the massive level of energy consumption found in the United States compared to other nations. It is a cultural theme of overindulgence and excessive consumption. The growth of the U.S. prison institution reflects these cultural values, as well as an indifference to consuming people as fuel for an expanding prison system.

## CHAPTER 2

# *Prisons and Crime*

THIS CHAPTER PROVIDES an overview of numerous issues that need to be considered in an examination of prison systems. These issues include exploring how philosophies, policies, politics, and economic factors drive the growth of prison systems, and whether there is a relationship between the growth of prisons and a reduction in crime. Before we can begin to examine whether a bigger prison system is better, we have to define what we mean when we ask whether one type of prison system is better than another.

For the purposes of this book, a better prison system is one that has a crime suppression effect, or one that reduces the level of crime in society. After all, isn't this why societies build and employ prison systems: to reduce crime? To be sure, crime reduction, whether through rehabilitation, deterrence, or incapacitation, has always provided the philosophical underpinnings for imprisonment (except if one adopts a pure retributive perspective, Newman, 1985). Indeed, if all society wanted to achieve was the simple punishment of criminal offenders, there would be better options or at least other alternatives to consider (Newman, 1985). In any event, the first criterion of a better prison system is that it should reduce crime. Thus, we can ask two questions about America's prison system. First, does the big prison system currently operating in America fulfill this goal? And second, has making the prison system bigger led to continual reductions in crime? We could add additional questions here, perhaps addressing the marginal gain in crime reduction that would occur for every 100 persons sent to prison. At this point, any additional questions can wait since asking and answering them is contingent on establishing the answer to the first two questions.

In addition to reducing crime, being better also implies that bigger prisons should do their task more efficiently than some other alternative.

That "something else" may be smaller prisons, or prisons organized around a different approach to crime and criminals than the current system, or even the use of responses to crime that do not involve imprisonment, such as adding jobs, enhancing the educational system, or improving life in other ways.

An additional criterion that we can consider is the cost of imprisonment. Why consider costs? It may be that prisons are equally as efficient as other crime control mechanisms. But, if the other mechanisms cost less, then they could be considered more effective because the unit costs (cost per crime) are lower. The "costs" of a system of punishment, however, are not restricted to financial issues. There are, for example, social costs involved when systems of punishment get too big (Clear, 1994), which may involve immeasurable impacts such as threats to democratic principles of social organization that may move society toward totalitarianism (Christie, 1994). There are also human costs to the offenders we lock up that we often disregard (Clear, 1994). These costs are not, however, limited to the offender. If we lock up and ignore large numbers of inmates, we create an even bigger problem than we started with—we create a population of alienated ex-offenders who might be more willing to resort to crime upon their release. There are also costs to the families of offenders and their communities that typically are not addressed when we examine the effects of imprisonment on society (Clear, 1994; Rose and Clear, 1998). Several of these aspects of "being better" will be touched upon in the pages that follow, but interested readers are directed to Todd Clear's research for more extensive discussion.

Even though being better implies that prisons are better than something else, this book cannot possible hope to provide the ultimate answer to the question of whether our big prison system is a better crime solution than some other system. It would be impossible to test the assumption relating bigger prisons to crime control everywhere, in every possible circumstance, or all its forms. To do so would require vast amounts of data on various historical periods, different cultures, and for a number of penal alternatives, some of which have not been fully or correctly implemented. Consider, for instance, that the data needed to address this question from a historical perspective are limited to the extent that recorded crime data are not necessarily available for the entire history of a prison system. For example, in the United States, the prison system dates to the late eighteenth century, while uniform crime data are available from the 1930s on. Likewise, the data needed to answer this question from a cross-cultural perspective are even more problematic in terms of availability. One need only check the data maintained by the United Nations Criminal Justice Network (UNCJIN) to establish this fact. Even if all the cross-cultural prison and crime data we desired were available, undertaking a study comparing the impact of imprisonment on crime would be a tremendously difficult task given the many factors that differ across nations that would need to be addressed because they might account for the presence or absence of a crime suppression effect of imprisonment or other crime control strategies. Researchers have identified numerous factors that affect the causes of crime, from personality constructs, to biological predispositions, to environmental pollutants, to family and friendship patterns, to economic, social, and political conditions that include unemployment, general economic factors such as recessions and stages of economic development, and economic inequality, to name but a few (Vold, Bernard, and Snipes, 2002). Research on the causes of crime has not, to date, produced definitive answers about the causes of crime, and thus testing the vast number of opposing viewpoints would be a daunting task.

Therefore it is important to limit the scope of this investigation into the effectiveness of prison to one location. And, while it is useful to limit the scope of the investigation to make it manageable, it will still be necessary to use data from other nations as the basis for making comparisons that illustrate the relative size the American correctional system. Despite the need for such comparisons, it is not the intent of this work to explain the factors that affect the size of prison systems across the various nations used for the purpose of comparison.

## NARROWING THE SCOPE OF THE INVESTIGATION

Given the large number of potential variables, and the extraordinary degree of variation in factors that might impact the relationship between crime and punishment across societies, history, and even individuals, it is necessary to simplify the task. Here, three strategies were employed to simplify the analysis of whether a big prison system reduced crime.

First, this analysis will not examine the impact of imprisonment on individuals. Imprisonment may affect individuals differently depending on a number of factors that vary across individuals, on how those factors interact, and on the strength of each factor (Agnew, 2005). For example, how a person was raised and socialized, an individual's personality traits, the strength of an individual's familial and community ties, her level of education, and so on, may all influence the effect of punishment on a particular individual. In addition to difficulties associated with accurately identifying and measuring these individual traits, it would be necessary to describe how these traits interact, and how the strength of different traits might affect the outcome. This would, at best, become cumbersome, and most likely would produce rather weak statistical models predicting the effect of imprisonment on an individual's potential future behavior. Such a study would also require enormous financial resources to accomplish, and a significant investment of time. Moreover, a big prison system might affect individuals differently than a smaller prison system, or some alternative to prison. Ideally, we would want to follow a sample of people over time as a prison system expanded. But it is now thirty years since the U.S. prison system began expanding, and we can't go back in time to construct such a study. The best we could do would be to examine the impact of different size prison systems on offenders using data from different states.

It is not only difficult to construct a study that could address all the potential sources of variation that may influence how imprisonment affects an individual, it is, more importantly, not necessary to know the answer. Rather, if a big prison system suppresses crime, evidence of a suppression effect ought to be seen in the aggregate level of crime in society; that is, in the summing up of all crimes committed by people in a society over a period of time. If imprisonment reduces crime, we can see this impact without needing to measure or know its impact on specific individuals. If we omit individual measurement as necessary, we can create a simple hypothesis stating that *as prisons get bigger and more people are incarcerated, crime should decline in a society.* Thus, it makes sense to determine if the level of imprisonment within a nation has a significant impact on that society's level of crime independent of the question of how imprisonment might affect specific individuals.

Second, the problem of controlling for a multitude of influences can be simplified by examining the aggregate relationship between crime and imprisonment in one historical period. By examining one time period, a number of historically contingent factors can be ignored because we eliminate their effects by restricting the scope of the study. Nevertheless, this strategy cannot remove the impact of all the factors that might influence the study's validity and generalizability. In many of the analyses that follow, a host of factors that may affect crime (e.g., employment rates, opportunity structures, etc.) are purposefully omitted, which creates a validity problem that must be acknowledged. Yet, if the level of punishment is the most important factor affecting the level of crime, it is not necessary to identify or control for alternative explanations since we are not interested in their effect; we are only attempting to establish whether the basic assertion that a big prison system controls crime could be true.

Third, the task of studying the relationship between crime and imprisonment can be simplified by restricting the study to one nation. To accomplish this goal, the United States was selected as the focus of this study. There are several factors that influenced this decision.

First, as an American researcher, I am more familiar with the U.S. prison system than with the prison system in any other nation. Second, as a citizen of that nation, I am concerned with the problems of crime and punishment that affect me most directly. Third, America presents a unique condition useful for testing the relationship between expanding levels of imprisonment and its impact on the level of crime. *That condition stems from the fact that the level of imprisonment in the United States has expanded each and every year from 1973 through to the present.* In theory, then, we have nearly perfect conditions to determine whether a consistent increase in imprisonment has an equally consistent impact on reducing crime. Indeed, these conditions are "quasi-experimental" to the extent that one condition of the investigation—the U.S. imprisonment rate—moves or trends only upward. As a result, if an expanding imprisonment rate acts as expected, then the crime rate *should always trend downward*. Finally, America has the world's largest prison system. If having a big prison system reduces crime, then this effect ought to be most evident in the United States.

It was noted that the United States has the world's biggest system of incarceration. But how big is the American prison system? It is useful at this point to introduce some data that speak to this issue.

## HOW BIG IS AMERICA'S PRISON SYSTEM?

In order to comprehend the size of America's prison system, we need something against which to compare it. We could use historical data for this purpose, and show the growth of America's prison system over time.

Doing so would help us understand the growth pattern of America's prison system, and how big that system is today compared to earlier time periods. For now, however, we are trying to understand the relative size of America's prison system compared to other countries.

The data in table 2.1 describe some facts about a sample of prison systems from forty-two nations. Before examining these data, it should be noted that International Centre for Prison Studies (ICPS) data have certain limitations. The most important is that the count of prison inmates represented in these data are not consistent because for some nations the data include counts of jail inmates. For example, the ICPS data for the United States and other major nations includes jail inmates. Other tables in this book will refer to incarceration data for the United States that exclude jail inmates. Having brought this fact to the reader's attention, let us return to a consideration of table 2.1.

First, let me draw attention to column 6 in table 2.1, which indicates the data year for each nation. Data for various nations were drawn from different years, and represented the most recent year for which data was available for any individual nation. Some might argue that the fact that data for each nation come from different years affects the observations and conclusions drawn from these data. It should be kept in mind, however, that the size of penal systems changes relatively slowly, and the small difference in years found in this table is not considered to be sufficiently large to alter the primary conclusions that will be drawn.

Second, it should also be noted that not every nation in the world is represented in table 2.1. Rather, this table contains a cross-section of nations from different areas of the world, and at different stages of development. An effort was made to display prison data from the majority of the world's largest nations, but also to give some idea of the size of prisons across different types of nations. It should also be mentioned that this table includes all the world's largest prison systems, and that the conclusions do not represent an intentional effort to exclude larger or include smaller prison systems.

Column 1 of table 2.1 displays the name of each nation in the sample, while the number of people incarcerated in each nation is found in column 2. Examining this table, we can see that the United States has the largest prison system in the world with more than 2 million inmates incarcerated in 2003.

TABLE 2.1

Incarcerated Populations Across a Sample of Nations (N = 42)*

| (1) Country | (2) Number of Inmates | (3) Imprisonment Rate** | (4) Number Institutions | (5) Avg. Size Institution | (6) Data Year | (7) U.S. Multiplier*** |
|---|---|---|---|---|---|---|
| United States | 2,033,331 | 701 | 1,709 | 1,190 | 2003 | 1.00 |
| Russian Federation | 874,300 | 611 | 1,010 | 866 | 2002 | 1.15 |
| Belarus | 55,156 | 554 | 37 | 1,491 | 2003 | 1.26 |
| Ukraine | 158,858 | 413 | 172 | 924 | 2003 | 1.70 |
| South Africa | 176,893 | 400 | 241 | 734 | 2002 | 1.72 |
| Panama | 10,630 | 367 | 73 | 146 | 2002 | 1.91 |
| Swaziland | 34,000 | 359 | 12 | 2,833 | 2002 | 1.95 |
| Mongolia | 7,256 | 279 | 28 | 259 | 2002 | 2.51 |
| Iran | 163,256 | 226 | 184 | 887 | 2002 | 3.10 |
| Poland | 83,113 | 215 | 156 | 533 | 2003 | 3.26 |
| Romania | 47,406 | 212 | 43 | 1,103 | 2002 | 3.30 |
| Chile | 33,098 | 204 | 145 | 228 | 2002 | 3.44 |
| Morocco | 54,288 | 191 | 47 | 1,155 | 2000 | 3.67 |
| Czech Republic | 16,643 | 162 | 34 | 490 | 2003 | 4.33 |
| Brazil | 248,989 | 161 | 922 | 270 | 2003 | 4.35 |
| Mexico | 114,765 | 156 | 44 | 2,608 | 2000 | 4.50 |

(continued)

TABLE 2.1 (continued)

| (1) Country | (2) Number of Inmates | (3) Imprisonment Rate** | (4) Number Institutions | (5) Avg. Size Institution | (6) Data Year | (7) U.S. Multiplier*** |
|---|---|---|---|---|---|---|
| Lesotha | 3,000 | 143 | 14 | 214 | 2002 | 4.90 |
| England/Wales# | 73,040 | 139 | 138 | 529 | 2003 | 5.04 |
| Spain# | 54,341 | 133 | 85 | 639 | 2003 | 5.27 |
| Columbia | 54,034 | 126 | 168 | 321 | 2001 | 5.56 |
| China | 1,512,914 | 117 | 698 | 2,168 | 2002 | 5.99 |
| Canada# | 36,024 | 116 | 211 | 171 | 2003 | 6.04 |
| Australia# | 21,819 | 112 | 98 | 237 | 2002 | 6.26 |
| Kenya | 35,278 | 111 | 92 | 383 | 2003 | 6.32 |
| Argentina# | 38,604 | 107 | 116 | 333 | 2001 | 6.55 |
| Italy# | 56,574 | 100 | 205 | 276 | 2002 | 7.01 |
| Germany# | 81,176 | 98 | 222 | 366 | 2003 | 7.15 |
| Austria# | 7,745 | 95 | 29 | 267 | 2003 | 7.38 |
| France# | 55,382 | 93 | 185 | 299 | 2003 | 7.54 |
| Netherlands# | 14,968 | 93 | 79 | 189 | 2001 | 7.54 |
| Turkey | 64,173 | 90 | 562 | 114 | 2003 | 7.79 |
| Ireland# | 3,378 | 86 | 17 | 199 | 2002 | 8.15 |
| Greece | 8,500 | 80 | 25 | 340 | 2002 | 8.76 |

TABLE 2.1 (continued)

| (1) Country | (2) Number of Inmates | (3) Imprisonment Rate** | (4) Number Institutions | (5) Avg. Size Institution | (6) Data Year | (7) U.S. Multiplier*** |
|---|---|---|---|---|---|---|
| Venezuela# | 19,554 | 76 | 29 | 674 | 2003 | 9.22 |
| Sweden# | 6,506 | 73 | 83 | 78 | 2003 | 9.60 |
| Finland# | 3,617 | 70 | 28 | 129 | 2002 | 10.01 |
| Switzerland# | 4,987 | 68 | 167 | 30 | 2003 | 10.31 |
| Denmark# | 3,150 | 59 | 56 | 56 | 2001 | 11.88 |
| Norway# | 2,666 | 59 | 43 | 62 | 2001 | 11.88 |
| Japan# | 67,255 | 53 | 190 | 354 | 2002 | 13.23 |
| Nigeria | 39,368 | 33 | 147 | 268 | 2002 | 21.24 |
| India | 304,893 | 29 | 1,058 | 288 | 2002 | 24.17 |
| Mean/Avg. | | 180.2 | 228.6 | 588.4 | | |

* Data for this table were extracted from the International Centre for Prison Studies website (http://www.prisonstudies.org). These data include both prison and jail populations. These data (see column 6) represent the most recent year for which data were available at the time this table was created.

** The rate of imprisonment is a standardized measure that allows for direct comparison of the size of a prison system. The imprisonment rate is per 100,000 population within a country, and is calculated as follows: (prison population/country population) × 100,000.

*** The U.S. multiplier compares the U.S. rate of imprisonment to the rate of imprisonment in each nation. It is derived by dividing the U.S. imprisonment rate by a specific country's imprisonment rate. This number tells you how many times larger the U.S. rate of imprisonment is compared to a specific country.

# The nations marked with a # are more comparable to the United States from an economic, social, and cultural perspective.

## *The Number of Inmates Imprisoned Versus the Rate of Imprisonment*

The number of people incarcerated within a nation gives a rough approximation of the size and extent of a nation's prison system. To get a better picture of how big a nation's prison system is, the size of a prison system should be examined relative to the size of a country's total population. There is a great deal of variation in the number of citizens who live within the counties listed in table 2.1, and some countries may have large or small prison systems simply because they have a large or small number of citizens. Likewise, it is useful to examine the relationship between the size of a nation's prison population and the size of its general population because the effect of having a prison system that incarcerates 100,000 people might be very different in a nation with 1 million inhabitants versus a country with 10 or 20 million inhabitants. Furthermore, it should be obvious that the relationship between prison and population size affects the proportion of the population that can be or is incarcerated in any given nation. Thus, it is important to consider the imprisonment rate since this ratio provides some measure of a criminal's odds of being incarcerated for an offense.

To account for population variations as they relate to prison size, it is customary to create a measure called the *rate of imprisonment.* The rate of imprisonment provides a standardized measure of incarceration that can be compared across nations by making the populations of all countries appear equivalent. To create this measure, the number of inmates in a country is divided by the country's population, and then multiplied by 100,000. This calculation sets the population in each country to 100,000 for the purpose of comparison, and tells us how many people are in prison for every 100,000 people in that country. These data are found in column 3 of table 2.1.

Imprisonment rate data indicate that the United States has the highest rate of imprisonment among the nations in the sample. Thus, not only does the United States have the most inmates in prison, it also incarcerates more people per 100,000 citizens than any other nation in this sample. Using the data in column 3, it can be determined that the U.S. imprisonment rate is nearly 4 times (3.9) larger than the imprisonment rate of the average nation listed in this table.

Using the "average" imprisonment rate for the purpose of comparison is somewhat misleading because it lumps together a number of very different nations. Instead of comparing the United States to the overall average, let us instead compare its rate of imprisonment to a more equivalent sample of nations: "modernized" (and democratic) nations. The sample of nations in table 2.1 contains a subsample of 18 "modernized" nations (the nations marked with a # in column 1) that are more directly comparable to the United States economically, socially, and politically. Compared to this subsample, the U.S. rate of imprisonment is nearly 8 times (7.8) higher. This figure indicates two facts. First, the U.S. rate of imprisonment is not similar to the rates of imprisonment found in a sample of similar nations. Second, it should be clear that the U.S. rate of imprisonment is more similar to *the rate of imprisonment found in less developed nations*. These facts indicate that the reliance on incarceration found in the United States is at odds with the use of imprisonment found in similar nations of the world. Further, if we take the rate of imprisonment as an indication of a dimension of social repression, then the United States is well ahead of its peers.

### The Number and Size of Prisons

The size of a prison system could also be represented by comparing the number of prisons within nations. These data, displayed in column 4, indicate that the United States also has substantially more prisons than any other nation. For example, the United States has 69 percent more prisons than the nation with the next largest number of prisons, the Russian Federation.

The number of prisons within a nation may not be the best measure of the size of its prison system. Again, the number of prisons within a nation will have some relationship to how many people are incarcerated and perhaps to the number of people living within that nation. To take these differences into account, we could create a standardized measure of this indicator as well. Instead, let us examine an equally useful, alternative indicator of the size of a prison system that might also contain some clues about how prisons are used within different nations, and the philosophies that guide the use of prisons across these nations. That indicator is the average size of a prison within each nation. Data on the average size of a prison for each sampled nation is found in column 5. These data show that the average prison in the United States housed nearly 1,200 inmates. On this indicator, the United States ranks fifth, behind Swaziland, Mexico, China, and Belarus, nations that do not compare favorably to the United States in terms of economic development, living standards, or even in terms of political systems. Overall, the average prison in the overall sample holds approximately 588 inmates, meaning that the average U.S. prison is more than twice as large as the average prison found in other nations. We might also want to ask how the U.S. average prison size compared to the size of prisons in the subsample of "modernized" nations. This latter comparison group has an average prison size around 300, indicating that prisons in the United States are typically 4 times larger than prisons found in nations with equivalent social, economic, and political conditions.

### Calculating the U.S. Multiplier

Finally, column 7 presents a statistic I call the "U.S. multiplier." The U.S. multiplier is derived by dividing a country's rate of imprisonment by the U.S. rate of imprisonment. A country that had an imprisonment rate equal to the United States would have a multiplier of 1.00. Countries with larger rates of imprisonment would have multipliers smaller than 1.00, while countries with smaller prison systems will have multipliers greater than 1.00. Since the United States has the highest rate of imprisonment, this multiplier indicates how many times larger the U.S. rate of imprisonment is than the rate of imprisonment in each individual nation. Thus, for example, if the U.S. multiplier is 5.00, then the rate of imprisonment in the United States is 5 times higher than the rate of imprisonment in the particular country being examined. (Note: the U.S. multiplier can be converted into a percentage by multiplying it by 100.) As can be seen in column 7, the U.S. multiplier's range is between 1.15 and 24.17. Thus, some countries come close to the United States in terms of prison size. The vast majority, however, have much smaller prison systems.

The data in table 2.1 should cause us to pause and ask, Why is the U.S. use of imprisonment so much higher than in the rest of the world? Much more data is needed to address this question. What we know at this point is that the U.S. prison system is big: the biggest in the world. If you believe in ideas like deterrence or incapacitation, then the relationships noted in table 2.1 might cause you to assume that the rate of criminal offending in the United States must, because of all this punishment, be

much lower than the rate of crime found in other nations. Without going into great detail and producing all the crime data for each nation, let
me simply indicate at this point that this assumption is not correct (for
more extensive discussion, see Marc Mauer's 2003 paper "Comparative
International Rates of Incarceration"). This is an important assumption
to expose because Americans commonly assume that having a big prison
system accomplishes the goal of reducing crime. This crime reduction
assumption is shared by many policy makers who occupy decision-mak-
ing positions through which they are able to influence the goals and
growth of the American prison system.

Having reviewed some data that provides a picture of how large
America's prison system is, we can begin to examine the assumption that
increasing the rate of incarceration should cause a reduction in crime.

## COMMON ASSUMPTIONS MADE
## ABOUT PUNISHMENT AND CRIME

In this section, some of the more common assumptions that link
punishment and crime are examined. Particular attention is paid to assumptions linking the growth and use of imprisonment to reductions in
crime through deterrence or incapacitation.

### Why Should Locking Up More People Reduce Crime?

Longstanding theories of behavior assert that punishment can change
behavior. Since the late eighteenth and early nineteenth century, these
theories have occupied a central place in criminological thinking. In the
early nineteenth century, Jeremy Bentham asserted that increasing the
costs of crime could deter criminals. Punishment is one such cost. This
idea has popular appeal, and many Americans believe that a bigger prison
system that locks up more offenders reduces crime. In theoretical terms,
the crime reduction that occurs through imprisonment involves either
incapacitation or deterrence. Technically, incapacitation and deterrence
are two different effects that can result from imprisonment, though they
may overlap and be difficult to distinguish.

Incapacitation is the term used to describe the effect of preventing offenders (usually repeat offenders since they are often the targeted
group) from committing crimes *while incarcerated*. That is, being locked
up prevents the offender from preying upon people in the free world.

Deterrence, in contrast, either dissuades the criminal offender who is locked up, or other potential offenders, *from engaging in future acts of crime because they fear the consequences* of punishment. Although these two effects are different theoretically and technically, it is difficult to distinguish incapacitation and deterrent effects, and to determine which might have contributed to a decline in crime (Kessler and Levitt, 1999). If, for example, we lock up an offender and the crime rate goes down, did it go down because the offender can't commit crimes while he is imprisoned? Or did it go down because when we imprisoned the offender it deterred others from crime? To know this, we would need to have fairly detailed information about the behavior of offenders that are imprisoned, including the number of crimes they committed for which they were not apprehended, and the behavior of the population of free offenders. We would also have to assume that the behavior of these offenders would not have changed in any way if they had not been incarcerated, or that a lack of incarceration would not produce a reduced crime rate among offenders who were not locked away. Likewise, to know if prisons actually deterred potential criminals other than the offender, extensive information about their behavior would be required. In addition, to establish if imprisonment of others really affected the behavior of potential criminal offenders, we would need to survey persons whose criminal behavior is known, determine if they have ceased this behavior, and ask them what role the imprisonment of others played in their decision to desist from crime.

Because we don't have this kind of extensive information on criminals, it is difficult to say with any certainty that imprisonment deters crime, or whether it suppresses a specific number of crimes through incapacitation. And, if prisons really worked the way we think they do, wouldn't both of these results occur? Wouldn't we incapacitate the incarcerated offender *and* deter other potential offenders from committing crimes through imprisonment? *If this were true, then having a big prison system ought to have a very large effect on crime since two different groups of offenders are being affected: the offender and other potential offenders.* In other words, if both deterrence and incapacitation were the result of incarceration, wouldn't the frenzy to lock up offenders that characterized the American prison system over the past three decades quickly extinguish crime in society? The answer would be yes, *if* incapacitation and deterrence worked as advertised. While crime has gone down in recent years, and "get tough" policies like increased rates of imprisonment have gotten credit, crime did not decline throughout most of the past thirty years, a period of time when imprisonment rose consistently.

Why didn't crime continually decline as imprisonment rates rose in the United States? One reason, which is the subject of much criminological inquiry into the etiology or causes of crime, is that criminals are constantly being produced by forces outside the threat and application of punishment. Evidence generated by studying the causes of crime suggests that incarcerated criminals are replaced by new criminals. If this were not true, if no new criminals were produced, crime would, at some point, be extinguished as criminals aged and died. If punishment was all that a society needed to reduce or eliminate crime, we would expect that the nation with the world's biggest prison system would have very little crime. But the level of punishment is not the sole determinant of crime, nor, perhaps, even the most important. For the reasons noted below, there are grounds to suspect that incapacitation and deterrence do not operate as advertised.

### Bigger Prisons, Less Crime?

Not only is it difficult to distinguish the effects of incapacitation from those attributable to deterrence, it is not possible to determine how big we should expect the effects of either to be ahead of time. That is, before we incarcerate people and assess its effect on the crime rate, we don't actually know if incarcerating people will reduce crime. The idea that imprisonment reduces crime is an assumption or a hypothesis about the effect of incarceration.

PREDICTING THE EFFECTS OF INCARCERATION ON CRIME. Indeed, the inability to predict how much of a crime reduction effect can be expected from raising the rate of imprisonment is perhaps one of the most perplexing things about the use of punishment as a deterrent or as a method of crime reduction through incapacitation. How many crimes should be eliminated through deterrence or incapacitation? More specifically, we might ask, how many crimes should we expect to be repressed by locking up one extra inmate? Should this effect be consistently evident across all types of offenders? Or are some kinds of offenders more difficult to

deter? Will incapacitation and deterrence effects emerge regardless of social conditions? Or are deterrent and incapacitative effects conditioned
by social and economic conditions? And, if the effect appears to be tied
to social or economic conditions, can we be sure that the observed effect
can be attributed to the deterrent or incapacitative effects of incarceration instead of social and economic trends?

The problem of predicting the effect of locking up more inmates
is complex, and would require an elaborate statistical model. The results
derived from such a model would also vary depending on the data that
were used for calculating the outcome, and the assumptions about behavior those statistical models included. For example, a simple model
with only a few variables may show that incarceration has a large effect on the rate of criminal offending. It is quite possible, however, that
in a more complex model that adds the effect of social and economic
factors, the effect of incarceration on the rate of crime might become
attenuated. Further, the more of these "other" variables that get added
to the model, the smaller the effect of incarceration on crime might
become. If this were indeed the case, then we would be able to show
that there are social and economic factors that override the effects of
incarceration on crime rates.

VARIATION IN EFFECTS OVER TIME AND PLACE. We also need to consider that research results that provide evidence of a deterrent or incapacitative effect may produce this result because they examine a very
limited time frame, or data from specific locations. For instance, research
studies that have employed data from the 1990s can demonstrate a small
deterrent or incapacitative effect on crime (see chapter 1). In recent
years, these kinds of studies have been taken as valid evidence that deterrence and incapacitation work. Likewise, data from some states, but
not from others, will show a deterrent or incapacitative effect. Longer
trend data, however, as this book will demonstrate, does not show the
same deterrent or incapacitative effects of imprisonment. Over the long
run, or since 1973, the large prison system America has built has not
produced consistent deterrent or incapacitative effects. At best, the results are mixed. These mixed results are not often acknowledged. In fact,
the assumption that imprisoning offenders reduces crime is so widely
accepted that it is rarely challenged. Likewise, if asked to come up with

suggestions for reducing crime, many members of the general population would respond that more police, longer prison sentences, and sending more people to prison would do the trick. What most people fail to understand is that punishment, or lack thereof, isn't necessarily the most important determinant of crime, and that the effects of incarceration may not be uniform or have similar effects across time, places, or people. In other words, the fact that imprisonment effects vary and are inconsistent is not considered by deterrence research.

Take politicians as an example. You never hear a politician say: "It is my intention to push for an expansion of our prison system because there is a 50 percent chance that doing so will reduce crime. That also means that there is a 50 percent chance my plan won't work." Rather, what politicians often do is suggest that they are in favor of raising the rate of incarceration because *it will lower crime.* What they are offering the public is what they believe the public wants to hear—that putting more people behind bars will make the public safer. Likewise, you never hear a politician who is attempting to gain your vote by offering his (and it's usually a man) views on how to reduce crime tell you exactly how much crime will be reduced by following his plan. Has anyone specifically said: "I am going to send 20 percent more people to prison because this will reduce the crime rate by 30 percent"? No, because, as I will demonstrate, there are no clear-cut answers such as this when we attempt to rely on the prison as a cure for crime. As a criminologist, I can tell you that we can't predict how much raising the rate of imprisonment will lower crime. Why? Well, we don't really know why exactly. What we do know is that the relationship between crime and punishment doesn't work the way we expect it to work; crime isn't simply a response to how much or how little punishment there is in a society. In fact, as research indicates, fear of punishment is only a minor source of compliance with the law (Tyler, 1990). Crime is the result of the interaction of numerous processes. The majority of factors that can be identified as causes of crime—poor economic conditions, deteriorated neighborhood conditions—will be unaffected by how much punishment society applies. That is, raising the rate of incarceration is unlikely to lower crime *if crime is caused by factors that incarceration does not or can not address.* Punishment doesn't reduce poverty, create jobs, or eliminate the problems of impoverished neighborhoods where we see the kinds of crimes that punishment is supposed to address.

WHEN ARE PREDICTED EFFECTS EXPECTED? As evidence of our inability to predict what will happen when we raise the rate of imprisonment, consider what actually happened to crime in the United States between 1973 and 2002, the thirty years when imprisonment grew every year. During this period, crime increased and decreased almost an equivalent number of times as the imprisonment rate rose. This simple observation, that crime can and has risen even while rates of incarceration are on the rise, leads to the conclusion that either outcome—a crime reduction or an increase in crime—was equally likely. In fact, as will be demonstrated in a later chapter, the relationship between increased rates of incarceration and crime resembles a coin toss: there are two outcomes, and neither is statistically more likely. We can see a similar pattern when we look across states or regions within the United States.

Why can't we predict the outcome when it seems so logical that crime should decline when we incarcerate more criminals? Consider again the simple idea of incapacitation: the more criminals we put behind bars, the fewer crimes they can commit. If this is true, then big prisons are an easy solution to the crime problem to the extent that all we need to do is lock up all the criminals. The appeal of such a straightforward and simple solution to crime is extremely compelling. Following the logic of the incapacitation strategy, the increase in incarceration that occurred in the United States since the early 1970s should have made crime drop like a rock falling from the Empire State Building, since we now incarcerate over 1 million more people than we did in the early 1970s. To illustrate this point, let us consider a fictional example.

Say that in a given year, the state I live in locked up 10,000 criminals who had committed an average of 5 crimes apiece. It seems logical that I could expect the number of crimes to be reduced in the next year by 50,000 (5 ★ 10,000) as long as I don't release anyone from prison, since I have incapacitated so many repeat offenders. But incapacitation never works this way, or this well, because there are two primary flaws in this approach to crime control.

First, we don't lock up criminals for life, meaning the suppression effect can only last as long as a prison sentence. So, why not lock up criminals and throw away the key? The answer is simple. First, not all the crimes that are committed in a society are severe enough to warrant such a weighty penalty. Second, doing so would be financially prohibitive and create an even bigger prison system than we have now. In fact, if society were to carry out such a program, it would soon find that more Americans would be behind bars than would be free. We probably can't lock up all the criminals because, as self-report studies indicate, the majority of people in society have committed a crime at one time or another, and we would end up with 100 million people or more behind bars. Thus, we have to limit our "lock 'em up" aspirations, and concentrate on the serious, repeat offender (as you will find out later, our big prison system holds its fair share of people who do not fit this category, but, rather, holds many more first-time offenders than might be expected). As a result, the incapacitative effects of an imprisonment strategy can only go so far.

Second, this strategy doesn't work in the long run because when society incarcerates some offenders, others come along to take their place. In other words, there appears to be a "replacement effect." Why? Because incapacitation does not address the social and economic conditions that influence people to commit crime in the first place. If, for instance, criminals turn to crime because they cannot find meaningful work in their community, and incapacitation does not enhance the prospects for employment within the community (in fact, to reduce the unemployment rate significantly, imprisonment rates would need to be several times higher than they are now), then how does incapacitation address factors that generate criminal populations? You could select any potential cause of crime you like and substitute it into this example: poor parenting; lack of strong nuclear families; poor social bonding; high dropout rates and poor school performance, and so on. None of these problems are addressed by locking up more people in prison. Or, we might want to think about the problem this way. For the purposes of this example, assume any cause for drug use you prefer, and assume that policy makers attempt to reduce drug use through interdiction strategies and aggressive policing tactics that target drug sellers. When society attempts to lower the rate of drug use crimes by locking up more drug traffickers, we can expect that someone will take the trafficker's place, especially if the demand for drugs remains high and nothing has been done to combat the factors *that caused the user's* behavior. Likewise interdiction doesn't reduce the demand for drugs, since interdiction does not address *the causes of drug use.* The point: punishment does not alter the general behaviors associated with the use of drugs, or the illegal sale of drugs, because the punishment does not change the conditions associated with either behavior.

How Much Should Crime Decline? Think about this: according to the International Centre for Prison Studies, in 2003 the U.S. system of incarceration became the first modern penal system to incarcerate over 2 million people. In contrast, in the early 1970s, the U.S. prison system incarcerated less than 200,000 people. It would appear obvious that if the incapacitation approach were the answer to the problem of crime, and we now incarcerate ten times as many people as we once did, the level of crime should be very low today compared to the early 1970s. Exactly how much lower should the crime rate be today compared to the early 1970s as a result of locking up so many more people might be hard to pinpoint. Theoretical positions would lead us to believe that the reduction should be quite substantial, especially given the size of the increase in imprisonment that has occurred in the United States over the past thirty years. Typically, however, we can only "know" the answer to this question by looking at empirical data that compares trends in crime and punishment. So, what do these empirical data have to say?

Here, for example, is what we do know from police arrest data: in 1971 there were 897.1 crimes per 100,000 people in the United States, while the rate of incarceration was 95 per 100,000. In 1981 there were 1,070 crimes per 100,000 American citizens—a 16 percent increase— while the incarceration rate had increased by about 62 percent to 154 per 100,000. By 1991 the crime rate had increased to 1,198.8 per 100,000 people, which amounted to a 12 increase since 1981, and a 33.6 percent increase since 1971. At the same time, the imprisonment rate rose to 313 per 100,000, constituting a 103 percent increase since 1981, and a 229 percent increase over 1971 levels (incarceration data appear in table 3.1; for arrest data, see table 4.2004 in the Sourcebook of Criminal Justice Statistics online). Thus, crime was rising along with substantial increases in the use of imprisonment. Let us fast-forward to 2001, when the arrest index was 807.3 per 100,000 people, or 10 percent lower than the 1971 rate where we began this example. The imprisonment rate, however, stood at 498 per 100,000, an increase of 424 percent since 1971. In other words, over these three decades, multiplying the imprisonment rate by more than 4 times reduced crime by only 10 percent. The biggest crime reduction over this period, which were especially evident in the 1990s, was a reduction in property crimes, which decreased from 721.4 per 100,000 in 1971 to 581.8 per 100,000 by 2001. Over the same time period, there were more violent crimes—28 percent more, in fact. So, prisons, which are supposed to protect us from the worst offenders through incapacitation or deterrence, did not seem to work on the population of the worst offenders. Overall, it took a large increase in imprisonment over this time span—over 400 percent—to lower the aggregate crime rate by just 10 percent, which comprised two opposing trends: a reduction in property crime and a rise in the rate of violent crime.

In sum, increasing the rate of incarceration (by more than 400 percent) between 1971 and 2001 *eventually* appeared to reduce crime by 10 percent from its 1971 level. At the same time, we must consider that the crimes most affected were property crimes, not violent crimes. These simple facts indicate that increasing the number of people we incarcerate is not the answer to the problem of crime: very large increases in imprisonment over an extended period seemed to lower the crime rate slightly, assuming no other conditions that may cause crime had changed. These simple facts also seemed to indicate that we have been mislead by following this course of action—a course of action that claims that a rising rate of imprisonment significantly reduced crime (again, perhaps because the causes of crime seem to lie somewhere outside the crime-punishment nexus).

What I have left out of the discussion above is the question of whether prisons deter potential criminals. All we need to do is substitute the word "deterrence" into the few paragraphs above to get our answer. A big prison system ought to, in theory, deter a lot more people than a small prison system because the threat of punishment has increased along with the size of the prison system. If we take the rate of incarceration as a measure of the odds of imprisonment, we can see that the increased odds of incarceration that accompany a big prison system had little impact on crime. The increase in the imprisonment rate from 1971 through 2001 of 424 percent (that is, an increase in the odds of being incarcerated for the U.S. population) is related to only a 10 percent reduction in crime. Looked at another way, we could say that: (1) locking up 403 more people out of every 100,000 people reduced crime by 90 per 100,000; or

(2) in order to eliminate one hundred crimes through imprisonment, 448 additional people would have to be incarcerated; or (3) to deter one crime, 5 people needed to be incarcerated. If we were to factor in the cost of building more prison space, this crime reduction mechanism would be quite costly—between $700,000 to $1.25 million per crime, depending on the construction and incarceration costs estimates that are used, and whether we consider the additional costs imposed on police and the courts. Thus, to eliminate 100 crimes would require locking up 448 offenders at a cost of between $314 and $560 million. Extrapolating from this estimate, reducing crime by 1,000 crimes would cost $3 to nearly $6 billion; for 10,000 crimes, the cost would be staggering: $30 to nearly $60 billion. To be sure, this estimate assumes that the effect of incarceration is constant, and that lower or higher levels do not produce significantly different results because the estimate averages the crime reduction impact and costs.

To make a long story short, we should have less crime if the costs of punishment have been extended or made more weighty by incarcerating more people, and the effect of punishment was more important than other factors that influence crime. As noted, however, this deterrent effect is minimal over the long run as evident in America's experiment with its expanding prison system since 1973. To be sure, there are time periods or short-run aberrations within the long run of the big prison period where deterrence appears to be at work. But, why should deterrence work in some parts of this period and not others? The deterrence theorist has an explanation for why this deterrent effect didn't happen throughout the entire time period: we didn't raise the level of punishment enough in the early portion of the expansion period to deter criminals. As later evidence will illustrate, this isn't true—in fact, when crime began to decline, the annual average rise in incarceration was lower than it had been in previous years. And, while the rate may not have been "high enough," we did incarcerate more people even during this earlier period of prison expansion than at other points in time. Why wasn't the crime rate also lower in comparison? Again, the deterrence theorist, believing in the power of deterrence theory and the value of punishment over other factors, argues that while we incarcerated more people and had increased the probability of punishment, either we had not increased the probability of imprisonment enough, or the sentences people received were not long enough. In effect, deterrence theorists are saying that having the biggest prison system in the world and being among the world leaders in average prison sentence length isn't enough to stop crime in America.[1] Yet, what these theorists don't tell is why small prison systems and lesser sentences coexist with lower crime rates in other nations.

We cannot, however, simply dismiss the point deterrence theorists are making—that deterrence doesn't work because there are other "disturbing" factors that limit its effect. We must recognize that they may be right, but not for the reason they believe. The problem is that while we can control the level of imprisonment and the length of prison sentences, *we have not done a good job of controlling other factors that may also influence or contribute to the causation of criminal behavior.* Thus, we must recognize that raising the rate of incarceration or punishment may not stop people from committing crime when other factors, such as the rate of unemployment, growing economic inequality, and shrinking relative wages for low-income groups, characterize a society's economic system. Punishing people for committing crimes doesn't erase the population's desire to make a decent living, perhaps at least not until the level of punishment is extremely severe.

In sum, a bigger prison system doesn't necessarily reduce crime. It doesn't necessarily deter people, and it doesn't necessarily generate an incapacitation effect. In this sense, a bigger prison system isn't necessarily good for society from a crime reduction or a cost-benefit perspective. But big prisons are good for some people in society. And this group who benefits from big prisons may have a say in how big America's prison system has become.

## WHO DOES OUR BIG PRISON SYSTEM BENEFIT?

The question of whether a bigger prison system is better depends on whose interests or whose perspective we employ to make this judgment. For example, from the perspective of the politician who might wish to point to some highly visible evidence that she has done something to control crime, a bigger prison system may indicate toughness on crime. Big prisons, in other words, can be a valuable and visible political tool that can assuage the public's feelings that something needs to be done about crime.

*Politicians and Public Demand*

When presented with a politician who wants to reduce crime by providing expanded economic opportunities and one who wants to reduce crime using more punitive responses, the public will tend to side with the latter politician. This occurs because of the all-too-common assumption that more punitive penal policies will serve the purpose of reducing crime. Yet there is little evidence that such policies are actually very effective, or consistent in their effect. And the public does not demand evidence that prisons are actually doing what they are supposed to do (or at least what politicians claim they can do). Thus, we cannot lay all the blame for our predicament on politicians; they can, however, share the blame with the general public.

The general public demands politicians do something. The public has no expertise in the area of crime control, and they tend to rely on their gut instinct rather than research. When it comes to crime, that gut instinct says that more punishment will reduce crime. Indeed, more punishment may reduce certain behaviors, but it also tends to create other problem behaviors. Overly punished dogs, for instance, will tend to become neurotic or overtly aggressive. It is not hard to imagine that similar responses might emerge in human populations that are punished too severely, or which live under the constant threat of punishment.

The public also believes (hopes?) that politicians are employing the advice of experts before they make decisions about the best policies that can be enacted to reduce crime. The problem is that the public acts on faith: faith that their elected leaders will do the right thing and will either read research or consult with researchers who have studied a particular problem. Because they are acting on faith, they do not exert any energy toward finding out whether the policies their elected officials have set into place are actually producing the desired effect. In a democracy, government can only be effective when the citizens are informed. An informed public might question whether supporting a bigger prison system is a useful crime control strategy, whether such an approach is fiscally responsible given the enormous cost of our big prison system and its low rate of return, and whether we ought to spend more money on questionable crime control strategies given the budgetary problems most states and our federal government encounter.

But, facts are often overcome by assumptions that appear appealing in the face of lack of knowledge, such as the one that says more prisons will produce less crime.

Politicians aren't the only beneficiaries of big prisons. Another often unseen and unimagined group benefits from our big prison system: entrepreneurs who invest in building, operating, and providing services to prisons. It should come as no surprise that if you were one of the many entrepreneurs that has taken advantage of the tremendous growth of the prison system by supplying services needed to operate prisons, you might also think that a bigger prison system is a better prison system. Our big prison system offers billions of dollars in profit to the private sector. But for the average American citizen concerned with reducing crime and the efficient expenditures of their tax dollars, a bigger prison system isn't necessarily better. In fact, bigger is probably a worse choice. But the public's interests are not all that counts when it comes to determining how big America's prison system ought to be, or how tax dollars get spent. We will return to this issue in a later chapter.

## BIG PRISONS AND BIG SPACES

It may seem silly or inconsequential to consider the amount of space prisons occupy. But a big prison system takes up a big space, unless, of course, you build high-rise or tower-style prisons. Because the average American prison is typically large (holding, on average, nearly 1,200 inmates, more than twice the average size of the prison systems for the various countries listed in table 2.1), and because big prisons typically require a good deal of space, they are located away from major population centers. The problem with this approach to building prisons is that the majority of criminals come from urbanized areas. Building big prisons in far away places creates transportation issues, potential service delivery problems, and can also be a source of isolation for inmates that results in severed ties to family and community, and increases the probability that, once released, the inmate will return to crime. From a security standpoint, however, locating prisons far away from urban centers makes some sense and cuts down on any immediate threat an escape may pose. But, in reality, few inmates escape from prison (approximately 8 out of 100,000 inmates, or 1 of every 12,500 inmates, or .008 out of 100 inmates).

In the United States, bigness and security issues have occupied a privileged position over other potential goals when it comes to operating and designing prisons. In other words, privileging security and bigness issues prevents the U.S. prison system from addressing other important problems such as the location of prisons, the costs of imprisonment, or energy issues (see chapter 8). There are several other related issues that bigness and security override. For example, consider the fact that the majority of people who are sent to prison will one day be released back into society when their sentences are completed. These inmates will face the difficult task of reintegrating themselves back into the community, a process that is essential if we expect them to refrain from crime in the future. Ex-inmates will need jobs, and will need to reestablish themselves in society in a legitimate way if they are to succeed and avoid returning to crime. In other words, the problem that is created by maintaining a large, isolated prison system may also explain why prisons are not a very effective mechanism for accomplishing the goal of deterrence. The ex-offender weighs the evidence, which in this case may involve the ability to obtain a decent standard of living, against the odds of going back to prison. For the unemployed offender living in undesirable housing in an economically disadvantaged and physically deteriorated neighborhood, the prospect of going to prison may be looked upon as equivalent. This is exactly what the American public fears when it calls for longer prison sentences, stark prison conditions, and bigger prisons. What is excluded from crime policy considerations is the alternative solution: improving the social and economic conditions that produce the average street offenders in the first place.

The difficult task of reintegration is compounded by having a criminal record, which reduces the opportunity for employment and helps to ensure a return to crime. In addition, the ex-inmate's reintegration into the community is affected by the isolation from community and family they may have experienced while they were imprisoned. Inmates locked up in large, out-of-sight prisons often lose touch with family and community members who might aid in the reintegration process. Because we concentrate on locking up so many people in just such a fashion, we lose sight of the roadblocks this system creates for ex-inmates, and fail to offer services needed to assure that inmates do not return to crime. Down the road, as the number of people released from prison rises—and it will rise because we have put more people in prison and someday they will get out—we may begin to see that the crime rate also rises as a larger number of ex-inmates fail to be reintegrated into society.

The big spaces big prisons take up become problematic for other reasons that are not often considered. As the number of prison facilities grow, finding suitable locations for these facilities becomes more difficult. Responding to environmental issues, there is now greater emphasis on protecting the remaining natural areas in the United States. This fact, coupled with the expansion of the population and its broader distribution over the American landscape makes it harder and harder to find isolated locations to build large prisons. As we continue to expand the number of prisons, we can expect to encroach on either wilderness areas or the space taken up by existing communities. In time, the "not in my backyard" public attitude that is commonly voiced concerning the location of other noxious facilities, such as landfills, waste sites, and facilities that treat, store, and dispose or produce hazardous materials, will be imported into the correctional system debate. To be sure, the middle class, with its heightened fear of crime, and the group most often associated with supporting "get tough on crime" approaches, may continue to call for prisons, while simultaneously arguing that these facilities not be placed in locations that violate their sensibilities, or lower their property values.

## FUELLING THE SYSTEM

Policy makers who have helped build our big prison system have been shortsighted in a number of ways, some of which have been discussed above. It is plausible that at least some policy makers have considered these issues. But there is a large problem looming on the horizon that policy makers have probably not considered, which we will later examine in greater detail—the impact of the end of the fossil fuel era on our nation's ability to continue to operate its massive prison system.

For those unfamiliar with the idea that the fossil fuel era is coming to an end, or has reached its midway point or peak, there is a growing scientific literature addressing this problem. The idea that there was a limited amount of fossil fuel in the ground and that consumption demands could one day empty the world's oil reserve was, for much of the twentieth century, regarded as foolish. This was true despite the fact that evidence of this possibility had been discovered in the 1950s.

This literature will be reviewed more fully later. For now, it is useful to bear in mind that the big, isolated prison system the United States has built will be difficult to operate and will become much more costly than it is now as fossil fuel supplies dwindle and the price of oil rises. Policy makers will need to address the size of our prison system and mechanisms for coping with the population we have incarcerated in an era where fossil fuels become increasingly scarce. Either we plan for this future now or face the consequences later. And, if not foreseen, those consequences could be dramatic and involve mass riots in large prisons where inmates are denied heat, and where security has been threatened by the lack of fossil fuel needed to operate security devices.

## Conclusion

A big prison system, such as the one operated in the United States, is a big problem for a number of reasons. Big prisons produce big anticipation that they will reduce crime. The relationship between the expansion of the American prison system and crime will be addressed later in this book. A big prison system also produces financial burdens. How much do we spend on our big prison system? How much should we spend? When we spend more on prisons, where does the money come from? We will examine these issues in a later chapter.

It is estimated that *about 25 percent of all prisoners in the world today are housed in American prisons and jails.* Given the large number of inmates in U.S. prisons, we should expect that our country would have very low rates of criminal offending. Compared to other nations, however, it does not. This fact should make us wonder why our country has selected such a different response to crime than most other nations of the world.

The big prison policy that has driven the American response to crime has not, despite its proponents' claims, met the challenge. And, hidden behind the big prison system, lay potentially big problems that will emerge as the predicted world oil shortage inches its way closer and closer.

In this chapter, the idea that our big prison system is an ineffective crime control model has been introduced. This chapter also introduced the idea that America's big prison model has benefits outside its purported crime control function. One such function is economic, and it seems that the continued growth of our system of imprisonment is also being driven by private sector interests in the prison system that have emerged over the past two decades.

In order to understand each of these issues more fully, additional analysis of each of these points is in order. The next step is to examine the growth of the American prison system, its relationship to crime control, and the growing interest of the private sector in the continued expansion of the system of imprisonment.

## CHAPTER 3

# The Growth of America's Prison System

THE UNITED STATES has the world's largest prison system. At mid-year 2005, federal and state prisons in the United States housed more than 1.4 million inmates (Harrison and Beck, 2006). Given the long-term and recent trends in imprisonment in the United States, we can estimate that the U.S. prison population will surpass the 2 million inmate mark before 2010. Only a decade ago (1994), the U.S prison system had just managed to squeeze in its one-millionth inmate. In 1986, the system incarcerated 500,000 inmates, which was twice the number of inmates incarcerated in 1976. To make a long (three decade) story short, in the previous twenty-seven years, the population in U.S. prisons has doubled three times. This rate of growth in imprisonment is unprecedented in the modern history (from 1925 on) of the U.S. prison system. Below, these trends in imprisonment are explored in greater detail.

IMPRISONMENT TRENDS IN THE UNITED STATES SINCE 1925

To get a better feel for these data, prison population growth for the United States is depicted in table 3.1 and figure 3.1. Take a moment to examine the table and graph, taking particular note of the trends you observe in the graph. What you will see may surprise you.

The story of the rapidly expanding U.S. prison population began in 1973. Shortly after 1973—1976 to be exact—there were 262,833 prison inmates incarcerated in American prisons, which was twice the number of inmates incarcerated in 1930. The fact that the number of inmates in American prisons had doubled between 1930 and 1976 is, in itself, rather unremarkable because by 1976 the U.S. population had increased by about 74 percent over its 1930 level. Still, while the population of

TABLE 3.1

*Rates of Imprisonment Per 100,000 Population, United States, 1925–2003*

| Year | Number Imprisoned | Imprisonment Rate | Imprisonment Index |
|------|------|------|------|
| 1925 | 91,669 | 79 | 82 |
| 1926 | 97,991 | 83 | 86 |
| 1927 | 109,983 | 91 | 95 |
| 1928 | 116,390 | 96 | 100 |
| 1929 | 120,496 | 98 | 102 |
| 1930 | 129,453 | 104 | 108 |
| 1931 | 137,082 | 110 | 115 |
| 1932 | 137,997 | 110 | 115 |
| 1933 | 136,810 | 109 | 114 |
| 1934 | 138,316 | 109 | 114 |
| 1935 | 144,180 | 113 | 118 |
| 1936 | 145,038 | 113 | 118 |
| 1937 | 152,741 | 118 | 123 |
| 1938 | 160,285 | 123 | 128 |
| 1939 | 179,818 | 137 | 143 |
| 1940 | 173,706 | 131 | 135 |
| 1941 | 165,439 | 124 | 129 |
| 1942 | 150,384 | 112 | 117 |
| 1943 | 137,220 | 103 | 107 |
| 1944 | 132,456 | 100 | 104 |
| 1945 | 133,649 | 98 | 102 |
| 1946 | 140,079 | 99 | 103 |
| 1947 | 151,305 | 105 | 109 |
| 1948 | 155,977 | 106 | 110 |
| 1949 | 163,749 | 109 | 114 |
| 1950 | 166,123 | 109 | 114 |
| 1951 | 165,123 | 107 | 112 |
| 1952 | 168,233 | 107 | 112 |
| 1953 | 173,579 | 108 | 113 |

*(continued)*

TABLE 3.1 *(continued)*

| Year | Number Imprisoned | Imprisonment Rate | Imprisonment Index |
|------|-------------------|-------------------|--------------------|
| 1954 | 182,901 | 112 | 117 |
| 1955 | 185,780 | 112 | 117 |
| 1956 | 189,565 | 113 | 118 |
| 1957 | 195,414 | 113 | 118 |
| 1958 | 205,643 | 117 | 122 |
| 1959 | 208,105 | 117 | 122 |
| 1960 | 212,953 | 117 | 122 |
| 1961 | 220,149 | 119 | 124 |
| 1962 | 218,830 | 117 | 122 |
| 1963 | 217,283 | 114 | 119 |
| 1964 | 214,336 | 111 | 116 |
| 1965 | 210,895 | 108 | 113 |
| 1966 | 199,654 | 102 | 106 |
| 1967 | 194,896 | 98 | 102 |
| 1968 | 187,914 | 94 | 98 |
| 1969 | 196,007 | 97 | 101 |
| 1970 | 196,429 | 96 | 100 |
| 1971 | 198,061 | 95 | 99 |
| 1972 | 196,092 | 93 | 97 |
| 1973 | 204,211 | 96 | 100 |
| 1974 | 218,466 | 102 | 106 |
| 1975 | 240,593 | 111 | 116 |
| 1976 | 262,833 | 120 | 125 |
| 1977 | 278,141 | 126 | 131 |
| 1978 | 294,396 | 132 | 138 |
| 1979 | 301,470 | 133 | 139 |
| 1980 | 315,974 | 139 | 145 |
| 1981 | 353,673 | 154 | 160 |
| 1982 | 395,516 | 171 | 178 |
| 1983 | 419,346 | 179 | 187 |

*(continued)*

TABLE 3.1 *(continued)*

| Year | Number Imprisoned | Imprisonment Rate | Imprisonment Index |
|------|------|------|------|
| 1984 | 443,398 | 188 | 196 |
| 1985 | 480,568 | 202 | 210 |
| 1986 | 522,084 | 217 | 226 |
| 1987 | 560,812 | 231 | 241 |
| 1988 | 603,732 | 247 | 257 |
| 1989 | 680,907 | 276 | 288 |
| 1990 | 739,980 | 297 | 309 |
| 1991 | 789,610 | 313 | 326 |
| 1992 | 846,277 | 332 | 346 |
| 1993 | 932,074 | 359 | 373 |
| 1994 | 1,016,691 | 389 | 405 |
| 1995 | 1,085,022 | 411 | 428 |
| 1996 | 1,137,722 | 427 | 445 |
| 1997 | 1,194,581 | 444 | 462 |
| 1998 | 1,245,402 | 461 | 480 |
| 1999 | 1,304,074 | 463 | 483 |
| 2000 | 1,321,137 | 469 | 489 |
| 2001 | 1,345,217 | 470 | 490 |
| 2002 | 1,380,516 | 476 | 496 |
| 2003 | 1,408,361 | 482 | 502 |
| 2004 | 1,433,793 | 486 | 506 |

The imprisonment index was derived by dividing the imprisonment rate in any given year by the imprisonment rate in 1973. The result is rounded to the nearest whole number. This calculation sets the imprisonment index in 1973 to 100, and represents the imprisonment rate in all years as a percentage of the imprisonment rate in 1973.

Data used in this table were extracted from The Sourcebook of Criminal Justice Statistics (http://www.albany.edu/sourcebook), and from data maintained by the National Institute of Justice (http://www.ojp.usdoj.gov/nij/). Note that like other crime and justice data, the imprisonment data listed here tends to be revised for up to five years as new information is received by government agencies that contribute to these count data. Thus, the figures represented here may not end up being the final government counts.

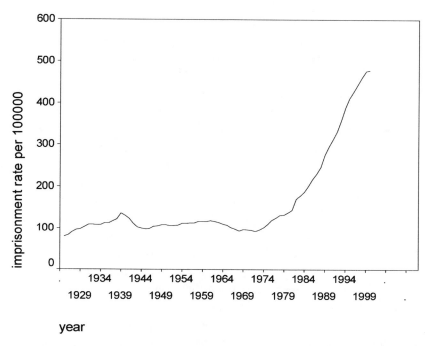

3.1. The Trend in the Rate of Imprisonment Per 100,000 Population for the United States, 1925–2000

the United States grew during this period, the rate of imprisonment was expanding at a greater rate than did population growth.

In terms of the rate of imprisonment, the total increase from 1930 through 1976 was 15.4 percent over nearly 5 decades. During this 46-year period the rate of imprisonment grew from a modest 104 inmates per 100,000 population (1930) to 120 inmates per 100,000 (1976). On average, that amounted to an annual growth rate of only 0.34 percent. Still, for this 46-year period, the growth of imprisonment exceeded the growth of the U.S. population. The margin of difference was significant, but not tremendous. And, despite prison population growth that exceeded general population growth, the rate of imprisonment increase was a modest 16 inmates per 100,000 American citizens over this time period.

The year 1973 marked the beginning of a period of expansive prison growth, regardless of how this growth is measured. During a substantial portion of this period, the rate of prison growth would far exceed population growth in the United States. Under such conditions, the probability of being incarcerated grew tremendously. One would expect, therefore, a persistent decrease in crime if prisons generate deterrent or incapacitative effects.

Why would the imprisonment rate grow more quickly than the population? One possibility is that prisons, which are typically seen as a response to crime, expanded as crime grew. In turn, crime grew exponentially as the population expanded. Another possible explanation has to do with a change in penal policies and punishment practices endorsed by policy makers. In other words, the increase in imprisonment was not simply driven by population growth alone, but was also a measure of our nation's response to crime. If this is the answer, we must also ask why policy makers chose a new penal strategy. Why did U.S. policy makers appear to suddenly decide to increase the rate of incarceration? Finally, the growth of the prison system might also indicate the possibility of some type of long-term social or economic problem outside of crime that required a more extensive application of formal social control. These three explanations constitute the primary mechanisms for explaining prison growth. All three have been used to explain various aspects of the growth of imprisonment in the United States. Each may contain some truth.

In order to explain why the U.S. prison system has grown at such a dramatic rate over the past three decades—in order to decide which of these explanations seems plausible—it is necessary to review some further details to put the rate of prison growth from the past thirty years into greater context, such as the long-term or historical pattern of prison growth. The long-term trend in prison growth provides a context against which the shorter-term growth of the past thirty years, and the 1990s in particular, can be assessed.

### Prison Growth Rates

As noted, the growth rate of the U.S. prison population was rather unremarkable over the five decades that spanned the mid-1920s through the mid-1970s. This period of time was marked by an annual average increase of less than one-half of 1 percent per annum growth in the imprisonment rate. During this period, the rate of imprisonment reached a high of 143 per 100,000 citizens following the Great Depression (1939).

For much of this period, however, the rate of imprisonment was maintained between the range of 104 to 118 inmates per 100,000 citizens. In addition, during this period, the rate of imprisonment fluctuated in both an upward and downward direction. As we shall see, this is an important characteristic of imprisonment before the mid-1970s—a characteristic that disappeared in the modern era.

In contrast to this earlier period, the rate of growth in imprisonment after the mid-1970s was substantially larger. This growth will be examined in greater detail below. For now, it is instructive to note that the annual rate of growth in the rate of imprisonment from 1972 through 2000 was nearly 15 percent per year compared to the less than 1 percent annual growth before the mid-1970s. It should also be noted that the annual average growth in the imprisonment rate before the mid-1970s was not only low, but at times it actually contracted—a tendency that is never apparent after 1973.

Growth rates can tell us a great deal about changes in the level of imprisonment, and can help identify periods during which the growth rate of the American prison system was unusually high. They can also be used to identify periods of stability and prison population decline.

GROWTH, 1925–1972. To begin, let us examine the growth in the rate of imprisonment from 1925 through 1972, focusing on three characteristics of annual imprisonment rates: growth or an increase in the imprisonment rate; contraction or a decline in the imprisonment rate; and stability or no substantial change in the rate of imprisonment. For purposes of this investigation, an increase in imprisonment is defined as a change in the imprisonment rate greater than 3 percent, while a decrease in imprisonment is defined as a contraction of more than 3 percent. When the change in the annual rate of imprisonment falls between plus or minus 3 percent, the rate of change is considered to be constant. Using these criteria, we discover that from 1925 through 1972, the annual rate of imprisonment increased twelve times, decreased nine times, and remained constant twenty-seven times. The largest increases were recorded during the 1930s, and probably reflected dramatically transformed social and economic conditions associated with the Great Depression.

The greatest decreases in imprisonment occurred during World War II. From 1940 through 1945, the rate of imprisonment declined from

131 per 100,000 to 98 per 100,000, or by slightly more than 25 percent in a short period, offsetting the imprisonment rate gains that occurred in the previous decade.

Following World War II, the imprisonment rate was relatively steady from 1949 through 1962. During this period, the imprisonment rate increased from 109 to 117 per 100,000, or by 8 per 100,000 in a 14-year time span. Looked at another way, the rate of imprisonment grew by slightly more than 7 percent in 14 years, or by approximately one-half of 1 percent per year.

Beginning in 1962, another period of contraction is seen in the rate of imprisonment. From 1962 through 1972, the rate of imprisonment fell from 117 per 100,000 to 93 per 100,000. This decline of 24 inmates per 100,000 population was slightly more than 20 percent. During this period, an important sub-trend is also visible from 1967 through 1973, when the rate of imprisonment fell below 100 per 100,000. The rate of imprisonment had only been that low in two earlier periods: from 1925 through 1929, just prior to the Great Depression, and in 1945 and 1946, during the end of World War II.

Relative to the current rate of imprisonment, which is around 500 per 100,000, the annual rates of imprisonment in the United States before 1973 appear small. By 1973, the rate of imprisonment stood at 98 per 100,000, or more than 5 times less than the rate of imprisonment in 2004. This marked the last time the rate of imprisonment in the United States would approach the level of 100 per 100,000. From this point on, the American prison system experienced substantial growth.

GROWTH, 1973–2000. As noted earlier, the U.S. prison population doubled during the forty-six years that spanned from 1930 through 1976. Due to the impact of population expansion, the increase in the rate of imprisonment was about one-half as large (approximately 52 percent). Over the next three decades (1976–2000), imprisonment would double two more times: By 1982, the number of people imprisoned was twice the number incarcerated in 1973; in 1992, the number imprisoned doubled the 1983 total. Based on current trends, it appears that the U.S. prison population total of nearly 850,000 in 1992 will again double by 2008. What is also remarkable is that the time it took the prison population to double contracted significantly. Before the 1970s, the prison population doubled once in forty years; since 1973 it doubled during the ten years from 1973 to 1983, and again during the nine years from 1983 to 1992.

This recent trend of the doubling of America's prison population is troubling. Quite clearly, the number of years it is taking for the prison population to double has shrunk. Forecasting from the trend evident from 1976 to 2003, we would expect the U.S. prison population to double about once a decade. If we take that trend as an indication of the future, then by 2035, there would be more than 16 million men and women in American prisons! That's a lot of people behind bars, and a lot of money to spend on a crime control strategy of dubious worth (Clear, 1996). It is unlikely that such a trend in the doubling of the prison population can be maintained, however, due to financial constraints, and emerging energy issues discussed in chapter 8.

Not only did the number of people imprisoned grow rapidly since 1973, so too did the rate of imprisonment. From 1976 through 2000, the rate of imprisonment grew by 315 percent (compared to the 402 percent growth in the number of people imprisoned). Compare these figures to those for 1925 through 1976 when the imprisonment rate grew by 52 percent, and the number of people in prison grew by 187 percent. To place these figures into greater context, we also need to consider the level of population growth in the United States. During the earlier period (1925–1976), population growth was 88 percent. In the latter period (1976–2000), U.S. population growth was much lower at approximately 26.5 percent.

These data on population growth clearly indicate that the expansive growth in imprisonment after 1976 is not simply a product of how rapidly the entire U.S. population grew. This observation is particularly relevant to age structure theories which state that crime and imprisonment trends can be traced to shifts in the age structure of the U.S. population. For example, some have claimed that the rise in crime and imprisonment in the 1970s and 1980s was related to a baby boom effect. That is, as baby boomers reached peak crime ages (eighteen through twenty-four), the number of people committing crime would increase, which would also swell prison populations. Moreover, one could conclude that after the population boom subsides, crime and imprisonment levels would decline. Thus, for example, the baby boom that occurred between 1947 and

1964 should affect both crime and imprisonment levels in later decades. Given that crime is most prevalent between eighteen through twenty-four, we would expect the baby boom effect to be registered on rates of imprisonment (or numbers imprisoned) by 1965 (1947 +18 = 1965), and continue through 1988 (1964 + 24) at the latest. In reality, the rate of imprisonment from 1965 through the mid-1970s was falling, as was the number of people imprisoned. In fact, the rate and number of people imprisoned fails to respond to the baby boom effect until nearly a full decade after this effect is expected, or at the tail end of the baby boom generation—which included a declining birth cohort size—reached the crime-prone years.

In addition, consider that the rate and number of people imprisoned not only lagged well behind the prediction we would generate using the baby boom population, but that the rate of imprisonment did not become lower as baby boomers aged. That is, if the baby boom affects crime and imprisonment, we would expect to see an increase in the rate of imprisonment by the mid-1960s, and a gradual decline in the rate of imprisonment after 1982, when the tail end of the baby boom genera-tion had aged beyond the crime-prone years. But, the number and rate of people imprisoned failed to decline as would be predicted from the baby boom effect. In fact, the imprisonment peak occurred too late, and, moreover, failed to decline in ways that would support a connection with the baby boom.

In sum, when looked at over the long run, the rate and number of people imprisoned in the United States can be divided into two large periods: 1925–1972, and 1973 through the present. The first period was marked by upward and downward swings in the use of incarceration. The latter period was marked by a persistent high rate of growth in imprison-ment not seen during the earlier time period.

### PRISON GROWTH: ANNUAL PERCENT CHANGES

The rather statistically unsophisticated form of trend analysis pre-sented above represents one way that changes in the rate of imprisonment in the United States can be tracked. To be sure, much more complicated methods can be used to express and assess imprisonment trends. These methods, however much they might reveal about nuances in imprison-ment trends, or specific turning points in these trends, are unnecessary for the present analysis. Simpler methods of assessing imprisonment trends can reveal much about the nature of this trend without unduly burdening the analysis with difficult statistical procedures.

For example, the changing rate of imprisonment in the United States can also be assessed simply by examining the number of times the imprisonment rate rose, fell, or remained relatively stable, as we did above, but using the entire series of data rather than each half of the data series. For the seventy-nine years from 1925 through 2003, there are seventy-eight changes in the imprisonment rate that can be derived (see table 3.2). These seventy-eight changes can be treated in several different ways.

To begin, let us calculate an annual percentage change. These percentages appear in column 2 of table 3.2. In column 3, the annual change is categorized into one of three types of change: an increase (+), a decrease (-), and no change (0). For the purposes of this classification, change is measured by any percentage increase or decrease, no matter how large or small the percent change. For example, even an annual change of as little as 0.1 is counted as an increase or decrease, depending on whether the rate of imprisonment rose or fell. Using this standard, we can then sum up the number of times each type of change is evident.

Of the 78 changes, 51 were increases (65.4 percent), 18 are counted as declining rates (23.1 percent), and a stable or unchanged rate was recorded 9 times (11.5 percent). There are a few interesting trends that emerge when the data is reclassified in this way.

First, we observe that all the years for which *declining or stable rates* of imprisonment are recorded *occurred before 1973*. Of the 48 times for which a rise in imprisonment was noted, 13 (27 percent) occurred before 1973, and 73 percent occurred after 1972. All the changes in imprisonment from 1973 through 2003 were marked by an increase in the annual rate of change in imprisonment.

Counting any level of change greater or less than zero as either a decline or increase provides some indication of changes in direction of the level of imprisonment. Technically, however, some of the changes are so small that they are insignificant from a statistical perspective. Without invoking the use of a precise statistical rule, let us reevaluate the changes in imprisonment by counting a 5 percent change in the rate of imprisonment as a meaningful change. This reclassification of annual changes in the rate of imprisonment is shown in column 4 of table 3.2.

TABLE 3.2

*Annual Percent Change, Rate of Imprisonment Per 100,000 Population, United States, 1926–2000*

| Year | % Change | Direction of Change | 5 % Direction of Change★ |
|------|----------|---------------------|--------------------------|
| 1926 | 5.0 | + | + |
| 1927 | 9.6 | + | + |
| 1928 | 5.5 | + | + |
| 1929 | 2.1 | + | 0 |
| 1930 | 6.1 | + | + |
| 1931 | 5.8 | + | + |
| 1932 | 0.0 | 0 | 0 |
| 1933 | 0.9 | – | 0 |
| 1934 | 0.0 | 0 | 0 |
| 1935 | 3.7 | + | 0 |
| 1936 | 0.0 | 0 | 0 |
| 1937 | 4.4 | + | 0 |
| 1938 | 4.2 | + | 0 |
| 1939 | 11.4 | + | + |
| 1940 | 4.4 | – | 0 |
| 1941 | 5.3 | – | – |
| 1942 | 9.7 | – | – |
| 1943 | 8.0 | – | – |
| 1944 | 0.3 | – | 0 |
| 1945 | 2.0 | – | 0 |
| 1946 | 1.0 | + | 0 |
| 1947 | 6.1 | + | + |
| 1948 | 0.9 | + | 0 |
| 1949 | 2.8 | + | 0 |
| 1950 | 0.0 | 0 | 0 |
| 1951 | 1.8 | – | 0 |
| 1952 | 0.0 | 0 | 0 |
| 1953 | 1.9 | + | 0 |

*(continued)*

TABLE 3.2 *(continued)*

| Year | % Change | Direction of Change | 5 % Direction of Change★ |
|------|----------|---------------------|--------------------------|
| 1954 | 3.7 | + | 0 |
| 1955 | 0.0 | 0 | 0 |
| 1956 | 0.9 | + | 0 |
| 1957 | 0.0 | 0 | 0 |
| 1958 | 3.5 | + | 0 |
| 1959 | 0.0 | 0 | 0 |
| 1960 | 0.0 | 0 | 0 |
| 1961 | 1.7 | − | 0 |
| 1962 | 1.6 | − | 0 |
| 1963 | 2.6 | − | 0 |
| 1964 | 2.6 | − | 0 |
| 1965 | 2.7 | − | 0 |
| 1966 | 5.6 | − | − |
| 1967 | 3.9 | − | 0 |
| 1968 | 4.1 | − | 0 |
| 1969 | 3.2 | + | 0 |
| 1970 | 1.0 | — | 0 |
| 1971 | 1.0 | − | 0 |
| 1972 | 2.1 | − | 0 |
| 1973 | 3.1 | + | 0 |
| 1974 | 6.3 | + | + |
| 1975 | 8.8 | + | + |
| 1976 | 8.1 | + | + |
| 1977 | 5.0 | + | + |
| 1978 | 4.8 | + | 0 |
| 1979 | 0.8 | + | 0 |
| 1980 | 4.5 | + | 0 |
| 1981 | 10.8 | + | + |
| 1982 | 11.0 | + | + |
| 1983 | 4.4 | + | 0 |

*(continued)*

TABLE 3.2 *(continued)*

| Year | % Change | Direction of Change | 5 % Direction of Change* |
|------|----------|---------------------|--------------------------|
| 1984 | 5.0 | + | + |
| 1985 | 7.4 | + | + |
| 1986 | 7.4 | + | + |
| 1987 | 6.5 | + | + |
| 1988 | 6.9 | + | + |
| 1989 | 11.7 | + | + |
| 1990 | 7.6 | + | + |
| 1991 | 5.4 | + | + |
| 1992 | 6.1 | + | + |
| 1993 | 8.1 | + | + |
| 1994 | 8.4 | + | + |
| 1995 | 5.7 | + | + |
| 1996 | 3.7 | + | 0 |
| 1997 | 4.0 | + | 0 |
| 1998 | 3.8 | + | 0 |
| 1999 | 2.6 | + | 0 |
| 2000 | 0.4 | + | 0 |
| 2001 | 0.2 | + | 0 |
| 2002 | 1.3 | + | 0 |
| 2003 | 1.3 | + | 0 |

After reclassification using the 5 percent rule, 25 of the changes are now counted as increases in the rate of imprisonment (32.1 percent), 4 of the changes are treated as decreases in imprisonment (5.1 percent), and 49 changes are treated as stability in the rate of imprisonment (62.8 percent). After reclassification, some of the trends noted in the data have not substantially changed. Here, for example, 18 (72 percent) of the positive changes in the rate of imprisonment occurred after 1972. Without the 5 percent rule, 73 percent of the positive changes in the rate of imprisonment occurred after 1972. Thus, using the 5 percent rule doesn't alter the original conclusion (it does, however, alter the count). However, several substantive differences between these two methods of determining change are evident.

First, for the period after 1972, 13 of the changes previously included as positive changes in the rate of imprisonment are now counted as stability because they involve less than a 5 percent change in the annual rate of imprisonment. Second, 10 of the positive changes in imprisonment before 1973 are now counted as stability for the same reason. Finally, 14 of the negative changes in imprisonment noted before 1972 are now counted as evidence of stability.

When we reassess this trend transformation, we again see that all the periods of negative growth in imprisonment occurred before the 1970s. The number of negative changes and positive changes diminishes, and the number of relatively stable rates of imprisonment, which were defined as between plus and minus 5 percent, increases. But, this method also has limitations. While it more accurately classifies individual changes in imprisonment from year to year (e.g., it eliminates counting very small changes as indicating a change in direction of the imprisonment rate), it provides a poor description of the trend in imprisonment across blocks of time. For example, when we use a 5 percent cutoff, we classify the change that occurred between each individual year from 1932 through 1938 (e.g., the change from 1932 to 1933; or from 1933 to 1934) as a year of no significant change in trend. However, over the entire span of these years (e.g., the change from 1932 to 1938), the rate of imprisonment rose from 110 per 100,000 to 123 per 100,000, or by 11.8 percent. Thus, while the yearly changes in the rate of imprisonment are insignificant when examined on an annual basis, the changes across a period of time as short as five years where annual change is stagnant can produce substantial changes in imprisonment. The annual assessment method, in other words, leads to an error when we try to assess the broader trend in imprisonment; and we cannot generalize the annual changes that were significant or insignificant into a larger conclusion about the change in imprisonment trends across a series of years. That is, when we aggregate the significant or insignificant annual changes, or when we look across a series of years rather than across each year, the annual trends of stability, contraction, and expansion in the rate of imprisonment are masked. They are there, but hidden by the form of analysis. But the reverse is also true: longer-term trends are masked by directing attention only to annual changes. This masking, for example, explains why it is possible to have annual changes that can be classified as no change, but have a long-term trend that depicts prison growth, as was evident from 1932 through 1938.

This raises a related issue that is important to the goal of this analysis. Should long-term or short-term trends be used to determine whether or not the rate of imprisonment affects the rate of criminal offending? For example, consider the data for the years 1996 through 1999 found in tables 3.1 and 3.2. During this period, the annual change in imprisonment was positive each year, yet the change was never greater than 5 percent, meaning that the year-to-year change in imprisonment was insignificant. Across the entire period, however, the increase in the rate of imprisonment was nearly 15 percent. The trend in crime for this period (measured as crimes known to police) almost mirrors the change in the imprisonment rate—about 15 percent fewer crimes are reported to police during this period where the rate of imprisonment rose 15 percent. Yet the annual changes for neither the crime rate nor the imprisonment rate are statistically significantly different from year to year. Thus, even though the crime rate was going down and the imprisonment rate was going up in the long run, it is unlikely that one trend has much to do with the other for two reasons. First, the annual changes are so small that they might represent random variation. This is especially true for the crime rate rather than the imprisonment rate, since the imprisonment rate can be seen as the result of a planned or socially engineered set of strategies, whereas the crime rate may not result from the same kinds of social forces. Second, for this period, the rise in imprisonment is almost exactly equal to the percentage decline in crime. This exact correspondence between these trends is unlikely, and, indeed, could not be justified by examining crime and imprisonment trends found at other points in history. As other evidence will detail, such a close correspondence between changes in imprisonment and crime rates is not typically observed, and should, therefore, be suspect, especially if these short-term data are being used to provide evidence favoring or disproving something about the relationship between crime and punishment.

Table 3.3 collapses the trends shown in column 3 of table 3.2 (+/- 5 percent change in the annual rate of imprisonment). This table lumps together consecutive years in which the annual changes were either stagnant

TABLE 3.3

Grouped Trends Using 5 Percent Change to
Indicate Growth (+), Stability (0), or Contraction (-)
in the Rate of Imprisonment

| Year(s) | Direction of Change | Number of Years |
|---|---|---|
| 1926–1931 | + | 6 |
| 1932–1938 | 0 | 7 |
| 1939 | + | 1 |
| 1940 | 0 | 1 |
| 1941–1943 | - | 3 |
| 1944–1946 | 0 | 3 |
| 1947 | + | 1 |
| 1948–1965 | 0 | 18 |
| 1966 | - | 1 |
| 1967–1971 | 0 | 7 |
| 1974–1977 | + | 4 |
| 1978–1980 | 0 | 3 |
| 1981–1982 | + | 2 |
| 19830 | 1 | |
| 1984–1995 | + | 12 |
| 1996–2003 | 0 | 8 |

(less than 5 percent annual change), negative (more than 5 percent reduction in imprisonment), or positive (more than 5 percent growth in imprisonment), and better illustrates the trend in oscillations in imprisonment. Examining table 3.3 we can isolate 15 groupings. The first group consists of the 7 years (1926–1933) during which the annual change in imprisonment across each year was 5 percent or greater; the second consists of the 7 years (1932–1938) during which the annual change in the rate of imprisonment was between + 4.95 and -4.95 percent; the third group consists only of the year 1939, when imprisonment rose by more than 5 percent; and so on.

One of the more interesting points table 3.3 draws our attention to is the grouping that occurs toward the end of this time span—the fifteenth grouping, which covers the years 1996 through 2003. Even though the rate of imprisonment rose consistently over this time period (from 427 per 100,000 in 1996 to 482 per 100,000 by 2003), the annual change across each year was less than 5 percent. Taken together, the change in the imprisonment rate across the entire 8-year period was 12.9 percent. Since 1973, these years (1996–2003) accounted for the smallest increases in the rate of incarceration. At the same time, the crime rate declined over this period, and the decline was quite significant—for example, crimes known to the police declined by 27.5 percent. So, it appeared, at least on the surface, that rising rates of imprisonment were related to a decline in crime. The problem with reaching such a conclusion, as shall be shown later, is that these short-term trends are not indicative of the longer-term relationship between incarceration and crime, and may present an aberration from the norm.

## PRISON GROWTH AND CRIME

As Jenni Gainsborough and Marc Mauer point out in their study "Diminishing Returns" (2000), by the late 1990s, leading policy analysts in the United States, among them Charles Murray, James Q. Wilson, and John DiIulio, were telling policy makers and the American public that the reason crime had gone down in the 1990s was the significant rise in imprisonment. What policy pundits like DiIulio, Wilson, and Murray left out of the story was that in 1991 the United States experienced its highest crime rate since 1980. The 1991 crime rate for offenses known to police was 5,898 per 100,000; the rate in 1980 was 5,950 per 100,000. Also omitted from this discussion was the fact that the decline in crime in the 1990s only took place following a decade and a half of rising imprisonment rates. What needs to be kept in mind is that the decline in crime experienced in the 1990s occurred after the rate of incarceration had risen each and every year since 1973 and crime had reached its highest point in a decade. In fact, from 1973 through 1991, the rate of imprisonment had risen by 226 percent, a significant increase especially when we consider that crime was on the rise throughout much of this period. If an increase in imprisonment was responsible for lowering crime, how did it happen that a nineteen-year period during which imprisonment rose persistently (1973–1991) could yield nearly *the highest level of crime seen during his period?* Moreover, given that crime had hit what might be a "natural" peak, it was likely to decline without modifying the response to crime significantly.

In the shorter term, the imprisonment rate had increased 125 percent between 1980 and 1991.Yet, over the same period, the rate of crimes known to police had declined by only 0.9 percent.The decline in crime over this period was statistically insignificant even though imprisonment rose substantially. Further, between 1991 and 1995, the period imprisonment proponents had focused their attention on, the rate of imprisonment rose 31.3 percent, while the rate of crimes known to police had declined by 10.6 percent. But it should be noted that the relationship between crime and imprisonment seen during this period was highly unusual, and no social scientist or policy analyst who understood the appropriate use of statistical modeling would focus on this one, short period in an effort to determine the effect of imprisonment on crime, or to determine policy for the entire United States.

As an example, consider how the following simple comparison might alter the conclusions we would reach about the relationship between crime and imprisonment in the United States. Let us begin with the 1991–1995 period, where imprisonment rose by less than 8 percent on average annually (7.75 percent). During this period, crime certainly fell. But the question is whether this trend is persistent enough—whether it can be found during other periods of time—to become the basis of crime policy.To make such a comparison, let us also consider the trends from the previous ten years, 1981–1991. During this period the annual average growth in imprisonment was 11.3 percent, higher than in the 1991–1995 period.Why, then, did crime decline more during the 1991–1995 period? Under what conditions could a larger annual growth rate in the imprisonment rate lead to a much smaller decline in crime? And don't these conflicting outcomes present the policy maker and social scientist with the kind of information that should lead them, at a minimum, to be skeptical about employing imprisonment to control crime?

Not only did the pro-prison policy proponents fail to explain how a 226 percent rise in imprisonment—both in the long run (since 1973) or in the shorter run (since 1980)—failed to stifle crime if imprisonment was a deterrent or a reasonable source of incapacitation. They also left out from their discussions of the crime reduction trend seen after 1991 the impact of improved economic conditions, the decline in racial salary inequality that had taken place under the Clinton administration, and the fact that crime tends to cycle, and that 1991 might perhaps mark some kind of upper boundary in crime,

Nevertheless, by the late 1990s, crime was down, and conservatives were giving credit to our big prison system (as well as to other crime policies, such as community policing and zero tolerance). Prison proponents made this claim often, and in very public forums, even though they did not have sufficient evidence that expanding imprisonment worked, or that other factors—especially factors they had failed to examine— might also have influenced crime rates.

For these reasons, the trends in crime and imprisonment in the period after 1992 become of great importance. During this period, the crime rate continued to shrink while the expansion of the prison system slowed. Why should this happen?

In fact, by 1992, the dramatic rise in imprisonment rates in the United States *had finally begun to slow* and, in some states, even reverse itself. At the same time that the imprisonment rate leveled off, and the annual rate of change in imprisonment was consistently *less than 5 percent,* for the first time in decades crime went down consistently from one year to the next, and not just once or twice. Beginning in the 1990s, crime went down eleven straight years, perhaps for the first time ever in U.S history, and at least since reliable crime data has been available. But could this result be attributed to a rising rate of incarceration?

To compound matters, the overall decline in crime across this latter period (1991–2002) was, as noted earlier, fairly large: a 30.2 percent overall decline in crimes known to police. What no one seemed to notice was that crime was going down the most when the rate of imprisonment started to level off, not when the imprisonment rate was rising the most from year to year.

During the early 1980s, the prison system grew very quickly, and was filled just as quickly. Crime, however, did not fall consistently, and in fact fluctuated on its way to the highest level of crime in modern American history. In 1973, the rate of crimes known to police was 4,154 per 100,000; in 1980, 5,950 per 100,000; in 1984, 5,038 per 100,000; and in 1991, 5,898 per 100,000. Crime oscillated while imprisonment rose substantially, from 96 per 100,000 in 1973, to 139 per 100,000 in 1980, to 188 per 100,000 in 1984, to 313 per 100,000 in 1991.

By the 1990s, prison growth was more controlled; annual changes in the rate of imprisonment were much lower than in the 1970s and 1980s. And suddenly, while the rate of imprisonment growth started to slow, while the growth of imprisonment was brought under control, crime went down. Could this just be a lagged effect? Was twenty years of prison expansion finally beginning to make a difference in the rate of crime? This explanation would be plausible only if the imprisonment rate had to cross some unknown ("magical"?) threshold before it became an effective crime control strategy. But, even if this were true, how could the trend in the United States be reconciled with the lower rates of crime and imprisonment found elsewhere in the world? And, with the lower rates of crime and punishment that coexisted earlier in the century even within America? Or with the fact that states with the highest levels of incarceration had the highest levels of crime? Or with the reverse observation that states with lower rates of incarceration had lower rates of crime? Extended discussion of these data are reserved for a later chapter.

Further, consider that the decline in crime that occurred since 1991 was much larger than the increase in the imprisonment rate. Crime shrunk by 30 percent while prisons grew by a more modest 17 percent. There was probably no other period in American history where such a large decrease in crime could be attributed to a much smaller increase in incarceration.

Given these trends in crime and punishment, the claim that a rising rate of imprisonment lowered the rate of crime doesn't appear to make much sense. Yet, by the late 1990s, policy consultants were assuring us this was indeed the case. Not only did they pronounce that imprisonment suddenly seemed to reduce crime, it worked better than ever before. Indeed, if one ignored the dramatic 7.6 percent drop in crime that occurred between 1982 and 1983, the crime decline of the 1990s was unmatched at any time over the prior 44 years. Interestingly, the decline in crime between 1982 and 1983 was preceded by 2 successive years in which the rate of imprisonment had increased by more than 11 percent *each year.* It should also be noted, however, that this crime decline also closely followed a peak in crime. But by the end of the 1990s, the conservatives were claiming that crime was being reduced by minimal prison growth. Furthermore, it seemed that each annual reduction in crime during the mid-1990s became evidence that conservative approaches to crime control worked, and no one questioned how anyone had arrived at this conclusion. No one, for example, seemed worried that a notable crime suppression effect could not be seen prior to this time, even though the rate of imprisonment had expanded continually. To be sure, as long as no one looked at the historical record, or noticed that low rates of crime earlier this century were accompanied by low rates of imprisonment, or noted that economic trends had been reversed in the 1990s, conservative "wisdom" on this issue could not be challenged.

Challenges to the conservatives' conclusions do, however, exist. Gainsborough and Mauer (2000) questioned the conclusion of conservatives and prison expansion proponents, and pointed out that "during the national decline in crime from 1991 to 1998, states with the *largest* increases in incarceration experienced, on average, *smaller* declines in crime than other states. The 'above average' states increased their rate of incarceration by an average of 72 % and experienced a 13 % decline in crime, while the rate of incarceration in 'below average' states rose by 30 % and crime rates declined by 17 %" (4). In other words, crime declined more in states where the imprisonment rate rose at a reduced rate. As a result, it is difficult to conclude that the rise in the incarceration rate alone was sufficient to reduce crime. As examples, Gainsborough and Mauer offer evidence on crime and incarceration rates from four states: Texas, New York, California, and Massachusetts. Of these states, Texas had the largest increase in imprisonment, 144 percent. Yet the level by which crime was reduced in Texas was similar to the reductions in crime experienced in New York, California, and Massachusetts, where the increase in imprisonment was substantially lower, ranging between 21 and 24 percent in Massachusetts and New York, to 52 percent in California.

Overall, "states that increased the use of incarceration the most in the period 1984–1991 experienced slightly less of a rise in crime than other states, 15 percent compared to 17 percent" (4). This 2 percent difference, which is inconsequential from a statistical perspective and could be due to random measurement error, had a substantial financial cost: "The estimated cost for additional prison construction and housing for this 2 percent gain was $9.5 billion" (4).

It is possible to draw more extreme cross-state comparisons than the ones offered by Gainsborough and Mauer using their data (table 1 in Gainsborough and Mauer; reproduced as table 3.4 here). For example, the rate of crime in West Virginia and North Dakota declined by 4 percent while the rate of imprisonment rose 131 and 88 percent respectively. Large increases in imprisonment and small declines in crime were also evident in Louisiana, Pennsylvania, Tennessee, Utah, Washington, South Carolina, Delaware, and Oregon. In contrast, substantial increases in incarceration rates in Nebraska (48 percent), Mississippi (74 percent), and New Mexico (42 percent) were associated with an *increased rate of crime*. And, Maine experienced a 19 percent decline in crime while its incarceration rate increased by only 2 percent.

Thus, examining these data further, we see that for 14 of the 50 states, or in more than 25 percent of cases, the general conclusion that large increases in imprisonment lead to substantial reductions in crime was not evident. Further, these 14 cases do not include the 9 states where the increase in incarceration was below the national average (that is, where the average rise in incarceration was less than 47 percent), and where the reduction in crime was substantially higher than average (i.e., there was a 20 percent or more decline in crime). Taken together, these 23 cases, or nearly half of all states, failed to confirm the claim that high rates of incarceration reduce crime. In fact, if we examine table 3.4 closely, we can see a trend which indicates that big increases in the rate of incarceration do not necessarily produce the biggest changes in crime. To do so, let us add two rows of data to Gainsborough and Mauer's table.

Instead of comparing state by state, since these comparisons can be challenged as biased by our selection of individual states, let us instead compare the average changes in the crime rates for the 21 jurisdictions (20 states plus the District of Columbia) that had average or above-average increases in the rate of incarceration (jurisdictions that had a 47 percent or greater increase in the incarceration rate) to the crime rates for the 30 states that had less-than-average increases in imprisonment. For the top 21 jurisdictions, the average increase in the imprisonment rate was 72 percent; for the bottom 30 states the average increase in imprisonment was approximately 30 percent. Logically, if prisons deter or incapacitate, we would expect to see the biggest state-level crime effects for the 21 jurisdictions with the largest increases in imprisonment. But, for the 21 jurisdictions with the largest increases in imprisonment, the average decrease in total crime was 12 percent, compared to the average

TABLE 3.4

*Changes in Incarceration and Crime Rates by State, 1991–1998, adapted from Gainsborough and Mauer (2000), Showing Percent Change in (1) Imprisonment, (2) Total UCR Crime Rate, (3) UCR Violent Crime Rate, and (4) UCR Property Crime Rate.*

|  | (1) | (2) | (3) | (4) |  |
|---|---|---|---|---|---|
| Texas | 144 | -35 | -33 | -35 |  |
| West Virginia | 131 | -4 | 30 | -7 | 21 Jurisdiction with above average increases in the incarceration rate |
| Wisconsin | 113 | -21 | -10 | -21 |  |
| Hawaii | 101 | -11 | 2 | -11 |  |
| North Dakota | 88 | -4 | 37 | -5 |  |
| Iowa | 79 | -15 | 3 | -17 |  |
| Mississippi | 74 | 4 | 6 | 4 |  |
| South Dakota | 72 | -15 | -15 | -15 |  |
| Montana | 69 | 12 | -1 | 12 |  |
| Idaho | 61 | -11 | -3 | -12 |  |
| Louisiana | 59 | -5 | -18 | -3 |  |
| Pennsylvania | 58 | -8 | -7 | -8 |  |
| Dist.of Col. | 57 | -18 | -30 | -14 |  |
| California | 52 | -36 | -35 | -36 |  |
| Vermont | 52 | -21 | -9 | -21 |  |
| Minnesota | 50 | -10 | -2 | -10 |  |
| Connecticut | 50 | -29 | -32 | -29 |  |
| Missouri | 50 | -11 | -27 | -8 |  |
| Oklahoma | 50 | -12 | -8 | -12 |  |
| Nebraska | 48 | 1 | 35 | -2 |  |
| Georgia | 47 | -16 | -22 | -15 |  |
| Kentucky | 45 | -14 | -35 | -11 |  |
| Illinois | 45 | -21 | -22 | -20 |  |
| Colorado | 43 | -26 | -32 | -25 |  |
| Tennessee | 43 | -6 | -2 | -7 | 30 States with below average increases in the rate of incarceration. |
| Indiana | 42 | -13 | -15 | -13 |  |
| New Mexico | 42 | 1 | 15 | -1 |  |
| Wyoming | 38 | -13 | -20 | -13 |  |

*(continued)*

TABLE 3.4 *(continued)*

|                | (1) | (2)  | (3)   | (4)  |
| -------------- | --- | ---- | ----- | ---- |
| New Hampshire  | 38  | -30  | -10   | -31  |
| Utah           | 38  | -2   | 10    | -2   |
| Washington     | 36  | -7   | -18   | -6   |
| Kansas         | 34  | -12  | -21   | -11  |
| Ohio           | 33  | -14  | -35   | -11  |
| North Carolina | 33  | -10  | -12   | -9   |
| Alabama        | 32  | -14  | -39   | -10  |
| Arkansas       | 31  | -17  | -17   | -17  |
| Florida        | 30  | -19  | -21   | -19  |
| Virginia       | 28  | -21  | -13   | -21  |
| Arizona        | 28  | -11  | -14   | -11  |
| Rhode Island   | 27  | -30  | -32   | -30  |
| New Jersey     | 25  | -33  | -31   | -33  |
| Delaware       | 24  | -9   | 7     | -11  |
| New York       | 24  | -43  | -45   | -42  |
| Nevada         | 23  | -16  | -5    | -18  |
| Massachusetts  | 21  | -35  | -16   | -39  |
| Michigan       | 20  | -24  | -23   | -24  |
| Alaska         | 20  | -16  | 7     | -19  |
| South Carolina | 16  | -7   | -7    | -6   |
| Maryland       | 14  | -14  | -17   | -13  |
| Oregon         | 14  | -2   | -17   | 0    |
| Maine          | 2   | -19  | -5    | -20  |
| AVERAGE        | 47  | -15  | -12   | -15  |
| Top 21         | 72  | -12  | -6.6  | -13  |
| Bottom 30      | 30  | -17  | -16.5 | -16  |

crime reduction of 17 percent in states with below-average increases in incarceration. In fact, what we notice is that the top 21 jurisdictions have, on average, experienced nearly 2.5 times the average increase in imprisonment when compared to the bottom 30 states, yet crime was suppressed more in the states with lower-average increases in imprisonment.

This trend is also evident when violent and property crimes are examined separately. Most interesting is the fact that imprisonment, which theoretically should protect society from the most dangerous criminals, appears to have less of an effect on violent crime than property crime rates for the 21 jurisdictions. This conclusion also holds when we compare the violent and property crime rates in the 21 high-imprisonment states to states with lower-average increases in imprisonment separately.

These data lead to the conclusions that: (1) the relationship between incarceration and crime is not clear, nor direct; (2) it is impossible to predict the extent to which crime will change knowing the change in incarceration; (3) the change in the level of imprisonment and crime is not proportional; (4) substantial crime declines are associated with smaller-than-average increases in the level of incarceration. From a policy perspective, these conclusions lead to a broader, more general conclusion, namely that the substantial investment required to increase the rate of incarceration is not guaranteed to reduce crime.

What should be made clear at this point is that these conclusions were not the story being told by conservative supporters of prison expansion. Indeed, rather than reflecting what was known about the relationship between imprisonment and crime that could be extracted from data from the two prior decades, or from data across states in the 1990s, conservative policy makers latched onto short term aberrations to present a rosy picture of imprisonment's crime suppression potential.

### Prison Growth: The Imprisonment Index

Another means of describing the growth and relative size of the prison system is to create a measure I call the imprisonment index (see the last column in table 3.1). Indexes are used in many different disciplines to provide an idea of how much something has changed over time by anchoring the measure of change to a specific level of the trend being studied, or to a specific year in the trend. A widely known example is the Consumer Price Index. The same idea can be used to construct an imprisonment index.

The imprisonment index was derived by dividing the imprisonment rate in any given year by the imprisonment rate in 1973, and multiplying the result by 100. Thus, for instance, the index of imprisonment in 1973 would be 96 / 96 $\star$ 100 = 100. This calculation standardizes the imprisonment rate by its level in 1973, and allows the imprisonment rate in all other years to be compared against the 1973 rate. For example, if the imprisonment index in another year was greater than 100, then we know that imprisonment in that year was higher than in 1973. An imprisonment index of 200 indicates that the level of imprisonment was twice as high as in 1973; an index of 300, three times as high as in 1973; and so on.

The imprisonment rate in the year 1973 was selected as the standardization marker because it marks the year when the prison system in the United States began it precipitous expansion. In effect, this standardization allows the level of imprisonment in each year to be interpreted as a percentage of the rate of imprisonment in 1973. For the sake of simplicity, this index is rounded to the nearest whole number.

The imprisonment index also provides another mechanism for assessing trends in imprisonment in the United States, but this time, relative to 1973. For the seventy-nine years represented in table 3.1, imprisonment was below the 1973 level of imprisonment only six times, at the 1973 level three times, and above the 1973 level seventy times. The highest imprisonment index before 1973 occurred in 1939 (the index measure for 1939 is 143) in the aftermath of the Great Depression, and was not surpassed until 1980, following the economic recession that characterized much of the 1970s, indicating a possible connection between incarceration and economic conditions (see chapter 5 for further discussion).

Using the imprisonment index to gauge the growth of imprisonment and restricting our view to years after 1973 reveals that the only times in which this index doubles is from 1973 through 1985, and again from 1985 through 1995. When we examine the entire series, we see that the imprisonment index doubled from 1925 through 1982, a fifty-seven-year period. Looking ahead from 1982, we see the next doubling point in 1993, just eleven years later. This compression in the doubling of the imprisonment index confirms the earlier analyses that indicated the existence of elevated rates of doubling in the use of imprisonment since 1973—the portion of the data that corresponds with America's imprisonment binge. The rate of doubling indicated by this index also demonstrates that most of the growth in the U.S. prison system occurred since 1980.

Finally, this index can be employed to consider the imprisonment differences between 1925 and 1973, and 1973 and 2003. The 2003 imprisonment index of 502 indicates that the use of imprisonment had increased by a factor of 5 over the 1973 level. The 1925 index level indicates that the use of imprisonment that year was 82 percent of the level of imprisonment in 1973. Thus, the 1925 and 1973 levels of incarceration were not extraordinarily different, while the difference between the 1973 and 2002 imprisonment index was substantial.

There are a number of other questions that can be addressed using this index. Specifically, is there a relationship between the imprisonment index and the level of crime? Let us, for the moment, focus on the period since 1960, and examine the relationship between the imprisonment index and an index of crimes known to police.

An index of crimes known to police can be created in the same way we created an imprisonment index. The rate of crimes known to police per 100,000 population in 1973 is the denominator, and the rate of crime known to police in any given year is the numerator. Thus, the crimes known to police index will, like the imprisonment index, be set to 100 in 1973. Table 3.5 shows these data for a select sample of years since 1960.

Consistent with earlier findings, table 3.5 demonstrates that the magnitude of change in the imprisonment rate (measured relative to the 1973 index) has no obvious suppression effect on the level of crime (relative to the 1973 crimes known to police index). In fact, this table illustrates a point that is in contention when debating whether the level of imprisonment affects crime. Ironically, the level of imprisonment *before* 1973, when the rate of incarceration started its annual rise, appears to indicate a crime suppression effect. That is, "higher" rates of punishment prior to 1973 (in this case, 1960 and 1965) are related to lower rates of offending. This effect disappears for the period after 1973, and only reemerges in 2000 (or perhaps somewhere in between 1995 and 2000, since effects for individual years are not measured in is table). This table, then, raises the possibility that crime either has a "natural cycle," or that the cycling of crime is related to some factor(s) other than the use of incarceration.

The other trend that is evident in this table is that the change in imprisonment must be relatively large to demonstrate a crime reduction effect across a relatively short time period (e.g., the difference between 1980 and 1985, which is 45 percent; the difference between 1990 and 1995, which is 39 percent; or the difference between 1995 and 2000, which is 15 percent). Yet, this table also illustrates that increases in punishment do

TABLE 3.5

*Comparison, Imprisonment Index and Crime Known to Police Index,*
*Select Years, 1960–2000 (rounded to nearest whole number).*

| Year | Imprisonment Index (100=1973) | Crime Index | Change[1] (Imp/Crime) | Change, 1973 (Imp/Crim)[2] |
|------|------|------|------|------|
| 1960 | 122 | 46 | — / — | 22 / -54 |
| 1965 | 113 | 59 | -7 / 28 | 13 / -41 |
| 1970 | 100 | 96 | -12 / 63 | 0 / -4 |
| 1973 | 100 | 100 | 0 / 4 | — / — |
| 1977 | 131 | 122 | 31 / 22 | 31 / 22 |
| 1980 | 145 | 143 | 11 / 17 | 45 / 43 |
| 1985 | 210 | 126 | 45 / -12 | 110 / 26 |
| 1990 | 309 | 140 | 47 / 11 | 209 / 40 |
| 1995 | 428 | 127 | 39 / -9 | 328 / 27 |
| 2000 | 490 | 99 | 15 / -22 | 390 / -1 |

1. Percent change in index measured from the previous year listed in table (e.g., 1970 compared to 1965).

2. Percent change in index compared to 1973.

not necessarily lead to a reduction in crime. Consider for example that: (1) a 31 percent increase in the imprisonment index from 1973 to 1977 is associated with a 22 percent rise in the crimes known index; (2) an 11 percent rise in the imprisonment index from 1977 to 1980 is associated with a 17 percent rise in the crimes known index; (3) a 2 percent increase in the imprisonment index from 1985 to 1990 is associated with an 11 percent increase in the crimes known index. Thus, these data suggest that there is no clear and simple relationship between the level of incarceration and the level of crime.

Overall, the change in the imprisonment *index* between 1973 and 2000 was 390 percent, while the crimes known to police index shrunk by only 1 percent compared to 1973. Again, this trend indicates that the change in crime operates independently of imprisonment, and is not as clear-cut as imprisonment proponents pretend. Indeed, these data also suggest that the relationship between crime reduction and the expansion of imprisonment is extremely disproportionate. For the entire time period, a 390 percent increase in imprisonment yielded only a 1 percent reduction in crime. If this period average indicates the proportional relationship between crime reduction and prison expansion, a significant reduction in crime, say by 50 percent, would require an extraordinarily large increase in the use of imprisonment (if we assume that the relationship is linear, and can be represented by the ratio of 1:390, then we would multiply 390 by 50 to discover the needed percentage increase in imprisonment). Of course, it seems highly likely that this mathematical extension probably overstates the extent to which imprisonment must expand to reduce crime by 50 percent, because, at some point, prison expansion of such magnitude is bound to suppress crime simply because a large portion of the U.S. population would be locked away. Nevertheless, what these data indicate is that the actual relationship between the growth and contraction in imprisonment and crime rates since 1973 is unclear. The relationship that is discovered does not favor the view held by those who support deterrence or incapacitation.

## Crime and Punishment in New York City: A Case Study

More so than any other U.S. city, New York experienced a precipitous decline in crime during the 1990s, especially violent crime. Michael Jacobson, the former New York City commissioner of corrections and probation, who discussed this crime drop in his recent book *Downsizing Prisons: How to Reduce Crime and End Mass Incarceration* (2005), noted that "perhaps no other city in the world has received the kind of attention showered over the last decade on New York City after its recent and highly publicized reduction in crime" (106). As Jacobson pointed out, between 1993 and 2003, New York City's crime rate declined by 64 percent, which amounts to a very substantial crime reduction. Furthermore, the extent of this decline was so great that it alone accounted for approximately *one-sixth of the crime reduction experienced for the entire United States during this time period.*

According to Jacobson, the effort to explain New York City's dramatic decrease in crime "became a virtual cottage industry in New York criminal justice and criminological circles" (107). As Jacobson notes, much of the credit for this decline was given to Major Giuliani and his new police commissioner William Bratton. Bratton instituted a zero-tolerance policy that centered on suppressing minor crimes and felonies by expanding arrests, searches, and the execution of warrants. A statistical program was also used to identify crime hot spots so that these areas could be targeted for enhanced policing. Bratton was of the opinion that increased police action taken against low-level offenders would sweep up a larger proportion of serious future felons, and also send a message to those contemplating crimes that New York City would not tolerate criminal behavior.

As Jacobson points out, those who supported this view argued that expanded police activity increased arrests, and thus would also generate more punishment. Therefore, as the number of arrests for targeted offenses increased, so too should indictments, convictions, and prison and jail sentences. Jacobson, however, suggests that this traditional view of New York City's crime drop has a number of serious flaws.

To begin, the crime rate in New York began to decline *before* Giuliani and his new police commissioner could affect a change in New York City's crime policies. Indeed, statistics indicate that New York City's crime rate began its decline in the last two years of Mayor Dinkins's term in office. To be sure, that trend continued under Giuliani, but, because this trend was already underway, it cannot be solely attributed to new, Giuliani-era crime policies.

Furthermore, during the rapid crime decline in New York City, New York State's prison population grew at a much slower rate than would be expected given increased police activity in New York City. In fact, the state's prison population grew by only 5 percent, or at a rate that was well below those found in other states during this time period. Jacobson argued that the significance of New York State's prison growth has to do with a related fact—that approximately two-thirds of New York State prison inmates are derived from New York City. In addition, while New York State's prison population grew during this time period, it was not due to the influence of an increase in offenders sentenced to prison who came from New York City courts. In fact, from 1993 through 2001, the number of inmates New York City courts sent to New York State prisons declined by 42 percent. Thus, Jacobson argues, New York City's crime decline could not be attributed to a rising rate of incarceration among offenders from New York City.

It was possible, however, that because New York City's crime policy targeted minor offenses, that those offenders were receiving lesser punishments, such as terms in New York City's jail system. But New York City's jail population declined by 25 percent from 1993 through 2001. Thus, not only could the decline in crime not be explained by an increase in punishment, but trends for incarceration among New York City offenders defied the national trend. Nationally, prison and jail populations were expanding, with prison populations up 45 percent, and jail population growth near 39 percent for the time period under study. This lead Jacobson to conclude that New York City's crime reduction could not have been caused by incarcerating a larger number of offenders.

Finally, consider that during this period, felon indictments as a percentage of arrests made in New York City were also slipping. This ratio declined even though the number of felon arrests dropped. In 1993, 39 percent of felony arrests led to an indictment. By 2001, this percentage had decreased to 25 percent. Overall, fewer arrests were leading to indictment, and fewer offenders were being sent to jail or prison.

Jacobson's analysis of New York City's crime drop illustrates that crime reductions occur without resorting to an escalation in the use of incarceration. Indeed, New York City's crime rate declined alongside a modest increase in New York State's use of imprisonment—though the increase could not be attributed to the fact that New York City sent more offenders to prison—and a reduction in the size of New York City's jail population. When added to other evidence presented by Jacobson throughout his book, it should be evident that the relationship between a reduction in crime and the use of incarceration supported by deterrence and incapacitation arguments did not materialize in New York City. Furthermore, as we have seen from evidence provided earlier, crime sometimes expands along with the rate of incarceration, both at the national and state levels. Likewise, from cross-sectional data, it is also apparent that crime sometimes falls when the incarceration rates contracts. These distinct empirical results provide the kinds of evidence scientists employ when they reject theoretical proposition as untenable.

Indeed, in support of the conclusion that crime and imprisonment are unconnected, consider Robert Agnew's (2005: 189) summary on this point: the majority of evidence points to the conclusion that "punishment does not reduce offending and may sometimes increase it."

## CONCLUSION

Taken together, the various observations made above on imprisonment rate changes and prison growth helps us to sort out the prison expansion patterns, classify and corroborate the existence of growth patterns, and understand the shape and direction of prison growth (and contraction) patterns in the United States from 1925 through the present. These observations do not, however, explain prison growth rate patterns, they only help us identify periods that require explanation, and narrow down the types of explanations that may fit these data trends. Why, for example, have prisons grown so rapidly in recent years? What now needs to be addressed are some potential reasons for this dramatic rate of growth.

## CHAPTER 4

# Raising Questions About America's Big Prison System

IN THE PREVIOUS CHAPTER, the growth and size of the American prison system was examined in detail. That examination brought numerous facts to light, but it did not attempt to explain any of these facts in any detail. In this chapter, several questions are raised about America's prison system with the intention of exploring what lies behind American's big prison model.

## WHY DID PRISONS GROW SO FAST?

There are numerous reasons that can be forwarded to explain the rapid rate of prison growth in contemporary America. For any of these explanations to be viable, they must not only explain the pattern in imprisonment, but must also explain why policy makers and politicians have helped to carry out a plan of action that continually increased the size of America's prison system.

To be sure, policy makers' obsession with incapacitation and deterrent approaches—the idea that locking up offenders prevents them from committing crimes while incarcerated, or deters others from committing crime by example, is the most apparent explanation. Most assuredly, as Sutton (2004) noted, prisons could not expand unless their expansion was supported by government officials. But asserting that prisons expanded because of the decisions of policy makers is a less than useful or adequate explanation. Sutton's assertion does not, for example, help us understand the expansion of prisons because it fails to describe *why* policy makers decided that it was the right time to expand America's prison system, and why the expansion should be so dramatic and so long-lived. Thus, while it may be impossible to explain prison growth without reference to the preferences of and decisions made by policy makers (Clear, 1996), this explanation, when taken alone, is lacking to the extent that it fails to describe the forces that drive policy makers to endorse prison growth. Why, for instance, didn't policy makers choose some alternative mechanism to reduce crime?

Thus, the first question that needs to be addressed is: why did policy makers endorse the big prison model of crime control that characterized American prison policy since 1973? There are related questions that need to be addressed as well, such as: what forces act on politicians and policy makers that might explain their support for prison expansion? Again, there are numerous answers to this question, such as changing political agendas of Congress and the White House; the selection of crime policy agency heads who have staunch crime control positions; complex economic factors and interactions; increased economic inequality and class conflict; the greater visibility of the poor; (re)election pressures; increased racial segregation; crime rates; pressure from interest groups, entrepreneurs and lobbyists, and public opinion, to name a few. Each of these forces probably has had some impact on the growth of America's prison system. Economic factors, conditions, and influences probably play a much larger role than is generally acknowledged. These issues will be examined in a later chapter that lays out a materialist or economic argument to explains prison growth.

The decisions rendered by politicians are important, but so too are other factors. To address these factors, we must first explain why the expansive prison growth experienced in the United States might be a problem.

## WHY IS AMERICA'S PRISON GROWTH RATE A PROBLEM?

There are numerous factors that may affect prison growth. These factors include, but are not limited to, political conditions, economic factors and cycles, and public policy and opinion. It is unclear exactly how these forces work together to influence the growth of prisons. What we do know is that these factors most certainly appear to affect prison growth in America.

Which of these factors is most important for predicting prison growth? How much does each factor contribute? There are no unequivocal answers to these questions in criminological or public policy literature. That is, we cannot say with any degree of certitude that we know which factors drive prison rates. But, while it is unclear why imprisonment rates have grown so rapidly during the last thirty years, it is more obvious that the rate of prison growth that has characterized the last three decades is problematic. The recent tendency of the U.S. prison population to double repeatedly since 1973, for example, provides evidence of a very troubling trend for expansive prison growth in the United States. The prison population doubling trend is troubling for several reasons.

First, we must recognize that when crime or punishment in a society either grows or declines rapidly, this is a sign of trouble or social instability. This observation was offered long ago by Emile Durkheim, in his well known books *The Division of Labor in Society* (1893), *The Rules of Sociological Method* (1895), and *Suicide* (1897). To understand this view, we must recognize that Durkheim argued that crime was normal since it was found in all contemporary societies, and, consequentially, that a society without crime would be abnormal. In addition, if crime is normal and serves useful social functions (which we need not detail here; see Durkheim, 1893, 1897), the eradication of crime would ultimately disrupt social order. Following this observation, Durkheim wrote in *The Rules of Sociological Method* that:"crime, for its part, must no longer be conceived as an evil that cannot be too much suppressed. There is no occasion for self-congratulation when the crime rate drops noticeably below the average level, for we may be certain that this apparent social progress is associated with some social disorder." (72).

In the Durkheimian view, crime was not abnormal. All healthy societies had crime. This leads to the conclusion that crime is not a social disease, but rather a social regularity or fact. And, for Durkheim (1895: 73), if crime is normal and not a disease, then "punishment cannot be its cure, and its true function must be sought elsewhere."[1] How do these observations apply to recent trends in punishment in the United States?

In effect, the high rates of punishment that characterize recent decades in the United States, and the elevated level in the doubling of the rate of punishment evident over this period, indicates *that there may be some larger problem in society that is causing the United States to rely too heavily on the powerful form of social control represented by the prison.* Consider, for example, that crime *is not caused* by a lack of punishment. There are numerous examples that can be cited to support this claim. Consider, for instance, the very low levels of punishment and crime that are seen to coexist in other societies, including Japan, India, Turkey, and Greece. Each of these nations has an imprisonment rate that is nine to twenty-four times smaller than in the United States (see table 2.1). Each also has a much smaller total crime rate—rates that are five to eighty times lower than the one found in the United States. Indeed, if a lack of punishment caused crime—and we examined the trend in crime and imprisonment in the United States—we should see very high crime rates in the early portion of this century in the United States since levels of punishment were lower. But we see exactly the opposite: low rates of crime coexisted with low rates of incarceration earlier in the century, with the reverse situation in the latter part of the century. Moreover, given the vast difference in the level of punishment between, say, the year 2000 and 1925, one could argue that if this assumption was true—if you need punishment to keep levels of crime low—then rates of crime in the 1920s should be extraordinarily high compared to 2000. But, this is not the case. In fact, what we find is that before the 1970s, the United States had a low crime and a low imprisonment rate. To be sure, the rapid growth in the rate of imprisonment, especially during the 1980s, seems unusual with respect to both historical trends within the United States and levels of imprisonment found in other nations during the same era (see note 1 of this chapter for discussion).

A second related explanation for the rising rate of incarceration has to do with two combined assumptions. The first assumption is that punishment changes behavior, and that imprisonment, as a form of punishment, is capable of changing behavior. The second assumption is that it is substantially easier to control crime by manipulating punishment rather than by engineering or changing other social features that promote or reduce crime. That is, efforts to increase imprisonment may be preferred because they are believed to be an effective and less burdensome approach than increasing employment, or providing the kinds of livelihoods and living conditions that would produce less crime. While social and economic engineering are not easy, and are certainly not preferred, such policies would have shorter-term costs than those associated with the continuous expansion of the prison system.

Third, members of American society are often unwilling to entertain the idea that social and economic engineering is needed to reduce crime because this detracts emphasis from the long-cherished belief that criminals deserve to be punished because they choose to commit crime. The public, and possibly policy makers and policy advisors, seem to over-look the fact that social and economic changes aren't made in place of punishing criminals; they are made alongside punishment in order to reduce crime. Perhaps the problem is that the public tends to view eco-nomic and social policy changes designed to reduce crime as a reward that somehow benefits criminals. In reality, economic and social change is a reward to society as a whole to the extent that these programs can reduce the rate of criminal victimization for non-criminals, reduce fear of crime, and lower the costs associated with enforcing laws, homeown-ers and car insurance policies, and even health care costs associated with violent victimization.

The American preference for punishment over social engineering is shortsighted, and fails to consider the causes of crime to which many young people who grow up in deprived economic and social conditions are exposed. Social and economic changes that improve the life prospects of the poor, for example, are multigenerational. Punishment is not. If punishment is used to control crime, it must be administered continually both within and across generations. Social and economic programs that improve the life of a community by adding resources and jobs, in con-trast, are likely to have long-term, cross-generational effects.

Fourth, reliance on imprisonment may represent a reaction to the reform efforts that were prevalent during the 1960s (Cullen and Gilbert, 1982). Many people viewed prison reform as "coddling" criminals, and failed to appreciate its importance in preventing future criminal behav-iors.[2] To be fair, while the public supports punitive penal responses, there is also evidence that the American public supports rehabilitation efforts as well (Cullen, Fisher, and Applegate, 2000; see also, Cullen and Grendreau, 2000, 1989).Yet, it could be argued that the tendency toward punitiveness results from the willingness of certain segments of the public to interpret rehabilitative reforms as illegitimate forms of punishment, and of public officials to support and voice this view when they discuss crime control strategies. These two tendencies stimulate or at least coincide with po-litical efforts to enhance punitiveness. Thus, while the "punitive" public exists, punitiveness is not the sole attribute of American citizens' correc-tional values (Cullen and Grendreau, 2000). Punitiveness is, however, the value that is stimulated by: (1) responses to crime endorsed by politicians and public policy makers and consultants; (2) researchers who examine public punitiveness using selectively worded survey instruments that elicit more pro-punitive responses (for exceptions, see Cullen's various work on this topic); and (3) by economic and social circumstances that generate fear of perceived criminals among the middle class, and the desire for status separation by members of the lower classes (e.g., I may be lower class, but at least I'm not a criminal; see endnote 1 of this chapter).

Fifth, the American public and policy makers have not considered the long-term consequences and the future path that a reliance on a big prison system brings. What Americans will have to cope with in the very near future is a looming financial crisis that will be exacerbated by, among other issues, the coming oil crisis that will impede the functions of big prisons, and the growing racial effects America's big prison system generates. At some point, the tremendous financial cost of the "lock 'em up" approach to crime will impede our nation's ability to rely on "easy" and, as I shall demonstrate in later chapters, ineffective methods for controlling crime represented by imprisonment (see also Clear, 1994; Austin and Irwin, 2003). Americans must also come to grips with the growing proportion of the minority population housed in prison, and understand that relying on imprisonment will exacerbate racial tensions as the likelihood of imprisonment increasingly disrupts the life of a larger percentage of American minorities.

Sixth, Americans must accept the fact that punishment may not be a useful crime control strategy. The failure of imprisonment to effectively control crime may, as some argue, be the problem most often hidden behind the tremendous growth of imprisonment in the United States. If the growth of imprisonment cannot be shown to be an effective crime control strategy (in terms of the percent of crime that is suppressed, and its financial costs), then why do we continue to rely upon this strategy? In part, society relies on this approach for two reasons. First, despite all the evidence to the contrary, we continue to *believe* that incarcerating more people ought to lower the rate of crime. The logic of such an idea has widespread appeal. Second, imprisonment has come to serve purposes other than reducing crime. These "other purposes," described later in this chapter, drive imprisonment independently of any effect imprisoning people may have on crime. For now, we need to turn our attention back to the question of the relationship between prisons and crime control.

## Do Prisons Control Crime?

The experiment our nation has undertaken with respect to using imprisonment in an effort to reduce crime is a failure. There is little evidence that sending more and more people to prison works to control crime to any significant degree. In addition, the evidence that does exist has historically specific limits. In other words, the evidence that suggests that prisons control crime only applies to certain time periods, and does not apply consistently to the imprisonment trend that has been in effect in the United States since 1973. Nor does it apply across nations, nor across states within the United States, nor does it hold when we look at the low crime rates earlier in twentieth-century America. If this is true, why do we continue to believe that imprisoning more people controls crime?

In part, the widely held belief that increased rates of imprisonment reduce crime comes from a limited number of studies. Some of these studies have been produced by highly visible policy analysts, or by important crime control agencies (see Clear, 1996, for extended discussion). A number of these studies use short-term evidence to draw conclusions about the relationship between imprisonment and crime rates over the long run, or attempt to transform short-term relationships between crime and punishment into absolute, immutable relationships. The results from short-term studies that reach sweeping conclusions may lead us in the wrong direction. This is true because these studies focused on a rather limited period of time (e.g., the mid-1990s) during which imprisonment increased and crime decreased. These same studies fail to address or take into account the fact that social and economic changes or factors other than punishment that might have caused crime to fall during this period. In short, we need to pay serious attention to the fact that many studies that support the expansion of incarceration as a method for controlling crime, especially those written in the mid-1990s, are suspect because they are methodologically faulty (designed improperly) or reach conclusions that amount to overgeneralizations from the data that the researcher analyzed. To be sure, the kinds of methodological deficiencies and overgeneralizations evident in pro-imprisonment research from the mid-1990s are well known to social scientists. Indeed, these errors are the substance of classic research design guides, such as Campbell and

Stanley's (1962) classic work *Experimental and Quasi-Experimental Designs for Research.*

Evidence from pro-incarceration researchers has been challenged on numerous grounds (Clear, 1996, 1994). In addition to emphasizing the short-term effects of an increased rate of incarceration on crime to the exclusion of evidence on the long-term relationship between crime and incarceration, evidence from some states and even some regions within the United States appear to suggest that expanding the number of people incarcerated works to reduce crime. For example, studies using data from specific states may support the finding that an increased rate of incarceration drives down the rate of crime. However, the same result is not found across all states that have increased the use of imprisonment (Austin and Irwin, 2003; Mauer, 1999; Lynch, 1999; and chapters 6 and 7). Again, there are limits to the evidence that has been mustered supporting the suppression effect of imprisonment on crime across time and space. Why, for example, does an increased rate of incarceration appear to lower crime in some states but not in others? What are the other differences between these states that might account for a drop in crime that operate independently of incarceration?

The evidence of prison's effectiveness as a crime control strategy must be balanced against evidence from places and time periods which demonstrate that increasing the rate of imprisonment does not reduce crime. That is, we cannot pay selective attention to only a portion of the available evidence that demonstrates the effectiveness of imprisonment as a crime control strategy. Doing so is the basis of bad decision making and bad social policy. For example, as illustrated in an earlier chapter, many nations have much lower rates of imprisonment than the United States. They also have much lower rates of crime. Even within the United States, the states with the highest levels of imprisonment do not have the lowest rates of criminal offending, a finding that was examined briefly in the preceding chapter, but which will also be studied at greater length in a following chapter. Considering the various contradictory evidence, we would conclude that high rates of punishment and low rates of crime do not appear to be a "rule," especially if one considers international data or cross-state data. These findings raise two additional points.

First, the study of human behavior does not generate the same kind of rules we find in hard sciences such as physics or chemistry. In chemistry, for instance, the presence of two chemicals may yield a compound under known conditions. In contrast, we could argue that human behavior is not so precise because people aren't chemicals or physical properties whose behavior is determined by a set of given conditions. In addition, there is a tendency to argue that humans, unlike chemicals, have the ability to make choices. Sodium doesn't decide to bond to calcium to form salt; the outcome is determined by the nature of these chemical and the conditions of how they are combined. To be sure, not everyone placed in the same circumstance behaves in the same way. Indeed, this *is* true; but what we want to know is not that some people may behave differently, but rather how do most people behave in a given situation. Likewise, we could catalog a tremendous number of ways in which individuals might differ that could affect their behavior. These difference could range from common descriptive state data that include age, race, and gender, to family factors that include information about parents, siblings, and family cohesion and intactness, to achievement and status variables such as level of education and income, to name but a few possibilities. The point is that we might say that an individual's behavior cannot be predicted with any degree of accuracy—and by accuracy, I mean that mathematical or statistical models predict a high degree of variation in the predicted behavior, is correct more often than it is wrong, and does not simply produce statistically significant results for specific variables because of sample size. This may occur because people have consciousness and choose their own behaviors, or because of the vast variation across individuals, which, taken together, make each person unique. All these explanations are based on an assumption that *if* behavior can be explained, it can be best done by looking at variations across individuals.

On the other hand, it may be that we cannot predict human behavior because of the way in which human behavior is normally studied. In other words, it is possible that predictions of human behavior are not precise because we make the wrong assumptions or expect the wrong outcomes or measure the wrong variables. Further, when the expected outcome does not occur, instead of looking for an alternative explanation, we invent reasons that explain why we did not discover what we expected, and look somewhere else to confirm what we believed when the weight of the evidence suggests that we should come up with a new explanation. Thus, rather than declare the hypothesis invalid and discard the explanation as useless, it is retained in the hope that future research will justify what was believed to be true before the evidence was collected.

Second, why should we believe that findings from other nations are irrelevant to the relationship between crime and imprisonment in the United States? Are people in the United States different from people in the rest of the world in some important way? Do Americans make decisions differently than other people? Are Americans less rational than other people? Does this explain why rates of imprisonment are so much higher in the United States? Without belaboring this point, we could asks hundreds of questions about difference that focus on personality characteristics, family structures, educational attainment, and the like. To be sure, Americans—unless they are Native American—immigrated from other nations, and must, as a result, share things in common with people from other places. It is unlikely that people from different nations vary dramatically, especially biologically. There may be some difference between people from different nations—differences that are often recorded as "personality" differences. But when an entire nation of people can be differentiated from another nation by, for example, personality differences or preferences, these differences are not individual, but are cultural. In such a case, these differences have sociological relevance.

If we accept that people in the United States and other countries may be different, but that these differences are not between individuals but collectives, doesn't this imply that cultural and economic differences may be the sources of these differences? And, if we believe this is true, doesn't this also imply the possibility that cultural and economic differences affect the propensity for crime within a nation? Or even the propensity to rely on imprisonment as a solution to crime? Furthermore, if we reach this conclusion, does not this also imply that changing the cultural and economic conditions that differ between the United States and other nations may hold the answer to the crime or imprisonment problem?

In theory, if deterrence, social defense, or rational choice models are appropriate explanations of criminal behavior, then crime should decline as the rate of imprisonment expands. If evidence from the real world shows that this effect happens in some circumstance or place or at some points in time but not in most places, circumstances, or times, then we have grounds on which to question the effectiveness and correctness of the assumptions that are driving the growth of the prison system in the United States.

Let us assume, for the moment, that the expanding rate of imprisonment in the United States could actually be shown to reduce crime. We would have to ask whether we now have sufficient evidence to serve as the basis of policy. Most policies, crime policies included, are not determined simply on the basis of a policy's effectiveness in curing the targeted problem. That is true because there is a difference between a useful policy and a policy that can or should be implemented, or even a policy that someone wants to implement. Often, when the government's agents consider whether a policy should be implemented, they also consider the costs of implementing the policy, the cost effectiveness of the policy (the question of whether the costs of the policy reap sufficient rewards), and perhaps even if it would be feasible to implement the policy on some other grounds. In addition, they are also forced to consider the desires of interest groups that include lobbyists and those who donate to political funds.

Let us take a specific example that supposes that a crime gene were to be discovered. What is the policy implication of this finding? Genes do not, as most people think, determine a specific outcome; they may influence behavior, but they cannot be said to be the direct causes of behavior. In other words, the presence of a particular "crime gene" (if there was one) might make crime a more probable outcome, but the outcome is not definite, since, as genetic scientists have shown, genes can be influenced by the environment (Ridley, 2000; Burdon, 1999, 2004). This may be especially true for the connection between genes and behavior, where the gene may come into play only in specific environmental conditions. Despite these possibilities, how should the government act if there was a gene-crime connection? Should we test everyone born in the United States for the crime gene? Then what? Take these children from their parents? Lock them in secure environments from an early age? Sterilize parents who have produced children with crime genes? Would this be feasible economically? Would the costs of reducing crime represent a greater savings than the costs of the programs required to reduce crime? Would it be socially acceptable? Would enough crime be suppressed by these actions alone to justify their existence? While a gene-crime connection might be found, it would be unlikely to explain most crimes. Most crimes are property crimes. What kind of gene would make people steal? Anthropological evidence, for example, indicates that the human race spent the majority of its existence living in societies where property was unknown, where property equity was encouraged, or where the accumulation of goods and wealth was prohibited or undermined by social rules (Henry, 1965; Sahlins, 1972). Thus, it is unlikely that there is a property gene, or that acquiring property is part of human nature.

Here we have come to the crux of a difficult problem: even if increased rates of imprisonment appear to reduce crime, we can pose the question of effectiveness on cost grounds. How much should we spend to reduce crime by a specific amount? Would other policies reduce crime at a lower cost? Sometimes, these questions cannot be addressed directly because there are no real world examples of alternative solutions being practiced. When this happens, as is often the case with criminal justice policies, researchers insert assumptions or guesses about the cost and effectiveness of alternative crime control approaches. In this case, the basis for determining whether or not a policy ought to be employed depends entirely on the assumptions the researcher makes about the cost and effect of a nonexistent alternative. It should be clear that in such cases, altering the assumptions researchers employ changes the outcome and the decision about whether a policy should be followed.

The point is that assumptions have played, and continue to play, a large role in crime and justice policy in the United States. For instance, the big prison model employed in the United States is, as we have discussed, based on a crime reduction assumption. This, and many other assumptions that underlie the big prison system, are faulty. These faulty assumptions, while they fail to control crime, help to maintain prison growth. The issue of crime control and imprisonment is examined further in chapter 6 and 7.

### Promoting Our Failing Prison Approach

The idea that prisons fail as an effective crime control mechanism is not a widely held view among politicians, news agencies, the public, criminal justice agents, or by those who own businesses that rely on the income generated by our massive modern prison system. Nor does it appear to be a view widely held by academics, since the media publicizes the large voice of a minority of scholars who believe in the effectiveness of prisons, and politicians have thrust the same group of academics into the public limelight. Regardless of how it happened, what has happened is that American society shares a widely held belief in the effectiveness of prisons. Furthermore, this widely held belief has helped to promote prison expansion over the past three decades. Below, we examine how the assumptions about big prisons work at different levels of government.

### Federal Agencies

Agents of the criminal justice system promote the idea that bigger is better, and few are heard to exclaim that our experiment with rising prison populations really hasn't mattered all that much. Speaking to this point, Todd Clear (1996) discussed how federal agencies and federal appointees promoted research that supported prison expansion philosophies and have actively suppressed anti-expansionist research findings during the late 1980s and early 1990s. On this point, it is worth quoting Clear's discussion of how the U.S. Department of Justice reacted to Joan Petersilia and Susan Turner's reanalysis of a study comparing recidivism differences for California probationers and released inmates. The first study demonstrated that prisons were a more effective method for controlling crime than probation. As Petersilia and Turner's reanalysis showed, untenable assumptions helped to produce these results. The government's response to Petersilia and Turner's reanalysis is shocking:

> When Petersilia and Turner . . . reanalyzed the . . . database and found that, when compared to a matched prison sample, the probationers . . . actually had lower arrest rates than the prisoners, and that with time, even the incapacitation differences might wash out, the Department of Justice reaction to this analysis was quite different. Faced with a set of findings that refuted the punishment/control agenda, suggesting that the incapacitative effects of imprisonment may be washed out, over time, by its criminogenic effects, the Department [of Justice] refused to support its [Petersilia's and Turner's report] dissemination. Instead, the National Institute of Justice, which funded the study (expecting, no doubt, a different result) refused to allow it to be published under federal dollars and attempted to stop [the] Rand [Corporation, Petersilia's employer], from publishing it with its own money, claiming the research was flawed (Clear, 1996: 5–6).

Clear proceeded to note that:

> The extremely cautious handling of the second Petersilia study must be compared to the lavish acceptance of an internally commissioned

paper by Zedlewski. The study argued the implausible line that locking convicted offenders up is cheaper than leaving them on the streets, and that higher national incarceration rates are associated with reduced rates of serious crime. Never sent out for review to independent social scientists, the study was instead immediately circulated free-of-charge to elected officials throughout the nation—state legislators, governor's staff, law enforcement personnel, and so forth (1996: 6).

Clear then turns to answer the question of why governmental agents would react in such a manner to the results of Petersilia and Turner's study in comparison to Zedleswki's research (for further discussion, see also Greenberg, 1990). Why disseminate a non-reviewed, flawed piece of research over the Petersilia-Turner paper? Why attempt to suppress the Petersilia/Turner study? Wouldn't this cover-up reemerge to haunt the government? Clear noted that "the idea, undoubtedly, was to continue to fuel an official Federal agenda of prison building that was already beginning to face heavy criticism, even from political conservatives, due to the heavy costs of prison crowding" (1996: 6). Furthermore, it should be noted that while this kind of activity by government agents is disturbing, especially to academics who are attempting to discover important information that can help produce useful crime policies, these same activities are not viewed as newsworthy scandals. No one is charged when academic studies are promoted or suppressed, which explains why, for example, the Bush administration's attack on and suppression of science has been so successful (for discussion see the website of the Union of Concerned Scientists, http://www.ucsusa.org/scientific_integrity).

### Politics

Let us take a moment to further consider Clear's point: politicians, who have set into motion the gargantuan system of imprisonment now in place in the United States, cannot suddenly abort this effort, as if to say, "We were wrong." Imagine a politician who has supported prison expansion on numerous occasions confronted by the idea that prisons don't reduce crime. Do you expect this politician to suddenly change course and repudiate his original position? Theoretically, we expect that they should, since it is the duty of their office to act in the best interest of American citizens. Two things may play a role. One is related to the tendency of politicians to point out that their political opponents have, in the past, behaved differently, which makes them "wishy-washy." Apparently, Americans prefer candidates who stick to their positions rather than ones who revise their ideas as they gather new information. Second, rather than confront the problem that prisons are an ineffective crime control strategy head on, the politician is likely to invent an excuse such as the following: "We already have a big prison system. What are we to do with all those prison beds if we don't send people to prison? We have already committed extensive resources to this approach. In a few more years, we will be able to determine whether or not this approach is working." How many years must pass, however, before we know the answer to the question of whether prisons reduce crime? At this point, more than thirty years have already passed since the United States embarked on its great prison expansion experiment. Do we have to wait longer than the thirty years we have already waited? Does more time have to lapse before we can assess whether employing the bigger prison system model works? And won't the prison system get even bigger in the meantime? Won't we spend more money on a system that doesn't seem to meet its promise? Are we to believe that we will, in a few more years, be able to walk away from our big prison system when we couldn't do so on previous occasions when the prison system was smaller?

When I imagine the answers politicians give when faced with questions about the relationship between our expanding prison system and crime, I often think of someone whose house is on fire. When you see that your house is on fire, your natural instinct would be to try and extinguish the fire. Politicians know that throwing a liquid on a fire is supposed to extinguish it. So, they grab a liquid and start dousing the fire. But the liquid they are throwing is, itself, flammable. Nevertheless, they keep at the task, throwing the flammable liquid on the fire until there is nothing left to extinguish. In some sense, the problem of the burning house has been solved by throwing flammable liquids on it—the house has been reduced to ashes—only the solution isn't a useful one.

### From the Top: Presidential Politics

Todd Clear is not alone in making the claim that politicians drive criminal justice policies, and that they have used their influence and power to ignore sound research in order to promote their independent crime control agenda (i.e., independent in the sense that these agendas are not based on evidence or sound research; see Feeley, 2004; Ross, 2000). Well-known prison expert John Irwin notes that there is a rather long-lasting connection between crime and politics in the United States that has produced ineffective and inefficient crime policies. Irwin (2005) traces political influence over the crime control model to the mid-1960s, and specifically to President Lyndon Johnson, who was instrumental in the creation of the Law Enforcement Assistance Administration and the Safe Streets acts. In both cases, efforts were made to control crime by increasing crime control measures. Shortly following Johnson's effort came Richard Nixon's crime policies. During the height of public unrest associated with the civil rights movement and Vietnam War protests, Richard Nixon's conservative crime control strategy, which focused on enhanced conviction rates, helped boost him into the presidency. Increasingly, public opinion polls showed that the public fell in line with the conservative crime control view that emanated from the White House. Following this message, by the late 1960s and early 1970s, a majority of Americans began to associate crime with the disorder of African-American neighborhoods and lifestyles (for discussion, see Beckett, 1997).

Pushing this conservative crime control agenda of increased surveillance and punishment, Nixon launched the war on drugs, a recurring theme in America's crime control strategy since the mid-1970s. This targeted response helped accelerate the arrest, conviction, and incarceration of the poor and minorities (Austin and Irwin, 2003; see also chapter 6). The conservative crime control policies of the 1970s were bolstered by popular academic works (e.g., those of James Q. Wilson) that reinforced prevailing political responses to crime, and which tend to reflect political agendas through resources provided by federal funding agencies (Savelsberg, Cleveland, and King, 2004). As Irwin (2005: 230) notes, "These criminologists, many of whom occupied the most prestigious positions in leading universities and on government bodies, succeeded in supplying the government with a body of polished, academically sophisticated theories to support the government's new war on crime. These ideas focused attention on individuals who, because of bad genes or bad families, were deeply committed to criminal behavior."

The conservative campaign against crime was continued by Ronald Reagan, who, Irwin suggests, created crime policies that were "not being driven by public opinion but was attempting to manipulate it" (2005: 231). Like his predecessor, George H. Bush also manipulated public opinion about crime to facilitate conservative crime control strategies that maintained the focus on drug interdiction, drug crimes, and increased punitive responses toward criminals (Irwin, 2005). Ironically, while presidential candidates often discuss crime policy, and presidents have some influence over national crime policy (Oliver and Barlow, 2005), presidential campaign promises related to crime are less likely than other types of campaign polices to be implemented (Marion and Farmer, 2004).

### Crime News

Policy makers are not alone in the endeavor to promote conservative crime control strategies and keep the public's attention focused on penalties such as imprisonment as a crime cure. Newspapers promote popular opinion linking crime and punishment by, for example, quoting politicians, criminal justice agents, and academics who favor prisons. It doesn't take a Ph.D. to demonstrate the conservative crime bias found in news coverage, though there is significant scholarly research focused on this issue (e.g., Weitzer and Kubrin, 2004). Pick up any newspaper and read the stories it features about crime. There will be numerous stories about homicides, for example, even though homicides make up only a tiny fraction (less than a fraction of 1 percent) of the crimes that are committed in the United States. News stories are also likely to focus on gang and drug problems, and on solutions to these problems that promote locking up more offenders for longer periods of time. The question of how much more it will cost to lock up an even greater number of offenders, or who will pay for this costly response to crime, rarely make headlines. To be sure, a discussion of the costs of our modern prison system, and who profits from our approach to crime, should be front-page news.

### Profiteers

In modern America, there are some big corporations that profit from crime, such as Hailliburton—the same corporation Vice-President Dick Cheney worked for as CEO, and in which he continued to own stock while serving as vice-president. Halliburton, primarily known for its work in the oil industry, has a subsidiary, Kellogg, Brown, and Root, that, among other things, builds prisons. This kind of troubling connection between public servants and corporations that profit from punishment may help explain why the push for a bigger prison system has remained so entrenched in American politics, despite evidence that this approach has not delivered on its claim. Consider also that the corporations that now profit handsomely from crime by providing services and commodities and prisons to the government spend a good deal of money lobbying politicians to make sure that they don't change their minds about the need to expand our prison system. In short, there are now many reasons why prison expansion continues. Part of that reason involves the mechanism of support built around the prison as industry, an important idea that will be examined in chapter 5.

### Conservative Academic Support

The revelation that prisons are not an effective crime control strategy is not news to most academics who study this topic. This is not to say that there are not some academics who support prison expansion policy. Indeed, some academics have written the most publicly acclaimed and re-lied-upon studies and arguments in favor of prison expansion (for discussion and critique, see Clear, 1996). While the majority of academics would oppose prison expansion as an effective crime control policy, the position of pro–prison expansionist academics are favored by policy makers and politicians because they fit a conservative crime control agenda that the public believes will work despite its many failures. The "get tough" prison expansion proponents are also most likely to make news.

### Punishment and Reinforcement

From the perspective of the average person, the expansionist view also fits with a seemingly common-sense notion about the association between crime and punishment: that punishment alters behavior. Animal experiments are often cited in support of the "punishment affects criminal behavior" view. The idea that negative reinforcement affects behavior has, for instance, become part of popular vernacular. For example, say we want to stop a puppy from chewing on shoes. One approach to this problem, perhaps the most likely, is to spank the puppy each time it chews on the shoes. This works *if* the puppy is capable of mentally linking the spanking and shoe-chewing activity. In addition, this strategy would be more effective if it occurred while the puppy was actually chewing a shoe. It is unlikely, however, that the puppy is always caught in the act of chewing. Sometimes the puppy has chewed the shoe while you were out, and, in this case, the punishment occurs too long after the chewing for it to make an impression on the puppy. Its in the nature of puppies to chew things as their permanent teeth grow and take the place of baby teeth. So, punishing the puppy is unlikely to erase the chewing behavior.

The first reaction was to punish the puppy for doing something bad. But the puppy didn't really do anything bad, and simply took advantage of the circumstances its owner created. The owner left the puppy alone for too long, and left shoes where the bored puppy with growing teeth could find them. Thus, rather than punish the puppy, there are other solutions. The owner could make sure the puppy doesn't spent too much time alone. Or, the owner could secure her shoes. The owner may not like these options. None of these "teach" the puppy how it should behave, and the owner wants an alternative that involves some mechanism to alter the puppy's behavior. The owner doesn't want to change his own behaviors. One alternative would be to coat the shoes with a bad tasting (but harmless) substance so that the puppy would learn immediately that chewing shoes leads to a distasteful outcome.

This illustration is useful for two reasons. First, it clarifies the difference between negative reinforcement (the nasty tasting substance) and punishment (spanking). These ideas are often confused because, for example, the nasty taste response can be considered a punishment when in fact it might simply be a negative consequence. Punishments are not always negative reinforcements because they do not work to eliminate behaviors for various reasons (e.g., time lapse). Second, as noted, one difference between negative reinforcement and punishment involves time; negative reinforcers occur in conjunction with a behavior, while a punishment may occur long after a behavior has happened.

With this brief discussion in mind, what most interpretations of punishment omit from consideration is what animal studies really tell us about behavior. Often animal studies are interpreted as indicating the effective use of negative reinforcement. But what these studies tell us is that a better approach for changing behavior involves a system of reward-related behavioral modification. Rewarding appropriate behavior, it turns out, is a more efficient and longer lasting mechanism for creating behavioral change in animals than is punishment. The bigger problem, however, involves whether studies on animals can be assumed to apply equally well to humans. Without belaboring the point, we can say that of the three methods for changing human behavior—positive reinforcement, negative reinforcement, and punishment—punishment is the least effective on humans.

### Obeying the Law

Why do people obey the law? Is obeying the law an outcome associated with the penalties law supplies for transgression? While most people believe that punishment leads to law abiding behavior, research evidence suggests otherwise. In fact, research indicates that most people follow laws because they believe in their legitimacy, not because they fear punishment (Tyler, 1990). The average person, for instance, doesn't walk into a store and "case the joint" in order to determine if he might be able to successfully pull off a robbery without being caught or punished. On the contrary, the average person doesn't even entertain this idea, not because they are afraid they will get caught, or that they might go to prison, but because they have been taught that this isn't the right thing to do. People may respect what the law has to say about taking property in an illegitimate way; or they may respect the social contract implications of abiding by legal rules; or they may have other options for obtaining money that they and others perceive as legitimate, worthy, and honorable; or they may believe that there is no honor in occupying a criminal status. The point is that there are a host of reasons that cause people to obey the law. Punishment is not among the most powerful of these reasons.

To illustrate this point, consider a simple example. Most well-behaved children aren't well behaved because they fear their parents; they are well behaved because they respect their parents and others and understand that behaving well earns them respect. To be sure, this is not true for all Americans or for all children, and when systems that confer status for legitimate activities break down, or when they are weak or nonexistent, or when there is no reward for conforming, the legitimacy of laws that are part of that system become suspect and have little meaning. For some Americans, for instance, there may be no advantage to conforming because there is no reward. Similarly, some people may have few or no legitimate options to obtain the money or status they are taught is valued in American society, and so crime becomes a viable alternative (Messner and Rosenfeld, 2001). It is also possible that some children have not been taught to respect others, or how to employ legitimate pathways to earn the respect of others. Whatever the source of this problem (e.g., family, schools, the economy, job prospects), it will not be remedied by more punishment.[3] People who are restricted from achieving, who lack access to achievement means, or who are not taught appropriate methods for achieving, or who have been overexposed to achievement goals, may all turn to crime to attain those things—including status and feelings of self-worth—they cannot otherwise obtain. Punishment may force some people to avoid crime, but it is unlikely to alter the behavior of most people most of the time for the reasons reviewed above.

The failure of punishment and prisons as a mechanism for changing behavior is not, however, widely recognized. As a society, we still believe punishment works well. As a result, we continually increase the level of punishment in the hope that it will work. And we further increase its use the more crime rises. Thus, in the face of failing to control crime, we did not given up on punishment—rather, we extended its reach.

### Summing Up Failing Crime Control Strategies

Part of the crisis of imprisonment we are currently experiencing in this country is the result of desiring rapid, visible results from crime control policies that are wedded to punishment. Politicians, because they need the support of the public to remain in office, try desperately to produce the desired results. They give speeches about being tough on crime, and endorse crime policies they view as tough. The problem is that few crime policies create rapid and immediately visible results. And, if politicians cannot make results appear rapidly, at least they can make the results appear visible. The rising rate of imprisonment is one very obvious mechanism for making efforts to control crime visible even if it doesn't really control crime.

## IF PRISONS DON'T CONTROL CRIME, WHAT DO THEY DO?

To begin this section, it is necessary to recognize that there are certainly people who we can say "belong" in prison—people who, perhaps, cannot be reformed, who continue to violate the rights of others in the most egregious fashion. The problem is that not everyone who violates a law needs to be placed in prison to protect the other members of society. Imprisonment is a severe punishment. Outside of the death penalty, which most advanced industrial nations except the United States have abandoned, it is the most severe punishment that society can administer. As a result, the act of imprisonment should be viewed as society's *last line of defense* against criminals, not its first. If we accept that premise, we can reach some rational conclusions about who ought to be in prison. For example, if prisons are the last line of defense against criminals, we could justifiably envision the prison as an institution with no purpose other than the control of repeat violent offenders who show an inability to refrain from violence. We might even decide that there are a few other types of offenders that need to be imprisoned to protect society. It is plausible, for instance, that the prisons might be a useful last defense against big-time drug dealers or racketeers. If we were to implement these kinds of rational rules about who should be in prison, the current system could be slashed substantially to one-fifth of its present size—to about 300,000 inmates, the number of violent and high-level drug offenders currently housed in the U.S. prison system—which would represent a reasonably sized prison population. The last time the U.S. prison system was that small was in the late 1970s.

If we can accept the proposition that prisons are a last line of defense, then there is something wrong with a society that overuses imprisonment. In addition, there is evidence that the use of imprisonment in the United States doesn't protect society from the worst criminals.

Further discussion in latter chapters also examines the purpose of imprisonment, where the issue of imprisonment as a form of class and race control is discussed. As a prelude to those points, the next section describes those offenders who are the least likely to be found in the U.S. prison system: white-collar and corporate offenders.

## THE EXCLUDED OFFENDERS: CORPORATE AND WHITE-COLLAR OFFENDERS

To be sure, it can be conceded that the current prison system does protect us from some criminals and crimes, even if the act of imprisonment doesn't substantially lower the crime rate. We might even say that the functions of imprisonment reviewed above—protecting the public from repeat, violent offenders—are legitimate. It is, however, a giant leap from recognizing the usefulness of a more limited form of imprisonment compared to our current prison system, from recognizing that incapacitation may serve some function in society, to elevating that function to the status of a cure for crime.

In order to discuss what prisons do and who is found there, we also need to acknowledge who we don't find in our prison system. We rarely use prisons, for instance, to house wealthy criminal offenders. Somehow, being wealthy seems to make people less deserving of severe punishments like imprisonment. As a result, the majority of wealthy criminals escape imprisonment (Reiman, 2003). Yet, in terms of the severity of their offenses, the crimes committed by wealthy offenders make the crimes of the ordinary street criminals who occupy our prisons look small. White-collar crimes, for example, cost American citizens thirty to fifty times more than street crimes (Lynch, Michalowski, and Groves, 2000). To take a more specific example, Leigh et al. (2000) determined that a very conservative costs estimate for preventable workplace diseases and injuries amounted to $155.5 billion in 1992, or *approximately 10 times the cost of operating the entire criminal justice system in that year.* Despite these high crime costs, few white-collar criminals end up in prison, and when they do, they are confined in much nicer, federal facilities that have the kinds of amenities the general public thinks shouldn't be found in a prison setting. Furthermore, when financially successful offenders end up in prison for their crimes— crimes that truly undermine the moral, philosophical, and even democratic basis of American society (Flanagan, 2003; Huffington, 2003)—they are there for much shorter periods of time than the street criminal.

The financial crimes of the wealthy are big, much bigger than the ordinary property crimes committed by the common criminal (Frank and Lynch, 1992). It would be a mistake, however, to believe that financial crimes are the only kind of crime in which the wealthy engage (Friedrichs, 2004; Reiman, 2003). In fact, the wealthy commit a variety of violent crimes that cause greater levels of injury and death than can be attributed to the ordinary criminal (Reiman, 2003; Lynch, Michalowski, and Groves, 2000; Lynch and Frank, 1992; Burns and Lynch, 2004). The wealthy, however, are not punished severely when they engages in these acts.

What kinds of violent crimes do the wealthy commit? In addition to the ordinary acts of crime the wealthy commit that we typically fail to recognize—spouse abuse, child abuse, and drug abuse offenses—the wealthy also engage in acts that only they have the opportunity to commit. These acts stems from their positions as owners and operators of large corporations.

Most people understand that large corporations, like individuals, commit crimes, and few would object to the suggestion that corporations can act criminally. What many people do not believe, however, is that corporate crime is not only widespread, but that corporate crime also involves acts of violence.

There are a large number of infamous cases that can be reviewed to demonstrate the contention that corporate crimes are a source of violence (Friedrichs, 2004). Among these examples is the Ford Pinto case, which provides an excellent illustration of a case where a corporation knowingly disregarded public safety in its pursuit of profit (Cullen, Makstead, Wozniak, 1987). Building an argument about corporate violence through this method, however, is time consuming, and would require the needless repetition of numerous cases reviewed elsewhere in order to make this point. Instead, let us take an alternative approach that relies on comparing larger aggregate measures of harm. For this purpose, we concentrate on one violent outcome: death.

On average over the past decade, about 18,000 people die from homicide each year in the United States. These deaths represent serious consequences of crime. We should keep in mind that these crimes constitute less than one-half of 1 percent ($< 0.5$) of all crimes committed in the United States in a given year. In other words, compared to the total number of ordinary crimes that are committed, homicides, the most serious of these offenses, is a statistically rare act.

To make sense of the level of death caused by ordinary criminal violence, we need to compare this figure to some other measures of death. Since we are claiming that corporate crime causes a larger number of deaths, death caused by corporate crime constitutes an appropriate comparison group. Several indicators can be employed for purposes of comparison. A few of these are listed below:

1. OCCUPATIONAL DEATHS. It has been estimated that each year, somewhere between 70,000 to 120,000 people die from preventable occupationally related diseases, illnesses, and accidents (e.g., Leigh et al., 2000;

Reiman, 2003; Lynch and Michalowski, 2006). Note that this figure is about four to six times the homicide rate. Yet, politicians and the news media rarely focus on these deaths, or how they might be prevented. Because these acts are not treated as crimes nor featured in the news, the public fails to recognize that their jobs pose a greater threat to their health and well-being than the anonymous criminal they fear. In addition, it should be recognized that in the majority of cases, adhering to legal requirements would significantly reduce workplace-related deaths. In other words, the majority of occupationally related deaths result from violations of workplace heath and safety laws. In addition, a significant number of these deaths could be prevented if stricter regulations were in place. Leigh et al. (2000) estimate that slightly more than two-thirds of occupationally related deaths are due to occupationally related cancers, indicating that stricter workplace rules or better enforcement of existing rules could substantially lower the number of occupationally related deaths each year.

2. FAULTY CONSUMER PRODUCTS. Each year, 3,000 to 4,000 Americans die from the use of faulty consumer products. These deaths should not be pushed aside and treated simply as accidents. Numerous case studies reveal that corporations often knowingly market unsafe products (Friedrichs, 2003).

3. DANGEROUS PRODUCTS. Dangerous products, such as pesticides (which include pesticides, herbicides, rodenticides, and fungicides), cause several thousand deaths each year. These deaths are preventable to the extent that alternative, safer products could be employed to obtain similar results (Lynch and Stretesky, 2001). In addition, the warning labels placed on these products are written in complex language, and in rather small print, making it difficult for the average consumer to read the instructions and comprehend their content (Lynch and Stretesky, 2001).

4. UNNECESSARY SURGERY. Each year, a substantial number of Americans die from unnecessary surgery. These surgeries, because they are not required to save lives, can be viewed as crimes (Reiman, 2003). It has been estimated that there are approximately 16,000 deaths that result from unnecessary surgeries in the United States each year (Reiman, 2003). Many

unnecessary surgeries result from the way medicine is practiced within the current structure of America's capitalist medical enterprise, and thus should not be blamed solely on individual medical practitioners. Nevertheless, what should stand out is that doctors kill as many people each year as homicide offenders by engaging in unnecessary medical procedures. And it is highly likely that the number of such cases is underreported.

5. Exposure to toxic waste. Each year, approximately 60,000 Americans die from diseases and illnesses contracted from exposure to toxic or hazardous waste (Burns and Lynch, 2004). These deaths can be considered crimes because they are preventable, either through altering production or waste-disposal practices (Lynch and Stretesky, 2001). It should also be noted that this figure is likely to be underestimated for a number of reasons. In addition, it should be noted that millions of Americans are exposed to toxic waste in various forms. This level of exposure could be prevented through stricter enforcement of existing laws (Burns and Lynch, 2004). In addition, it is necessary to consider the unequal burden toxic waste exposure creates, especially on minority populations (for relevant discussions by criminologists, see Lynch, Stretesky and Burns, 2004a, 2004b; Stretesky and Lynch, 2003, 1999a, 1999b).

If we sum up these preventable deaths and compare them to the number of deaths by homicide, we can conclude that corporate violence causes considerably more death than ordinary street crime (see Reiman, 2003; Lynch, Michalowski, and Groves, 2000; Lynch and Michalowski, 2006; Burns and Lynch, 2004, for detailed discussion). Because society defines corporate violence as unavoidable and accidental, the deaths caused by corporations are not treated as criminal outcomes, and the persons responsible are not punished in the same way that we punish the ordinary street criminal (Burns and Lynch, 2004; Lynch and Stretesky, 2003; Stretesky and Lynch, 1999a; Lynch, Michalowski, and Groves, 2000; Frank and Lynch, 1992; Reiman, 2003; Friedrichs, 2003). The fact that our society fails to punish these serious acts of corporate violence should not be construed as an indication that corporate crimes are inconsequential acts. Rather, society's neglect of the crimes committed by its most powerful persons indicates another dimension of the relationship between power, economics, and punishment. What these facts about the costs and harms of corporate and white-collar crime indicate is that society's most harmful and dangerous criminals are not the subject of the criminal justice system's control process. Imprisonment is the punishment to which poor people are subjected, and others have argued that the American prison system is a substitute for the poorhouse (Goldfarb, 1969). In other words, one of the primary purposes of the prison has become to control the poor through either direct physical restraint, or through the threat of punishment, which echoes the sentiments of Ebenezer Scrooge, who lamented, "Are there no prisons? No poorhouses?" Scrooge would have no complaint to lodge if he lived in modern-day America.

One excuse often offered for treating white-collar and street crimi-nals differently has to do with assumptions that the level and kind of intent criminals form when committing these two acts is unique. The corporate offender, for example, is often excused when he harms the public because he did not intentionally target a specific individual. In contrast, the victim of an ordinary street crime of violence is a specific target, and the offender is viewed as intending to harm the victim. The difference here is semantic rather than real. The corporate offender, like the street offender, cannot carry out his offense without a victim. The corporate offender knows this is true. He intends to harm a victim to enrich himself or his corporation. He just doesn't have a specific victim in mind because he is even more callous than the street offender—for the corporate offender any victim will do; they are nameless and face-less. Furthermore, the corporate offender does not think of a victim, he thinks of a mass of victims, for this is the only way he can satisfy his unre-strained lust for more. In this respect, the corporate offender's crimes are more heinous than the act of the ordinary criminal because he does not care if his victim is John Smith, his neighbor, or John Smith's children. The concern is profit, and it doesn't matter who gets killed or injured to serve this end. Viewed in this way, corporate violence appear as random acts of violence, a subject that is often newsworthy when the offender uses a gun, or is easily identified as a given person, because the image of the latter promotes a myth of crime that encourages focusing on and fearing the poor offender (Reiman, 2003).

The other excuse for corporate crime is that in law, the corporation is treated as a person. But, we must recognize that in reality, corporations do not act on their own. Rather, it takes the conscious activity of indi-viduals to make corporations behave. In other words, behind every bad corporate act or every criminal corporation are individuals who intentionally choose criminal behavior. They can often do so without fear of punishment, as they hide behind the veil of the corporation.

If, as the above discussion suggests, the purpose of our big prison system is not the control of crime, nor even the control of only the most serious crimes in our society, what purpose does our big prison system serve? A small part of this answer has already been offered: prisons control the poor. But, to answer this question more completely, we must turn our attention to the lessons offered by materialist analyses of punishment.

## CONCLUSION

This chapter has reviewed some basic data about the American prison system, detailed its growth, and examined some explanations for why it has grown so much and so rapidly over the past thirty years. In a later chapter, further evidence will be offered to support the contention that the large prison system the United States has created is an ineffective mechanism for controlling crime both because it fails to reduce crime, and because any marginal level of crime reduction it may produce is generated at the expense of excessive financial costs.

This chapter also noted that, while the American prison system has become the largest in the world, it fails to incarcerate society's most dangerous offenders—corporate and white-collar criminals. Clearly, then, this system of punishment presents a legitimation problem of which the poor are quite aware: they get locked up while the rich use their resources to avoid incarceration, allowing them to proceed unimpeded on their life course, perhaps even able to achieve the lofty aspiration of occupying the White House.

## CHAPTER 5

# Explaining Prison Growth in the United States

## THE MATERIALIST PERSPECTIVE

THERE ARE A number of different mechanisms for understanding and explaining the extraordinary rate of prison growth experienced in the United States over the past three decades. It is common to read or hear explanations of the following kinds:

1. *Imprisonment responds to crime.* In this view, imprisonment expanded in response to a growing crime problem. As the problem of crime in the United States got worse, imprisonment grew at an increased rate both in an effort to incapacitate and deter criminal offenders.

2. *Imprisonment responds to public demand.* In a democracy, it can be argued that trends in imprisonment should follow public demand. Public demand models argue that the expanded use of imprisonment has been fuelled by public attitudes concerning punitiveness toward criminals. As public punitiveness expanded, so too did America's system of imprisonment.

3. *Political responses.* Similar to the public-demand model, one version of the political model argues that public demands for increased punishment encourages politicians to put in place enhanced crime control, which, in turn, accelerated the use of imprisonment. A second suggests that political interests may also reflect pressures and incentives that originate in the private sector. This position takes account of political campaign contributions, lobbying efforts, and other forms of industry influence.

4. *Perceived failure.* The perceived failure of rehabilitation models of the 1960s lead to a search for an alternative philosophy of punishment. The alternative model, social defense, which argues in favor of imprisonment as a means for incapacitating criminals, drove prison expansion for much of the period between 1973 and the present.

5. *Imprisonment, crime, and the age structure of society.* Imprisonment grows in response to crime pressures exerted by population growth and disruptions in population growth such as the baby boom years. As the proportion of the population that fell within the crime prone years (ages fifteen through twenty-four) increased, crime rose, and so too did the need for incarceration.

Other explanations, similar in form to those noted above could also be offered. The point is that each explanation interprets the prison expansion problem within a limited sphere of possibilities and sees the growth of imprisonment as the result of responding to crime, political matters and pressures, and public opinion. These are not the only kinds of explanations that may be relevant for understanding the growth of imprisonment over the past three decades. An interesting alternative explanation for the growth in imprisonment in the United States is provided by materialists, who concentrate on examining the association between imprisonment trends and economic conditions. This chapter explores this idea, and provides examples of how this approach can be employed to understand the growth of the American system of imprisonment.

## PRISONS AND MATERIALISM

Numerous studies of punishment have been written since Becarria first broached this topic from a "modern" theoretical perspective in his eighteenth-century book *On Crimes and Punishment*. Despite the number and the variety of studies of punishment, especially those concerned with penal philosophy, the first study of penal responses that employed the materialist perspective was not written until more than 170 years after Beccaria, in 1939. In their now-classic book *Punishment and Social Structure,* Georg Rusche and Otto Kirchheimer employed the materialist perspective to forward and illustrate the following hypothesis: *every system of production discovers punishments consistent with its economic goals.*

Rusche and Kirchheimer spoke of systems of production rather than societies as the primary unit of analysis because societies share common features and could be grouped together depending on how they are organized along economic, political, and social dimensions. Thus, rather than treat each society as unique, commonalities that link societies together can be used to help researchers discover patterns that connected them.

As materialists, Rusche and Kirchheimer focused on economic features of society, which included the primary mechanism for generating wealth (e.g, agricultural production, trade or artisan labor, industrial labor). An additionally important characteristic of an economic system is its class structure or ownership pattern. Patterns of ownership are important because they relate to several features of a society. First, patterns of ownership can be used to describe the distribution of economic, political, and social power within a society. Those individuals and classes that own the primary mechanisms for generating wealth have economic power. The people who form the owning class also tend to posses the resources and influence necessary to translate their economic power into political and social power. Second, ownership patterns are an important consideration because they tend to reflect the broader economic orientation (e.g., feudalism, mercantilism, capitalism, socialism) of the society in which they are found.

Examining the long run of history spanning from feudalism to capitalism, and a cross-section of nations, Rusche and Kirchheimer provided numerous illustrations of punishments that fulfilled economic goals within different societies. For example, imperialist nations that colonized far-off lands sentenced criminals to galley slavery to provide manpower for the great vessels used for exploration and conquest. Later in history, these nations also employed the practice of transportation, which involved giving criminals the option of receiving a severe criminal penalty (typically death) or transportation to a colony where the individual might have to also serve as an indentured slave and provide the labor needed to exploit colonial resources. During feudalism, where the majority of punishments befell serfs, punishments were more immediate, and were carried out in ways that did not rob landowners of the serfs' labor power (e.g., corporal punishment such as whipping) or the ability to generate wealth.

Early capitalist societies invented the workhouse as a criminal punishment. Workhouse incarceration served two purposes: providing free labor to fledgling capitalist industries, and resocializing recalcitrant workers to accept the new labor regimes that accompanied capitalism (Foucault, 1979). Two centuries later, capitalist nations turned to the prison as a form of punishment. Under capitalist economic arraignments, the prison provided several economically necessary conditions: physical control of the surplus population, the potential for the production of goods without labor costs (especially in the form of the industrial prison), and rehabilitation and resocialization of marginalized workers through the use hard work as part of the penal response.

Given its historical emphasis, Rusche and Kirchheimer's analysis depended heavily on qualitative evidence. Other researchers in this tradition have used both qualitative and quantitative data to support Rusche and Kirchheimer's contentions. Barnes and Teeters (1945), for example, applied Rusche and Kirchheimer's thesis to an analysis of the accumulation function of industrial prisons during the early part of the twentieth century. Specifically, their quantitative data addressed the growth of the industrial prison and the monetary value of its output. Foucault's widely read book *Discipline and Punish* (1979) provides an analysis of the changing nature and goals of punishment throughout history, and employs a rich and detailed form of historical-qualitative data. Furthermore, Foucault quotes Rusche and Kirchheimer approvingly in his analysis of the ideological role of the prison, and in his claim that the prison replicates the disciplinary order of capitalism.

Beginning in the 1970s, numerous researchers captured the insights of Rusche and Kirchheimer in analyses that examined the relationship between trends in unemployment and incarceration. More specifically, this research addressed the marginalization or labor market thesis found in Rusche and Kirchheimer's work. Simply put, this thesis stated that under capitalism, imprisonment expands to exert greater control over the economically marginalized segment of the working class. Others extended Rusche and Kirchheimer's thesis and examined associations between alternative measures of labor market conditions and their impact on punishment. Overwhelmingly, this research tended to support the views of Rusche and Kirchheimer.

The researchers who examined Rusche and Kirchheimer's theses were also materialists. Within criminology, these materialists were typically called radical criminologists (Lynch, Michalowski, and Groves,

2000). Radical criminologists not only share a commitment to materialism, they also share a commitment to critiquing and exposing the relationship between economic, racial, and gender inequality and various crime and justice issues. As far as prison trends were concerned, radical criminologists were also sensitive to examining the growing association between the expansion of the prison system and the rapid growth of African-American rates of incarceration. Beyond these issues, radicals also share a commitment to social and economic change as a mechanism for remedying social problems such as crime or growing rates of incarceration. Thus, radical scholars point toward economic solutions that will help minimize crime rates as well as our reliance on formal social control mechanisms such as the prison (Lynch and Michalowski, 2006).

At the same time that support for Rusche and Kirchheimer's perspective was strengthened, the nature of radical criminology was undergoing a transformation from within. By the mid-1980s, many of those who worked within the radical criminological perspective began a movement to shed this label, preferring to be referred to as critical criminologists.[1] The impact of this change in name signaled a redirection in the type of research the new critical criminologists were to carry out. The majority abandoned research into the association among economic conditions, class inequality, and crime and justice. Many were drawn into postmodern views. A significant and needed focus emerged on race and gender inequality. An important emphasis on working-class victimization and public policy was proposed by left-realists. These new, critical criminological variations drew increased attention (Lynch and Michalowski, 2006).

Given the broad appeal of this new movement, few researchers were left to continue the promising line of study suggested by radical or materialist perspectives, such as the one developed by Rusche and Kirchheimer. In effect, the materialist roots of critical criminology were increasingly abandoned. As a result, Rusche and Kirchheimer's influential view, which had mounted a substantial challenge to the orthodox view that prisons were a useful response to crime, drew less attention, though it remained a significant basis for critiques of orthodox explanations of the crime-punishment connection (for an opposing opinion see Sutton, 2004, 2000).

Over the past decade, the pronounced neglect of materialist views on crime and justice has lead to what could be defined as a crisis in critical criminological theorizing. For example, with Rusche and Kirchheimer's view now tucked away behind the scenes of the postmodern emphasis common to the critical criminological enterprise, it became incumbent on critical theorists to develop a new view of the modern U.S. prison crisis. How would critical criminologists explain American penal practices defined by warehousing and its expanded use of imprisonment?

For the most part, critical criminologists failed to take up this challenge, and the critique of prison expansion that was developed came primarily from liberal criminologists (Austin and Irwin, 2003; Clear, 1994). To be sure, a few researchers have continued to examine these issues employing a materialist framework (Greenberg and West, 2001; Greenberg, 2001a), while others have turned to race-based explanations, or to research emphasizing the association between the expansion of imprisonment and the war on drugs (Austin and Irwin, 2003; Mauer, 1999; Welch, 1999, 2004a, 2004b). And, to be sure, these views have helped us understand at least some of the problems behind the growing rate of incarceration in the United States. Still, it is my assertion that the contemporary prison problem we face cannot be addressed without a strong materialist theoretical base. Below, I clarify my position and rectify the neglect of materialist explanations of the modern problem of rapidly expanding rates of imprisonment in the United States.

MATERIALISM AND IMPRISONMENT IN THE UNITED STATES

In 1973, the rate of imprisonment in the United States began its long-term climb. While the growth in the U.S. rate of imprisonment has slowed in recent years, the number of inmates in U.S. prisons nevertheless reached record highs. How much did imprisonment grow during the thirty years following 1973? And how is this growth associated with economic conditions? These trends were reviewed in an earlier chapter, but a brief summary is useful for purposes of the discussion that follows.

In 1973, the rate of imprisonment per 100,000 citizens in the United States stood at 96. What was interesting about 1973 was that the rate of imprisonment that year was lower than the average rate of imprisonment from 1929 through 1967. From 1929 through 1967, the lowest rate of imprisonment, 98 inmates per 100,000 U.S. citizens, was recorded in 3 separate years—1929, 1945, and 1967.

It is important to understand the historical trend of the rate of imprisonment in order to appreciate the current level at which we imprison criminals. As reviewed in the previous chapter, reliable figures on imprisonment rates date to 1925. In that year, the rate of imprisonment was 79 per 100,000 population. By 1929, the rate had risen to 98 per 100,000, a rather substantial increase of 24 percent spread out across 5 years. From 1929 through 1939, the imprisonment rate continued to climb, from 98 to 137 per 100,000 (although there was a slight decline and a "steady state" in 1933 and 1934). The increase from 1929 through 1939 was nearly 40 percent, though the increase was spread out over a decade. Furthermore, this increase occurred during a period of adverse economic conditions marked by high unemployment rates that followed the Great Depression. From 1940 through 1945, however, the rate of imprisonment declined to its 1929, pre-Depression level of 98 per 100,000—a decline of more then 28 percent in 5 years. This decline in the imprisonment rate corresponded with enhanced economic performance of the U.S. economy linked to wartime production. During this period, unemployment declined sharply, the result of employment opportunities in war-related industries and the effect of the draft on the pool of available workers.

At the end of World War II, the rate of imprisonment once again began to ascend, probably in response to labor market shifts caused by the return of war veterans into the economy and the tightening of the labor market and economic opportunities. By 1950, the rate of imprisonment had reached 109 per 100,000. This was only a slight (11 percent) increase since 1945. The imprisonment rate remained relatively steady through 1956 (112 / 100,000). Over the next several years, the rate of imprisonment rose only slightly, to 119 per 100,000 in 1961. Overall, the imprisonment rate expanded only 9 percent from 1950 through 1961.

From 1962 through 1972, the imprisonment rate declined during a period of economic expansion and increased employment opportunities. By 1972, the imprisonment rate reached its lowest point since 1927 at 93 per 100,000. During this short period (1961–1972), the imprisonment rate declined by nearly 22 percent.

By the mid-1970s, however, the United States began to experience an economic recession and associated increases in the unemployment and interest rates. This period of economic difficulty was mirrored by growth in the U.S. prison system. From 1973 through 1979, the rate of imprisonment expanded from 96 per 100,000 to 133 per 100,000, nearly 39 percent. The importance of this latter period is that it would mark the last time that there was seemingly full concordance between trends in the economic system and trends in the imprisonment rate—at least from the traditional materialist view extracted from Rusche and Kirchheimer's work. That is, the economic recovery experienced during the late 1980s and 1990s did not have the expected impact on the incarceration rate—at least not the outcome that would be predicted by relying on the traditional interpretation of the Rusche-Kirchheimer thesis, which would result in a declining rate of imprisonment. Specifically, using the Rusche and Kirchheimer labor market model that had been developed during the 1970s (e.g., Greenberg, 1977), we would predict that the upward trend in employment that emerged in the recovering economy of the late 1980s and 1990s should cause the rate of imprisonment to decline. But the rate of imprisonment did not decline; it continued to rise in the face of expanded economic and labor market opportunities. This new pattern of continually expanding rates of imprisonment during a period of economic recovery became the crux of a dilemma for radical criminologists, one that they failed to explain, and which the new critical criminology failed to tackle as well (for an exception and discussion, see Michalowski and Carlson, 1999).

By 1980, the rate of imprisonment had reached 139; by 1990 it was 297 per 100,000; and by 2000 it was 478 per 100,000. In terms of percentage increase, the imprisonment rate expanded nearly 114 percent from 1980 to 1990, and by 60 percent from 1990 through 2000. For the entire period (1980–2000), the increase in the rate of incarceration was over 230 percent, while the increase in the raw number of inmates incarcerated was nearly 300 percent. During this period, the U.S. correctional system surpassed several milestones. The number of inmates topped 500,000 during 1987; the 750,000 level was passed in 1992; and the 1 million mark became history in 1995.

There is something deeply troubling in these figures. Why did the rate of incarceration expand from 79 per 100,000 in 1925 to 478 per 100,000 by the year 2000? What would cause the rate of incarceration to go up by over 500 percent during this period? These are interesting questions that are beyond the scope of the limited investigation taken up here. The concern here is with the latest period of incarceration and the reasons for such a rapid rise in the rate of incarceration in such a short period of time, from 1973 to the present. Let us also not forget that another point of this work is to answer the following question: why did the Rusche-Kirchheimer hypothesis suddenly stop making sense?

Before continuing, the failure of the traditional Rusche-Kirch-heimer hypothesis in modern circumstances demands some minor additional comment. The sudden inability of this thesis to explain a process it seemed capable of tackling for the centuries of data it had been applied to speaks to some of the differences between social science theories and natural science theories. On the one hand, the theories of natural sciences tend to deal with behaviors (if we can be allowed, for instance, to call how two chemicals react with one another a behavior) that do not change over time. As long as scientists know and control the surrounding environment (e.g., pressure, temperature, contaminants), the chemicals they are studying will react in the same way in the year 1850 as they do in the year 2000. If they did not, then very simple things we rely upon everyday (from our coffee pots to our computers) would not work as expected. Human behaviors are not so predictable because they occur in an environment that is not as controlled as the one in which the scientist's chemical reactions occur. Economic systems change; social relations change; political systems change; neighborhoods change; family relations change, and so on. Sometimes these changes in the human social, economic, and political environment are so great as to require new explanations.

### UP, UP, AND AWAY: IMPRISONMENT IN THE 1990S

As noted, the imprisonment rate became greatly inflated by the 1990s. The widely accepted explanation for this persistent growth of imprisonment suggests that conservative and punitive attitudes expressed by the public toward criminals caused politicians to adopt a "get tough on crime" approach (or even the other way around). Having heard their constituents, the exact meaning of the idea of "getting tough" was left up to politicians to determine. Politicians either thought or knew from experience that if they did not seem tough enough on crime, their constituents would be unhappy. Politicians responded in a variety of ways. President Bill Clinton, for instance, pledged money toward hiring new police officers. Legislators responded by passing enhanced sentencing laws that included widely adopted "three strikes you're out" and other career-criminal sentencing alternatives, as well as enhanced penalties and lesser standards for juvenile waivers to adult courts. At local levels, police chiefs, pressured by politicians to do something about crime, turned to zero-tolerance strategies to increase arrests. In addition, a more global war on drugs continued to attract attention, especially at the federal level.

To a large extent, these efforts were misguided in that they relied more heavily on political pressures than on knowledge concerning the impact of more severe punishments on crime rates. This effort can also be considered misguided to the extent that the US was not a society that could be considered "soft on crime." For example, by the 1990s, the United States already had one of the highest imprisonment rates in the world. In addition, the United States was also among the world's leaders in terms of average prison sentence lengths (Welch, 2004b). Despite an already-tough approach toward crime, however, the United States was also among those countries with high rates of criminal offending—especially when compared to other modern industrialized nations, and especially with respect to violent crimes. In spite of these facts, the hope was still held that sending even more people to prison would lower the rate of crime. To be sure, at some point, such a strategy must at least appear to work, and at some point the cycle of crime and imprisonment would be aligned. This alignment occurred during the 1990s. But what percentage of the population must be locked up to make imprisonment an effective crime control strategy? And, at what price, both in terms of human and financial costs? I will return to address a portion of this question later.

While there were visible and empirically based reasons to doubt that a "get tough" approach would reduce crime, or that this was a major reason other nations had low rates of crime (see Farrington, Langan, and Tonry, 2004), U.S. policy makers pushed the nation further in this direction. The public, spurred on by bad news about rising crime rates and political rhetoric about crime and punishment, continued to shift to the right in terms of their opinion about the solution to crime.

In part, the political response to crime in the 1980s and 1990s reflected both common sense and the desire to do something about crime. These policies, however, did not necessarily make sense from the perspective of what is known about the relationship between crime and punishment. Consider, for instance, that the crime rate in the United

States had risen annually from 1985 through 1991. But so too had the rate of incarceration. And then a funny thing happened: crime began to fall as sentence lengths increased, imprisonment rates rose, and tougher new crime control policies were implemented. What was funny or odd about this circumstance was that crime had not fallen during the previous decade when sentence lengths were expanding and imprisonment rates were growing each and every year. But, all of a sudden this strategy appeared to work, as if some magic threshold had been crossed. And crime didn't fall just once: it fell over and over again from 1991 through 1999. Whether through deterrence or incapacitation, or for some other unexplained reason, crime was falling. This association allowed proponents of "get tough" legislation and prison expansion to argue that their approaches were working to reduce crime. Prison expansion advocates took credit, but so, too, did sponsors of other "get tough" approaches, such as enhanced police enforcement, zero-tolerance policies, and three-strikes and career-criminal legislation. Since no one could pinpoint which of these policies—if any—was the real cause of the decline in crime, and since the decline in crime was so precipitous (27 percent overall from 1991 to 1999), there was more than enough credit to spread around.

To be sure, there was something different about the relationship between crime and punishment in the 1990s—or at least there appeared to be something different. The visible difference did not go unnoticed by academics, in particular Raymond Michalowski and Susan M. Carlson. Employing Rusche and Kirchheimer's thesis as their starting point, Michalowski and Carlson (1999) examined the relationship between unemployment rates and imprisonment rates (and in a separate analysis, crime; see Carlson and Michalowski, 1997) over a long historical period (four decades). They discovered that the relationship between unemployment and incarceration was "historically contingent." During this period, they argued, the relationship between unemployment and incarceration changed. While incarceration initially appeared to be a response to controlling marginalized populations, as Rusche and Kirchheimer suggested, this relationship appeared to be contingent on other economic factors as well. In particular, Michalowski and Carlson noted that the relationship between unemployment rates and incarceration rates since 1933 was conditioned by social structure of accumulation (SSA) effects. Employing

research by economists, Michalowski and Carlson suggested that economies passed through different stages of accumulation (SSAs). These stages
(expansion, consolidation, and decay), when taken together, form a "long
swing." But, during each long swing of the economy, specific phase characteristics could come into play that affected the relationship between
unemployment and imprisonment. Their analysis supported their hypotheses of: (1) a weak relationship between unemployment and imprisonment during the exploration phase of the economy from 1933–1947;
(2) a strong positive relationship between unemployment and imprisonment during the economic decay period, 1967–1979; (3) a weak or
nonexistent relationship between unemployment and imprisonment for
the 1948–1966 period of economic consolidation, which is marked by
economic growth and industrial contraction; and (4) an inversed relationship between unemployment and imprisonment from 1980–1992 during
the new expansion stage of an SSA based on a completed transition from
an industrial to a service economy.

Carlson and Michalowski's findings made it clear that applications
of Rusche and Kirchheimer's thesis did not form an ironclad law such
as the ones found in the natural sciences, and that the relationship between employment and incarceration was conditioned by other economic factors. This finding, which had been suspected for some time,
was a blow to well-entrenched radical explanations of penal trends that
drew directly on Rusche and Kirchheimer's labor market hypotheses,
especially those that converted the broader implications of Rusche and
Kirchheimer's theory into a narrow theory of the impact of unemployment on incarceration. Carlson and Michalowski did not, however, leave
radicals hanging. They offered an alternative explanation based on social
structures of accumulation and long cycles theory. To be sure, this was a
useful explanation because it demonstrated why imprisonment did not
respond to unemployment in the same way in every era of economic
development. The argument suggests that during this four-decade period, the U.S. economy passed through various stages of economic contraction, expansion, and exploration, which affected how imprisonment
would be used to control economically marginalized groups. To be sure,
this was a noteworthy contribution to the literature, and one way of
amending Rusche and Kirchheimer's argument. Below, I review some
of the economic conditions during this period, and offer an additional,

plausible explanation consistent with materialist interpretations. My view is not to be taken as a criticism, but rather as an extension of Carlson and Michalowski's approach.

## TRANSFORMATIONS IN THE U.S. ECONOMY

The economic transformation of the U.S. economy was driven by a contraction of the manufacturing sector and an expansion of the service sector. The contraction of manufacturing, which has characterized the U.S. economy since the mid-1970s, has been marked by several tendencies that have lead to a loss of jobs in the manufacturing sector. A key factor in job loss was the expansion of automation that culminated in the replacement of human labor with machine labor and the elimination of well-paying manufacturing employment. A classic example involves the U.S. automobile industry, once a mainstay of the economy, a leading manufacturing employer, and the heart of Detroit. Similar pictures can be found in the mining and steel industries.

In the steel industry, for example, new furnaces introduced in the 1960s decreased melt times to one-tenth their original level. More recent technological and production innovations at companies like Steel Dynamic (Indiana) have reduced the needed "man" hours per ton to 0.3, one-tenth the industry's average. Overall, the American Iron and Steel Institute (AISI) reports that labor productivity per ton of finished steel has increased by 70 percent since 1980. The introduction of continuous casting in the 1960s likewise reduced the need for labor, as it eliminated the four-step casting process previously employed in steel production. The introduction of thin-slab casting the late 1980s further reduced steel production times and increased productivity per worker.

AISI's description of the steel making process illustrates the role technology plays: "In today's steel mills, red-hot billets and slabs of steel glide down aisles of rollers, their progress silently monitored by electronic sensors. In climate-controlled glassed-in 'pulpits' above the refractory floor, highly trained experts observe computer monitors, confirming the steel's world-class quality and dimensional accuracy-always in pursuit of perfection" (American Iron and Steel Institute).

These innovations have helped U.S. steel manufactures compete with overseas producers, where labor costs can be anywhere form ten to thirty times lower than in the United States. And while steel manufacturers have been able to use technology to maintain profit margins, they have failed to consider the cost to the working class in terms of jobs lost.

American workers are often criticized for their lack of productivity. Moreover, the lack of productivity argument is often used to justify moving plants and facilities overseas, or serves as the basis for downsizing and other profit-enhancing schemes that take a slice out of the already shrinking job market in America. Table 5.1 demonstrates that declining worker productivity claims are false. Here we see productivity indexes calculated by the U.S. Department of Labor's Bureau of Labor Statistics for a selection of industries for which data are available from 1950 or 1960 onward. For all industries, with the exception of millwork, productivity gains have been substantial. It should be noted, however, that each of the industries shown in table 5.1 *has experienced a productivity gain,* and even if the gain cannot be considered substantial, it still indicates that American worker productivity has, contrary to widely publicized claims, grown.

Another important market force during this period was deregulation. In theory, deregulation increases competition within an industry and thereby forces improvements in efficiency that should lead to a lower price structure. In the words of Barlett and Steel (1996:106), "Removing government restrictions on the private sector would let free and open competition rule the marketplace. Getting rid of regulation would spur the growth of new companies. Existing companies would become more efficient or perish. Competition would create jobs, drive down prices and benefit consumers and businesses alike. In the real world, such rosy outcomes are less apparent."

But, as this quotation implies, this happy scenario has not been evident. In terms of pricing, for instance, consider the case of electricity deregulation in California. In 1997, the year before deregulation of energy providers in California, private providers generated 35 percent of California's electricity. By 2002, private providers' share of electricity generation expanded to nearly 60 percent. During this same period, *as public electricity generation was privatized, the price per kilowatt hour of electricity grew by 27.4 percent.* To be sure, this rise in price contradicted the claim that privatization is beneficial to the public to the extent that end price or costs are reduced. Furthermore, consider that at the same time that private electricity generation in California forced a rise in cost, *the nationwide average price per kilowatt hour (excluding California) remained*

TABLE 5.1

*U.S. Department of Labor, Bureau of Labor Statistics, Industry Specific Indexed Output Per Worker, Select Industries with Long Term Data, 1950–2000*

| Industry | Year | | | | | | % Gain |
|---|---|---|---|---|---|---|---|
| | 1950 | 1960 | 1970 | 1980 | 1990 | 2000 | |
| Flour/Grain | 29.3 | 43.0 | 64.9 | 93.4 | 106.0 | 151.5 | 417 |
| Malt Beverages | 12.6 | 16.5 | 30.3 | 63.6 | 106.4 | 121.6 | 86 |
| Glass Containers | 53.8 | 54.9 | 71.3 | 85.2 | 109.2 | 156.6 | 191 |
| Copper (Primary) | 22.2 | 23.8 | 29.2 | 35.7 | 116.9 | 163.2 | 635 |
| Aluminum (Prim.) | 32.6 | 54.6 | 60.8 | 73.4 | 104.5 | 114.9 | 252 |
| Metal Drums, Pails, & Barrels | 37.4 | 46.5 | 57.6 | 74.0 | 117.8 | 170.5 | 356 |
| Petroleum Pipelines | 13.3 | 29.9 | 75.2 | 88.8 | 102.0 | 141.4 | 963 |
| Coal Mining | | 42.4 | 74.9 | 59.5 | 123.6 | 219.0 | 417 |
| Milk, Liquid | | 29.1 | 43.4 | 74.2 | 106.0 | 111.0 | 281 |
| Soft Drinks | | 35.9 | 42.3 | 66.2 | 127.4 | 169.1 | 371 |
| Sawmills/Planing | | 39.9 | 60.2 | 67.0 | 98.8 | 128.6 | 222 |
| Millwork | | 81.2 | 105.4 | 93.3 | 95.8 | 93.0 | 15 |

*Information in this table was extracted from the U.S. Department of Labor, Bureau of Labor Statistics files, "Industry Labor Productivity and Costs Tables," "Output per employee" subseries: ftp.bls.gov/pub/special.requests/opt/dipts/dipts/iprsicdata.txt.

*constant.* Moreover, in determining consumer costs, other factors must also be entered into the equation. For example, costs to consumers in California were compounded by the fact that *privatization expanded electricity-related pollution by more than 15 percent,* while electrical generating capacity rose only 6 percent (for data related to the above, Energy Information Administration, U.S. Department of Energy, 2003). Data on capacity expansion and pollution levels indicate that the expanded role private industry was playing in providing electricity in California had other detrimental costs to the public that were not included in simple electricity price cost comparisons.

Lack of regulation has also generated huge financial collapses and larger national scandals associated, for example, with the bankruptcy of Enron. In other areas, deregulation has created a rash of related problems including innovative crimes. For example, the impact of banking deregulation not only lead to a plethora of bank failures, but numerous banking scandals with national repercussions (Calavita and Pontell, 1994; Calavita, Tillman, and Pontell, 1997; Black, Calavita, and Pontell, 1995; Tillman and Pontell, 1995; Tillman, Pontell, and Calavita, 1997).

Theoretically, from a free-market economic position, deregulation has been offered as a solution to a host of economic ills, and it is typically depicted as a "boon" for consumers. In retrospect, however, it is clear that deregulation will tend to favor the market position of large firms, which have greater price flexibility. Larger firms will use price flexibility in the deregulated market to squeeze smaller firms, or buy out and consolidate smaller firms; this will lead to lower long-term employment prospects, increased consumer costs, and enhanced profit margins for corporations.

Deregulation has been costly not only to consumers, but also to workers. Job losses in the airline industry, which was deregulated in 1978, totaled more than 50,000 by the mid-1990s. In the trucking industry, deregulated in 1980, the picture is even worse, with 150,000 jobs lost (Barlett and Steele, 1996). By increasing competition, deregulation has caused accelerated economic concentration in the airline and trucking industries, firm consolidation and closings, and lost employment opportunities. In 1979, the year before trucking deregulation went into effect, 186 trucking businesses closed their doors. In 1990, following 11 years of deregulation, the number of trucking business that shut down was at an all time high in one year, 1,581. Over the course of the 1980s, more than 11,000 trucking businesses were shut down. A similar pattern is seen in the airline industry (see Barlett and Steele, 1996).

Since the 1980s, globalization and outsourcing have become a major impediment to employment prospects in the United States. For corporations, globalization has numerous benefits, especially in terms of accessing the cheapest available labor pool. To do so, however, jobs must be moved to foreign nations, which has led to a long-term decline in manufacturing employment and aggregate manufacturing output in the United States (the decline in output is aggregate and is due to plant closings rather than a decline in worker productivity). In turn, diminished manufacturing output has caused an escalation of the U.S. trade deficit. For example, in 2004, the United States had a manufactured trade goods deficit of nearly $360 billion dollars, which is the result of exporting manufacturing jobs in a global capitalist economy and needing to purchase manufactured goods from foreign suppliers. More than one-third of the 2004 U.S. foreign trade deficit ($124 billion) was with China, a nation that has been expanding rather than contracting its manufacturing base. How far has the United States sunk in terms of world goods production? In 1950, 60 percent of products manufactured in the world were produced in the United States. By 1999, only 25 percent of manufactured goods originated in the United States (DuBoff, 2003).

To be sure, working people in the United States have felt the effects of globalization and outsourcing for decades. The impacts of these forces, however, have been magnified in recent years. For example, since 2000, 90 percent of jobs lost in the United States—some 2.7 million—were in the manufacturing sector, and by 2003, employment in the manufacturing sector was at its lowest point since 1958. It is increasingly evident that the extent of job losses in the manufacturing sector is a unique American problem (not that other nations do not experience a loss of manufacturing jobs, but the degree of loss appears greater in the United States), exacerbated not only by globalization, but also by an American political foreign policy agenda tied to corporate interests. In Canada, for example, where manufacturing trends have tended to follow those in the United States for decades, manufacturing employment has grown by 12 percent since the late 1990s while the United States experienced net losses in this area.

Whatever the exact causes of these job losses may be, what should be clear is that the manufacturing base in the United States has been eroded. At the same time, industrial or worker production values increased (see figure 5.1), which indicated that the U.S. manufacturing sector produced more value using fewer workers. Overall, however, the aggregate level of production has fallen as industries have outsourced production. Workers are either being displaced into lower paying service sector jobs or finding it harder to find decent employment, which explains the expanding U.S. inter-class economic disparity (for extended discussion see Wolff, 2002; Keister, 2000).

Within the United States, the impact of the decline of manufacturing was uneven geographically, and certain areas of the country were

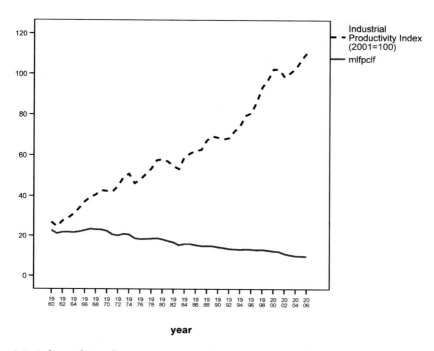

5.1. Industrial Employment and Index of Industrial Productivity (2002 = 100), United States, 1960–2006.* Industrial Employment is the number of workers in manufacturing divided by the number of workers in the civilian labor force.

much more intensely affected than other areas. For example, Detroit's economic base was devastated by the contraction of manufacturing, and jobs were lost to both intense mechanization of the automobile industry and the movement of auto-manufacturing plants to others states and countries. In some respects, the crisis presented by deindustrialization appears locally at the city or town level, while it is an indicator of a larger structural crisis (see Mills, 1959, for discussion of how individual or local troubles reflect larger social problems).

As one might expect, crime rose during this economic transformation as a growing percentage of the U.S. work force was displaced or marginalized by the shrinking manufacturing base. Two caveats must be noted about this general statement.

First, the relationship between economic marginalization and crime is not easily observable to the extent that economic marginalization is often inappropriately measured as a simple unemployment rate. Economic marginalization extends beyond unemployment, and can include partial and seasonal employment, as well as forms of economic exploitation found in wage-based economies where class membership defines owning and laboring options, as well as broad shifts in salary structures associated with the expansion of the service economy. To address these concerns, scholars devised empirical methods that measure marginalization in ways that are more consistent with the unique theoretical anchoring of radical criminology (as opposed to the theoretical anchoring of traditional, mainstream, or orthodox criminology; for discussion of these methods and examples of their empirical application in criminology see Lynch, 1987, 1988; Lynch, Groves, and Lizotte, 1994; Lynch, Hogan, and Stretesky, 1999; Nalla, Lynch, and Leiber, 1997).

Second, crime did not rise during the entire period under discussion; in fact, as noted earlier in this book, crime began to decline in the 1990s. Interestingly, *the decline in crime in the 1990s came at a time where employment opportunities had expanded and rates of wealth concentration slowed* (Wolff, 2002). The relationship between crime and unemployment is not uniform, linear, or always in the expected direction (e.g., as unemployment goes up, crime will increase; Michalowski and Carson, 1999). Again, this may be due to the fact that unemployment and economic marginalization are two different concepts that require different measures.

We must also consider what happened to the imprisonment rate. Following the predictions based on the Rusche-Kirchheimer hypothesis, we would expect the imprisonment rate to rise along with economic marginalization. The more specific hypothesis found in the research literature, however, links Rusche and Kirchheimer's model to unemployment rates, which leads to the hypothesis that unemployment and imprisonment rates should fluctuate together. By the mid- to late 1980s, as the economy began to recover from the high unemployment rates of the mid- to late 1970s, one would expect, therefore, that the imprisonment rate would decline. But, it did not; it continued to rise. How can this apparent discrepancy be explained? In part, the mild economic recovery in the 1980s was fuelled by an expansion of the service industry and the renewed opportunities for employment this sector generated. To be sure, the erosion of the manufacturing base was somewhat offset by growth in service sector employment, illustrated in figure 5.2.

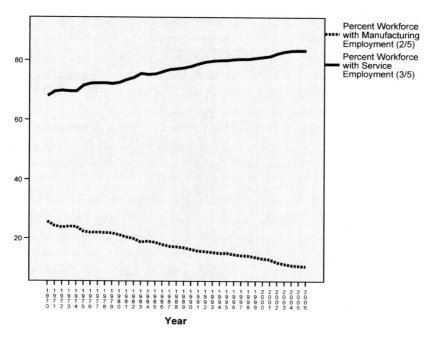

5.2. Service and Manufacturing Sector Employment, United States, as a Percent of Total Nonfarm Labor Force, 1970–2006

Nevertheless, and contrary to expectations, despite enhanced employment opportunities, crime continued to rise through the late 1980s. In part, this rise in crime can be traced to the lower standard of living among the working class. That is, while expansion of the service sector created new jobs, the jobs that were created were lower-paying positions. It could be argued that the reality of these jobs did not meet social expectations. Furthermore, the wage decline associated with the transformation from an industrial to a service economy indicates that a very broad form of economic marginalization was affecting even employed workers.

During the Clinton administration, the economy began to grow at an accelerated pace. This economic upsurge was, to a large degree, more imaginary than real, benefiting upper-income groups through the development of the high-tech computer industry and the proliferation of the "dot.com" market place. During this period, class inequality increased as accelerated economic activity tended to be concentrated, providing the greatest benefit to those who could invest in the stock market, as well as among the new high-tech entrepreneurs and their managing class. (This trend was very visible in certain markets and cities, such as Atlanta).

In the big picture, things looked better, and consumer confidence in the economy was high. When the big picture was broken down, however, we see that expanded economic fortunes had limited impact on the majority of workers, especially those at the low end of the income scale, who continued to lose ground once the effects of inflation were considered (Wolff, 2002).

Under George W. Bush's Republican leadership, the economy began to stumble. Unemployment rose, manufacturing declined further, interest rates were cut in an effort to stimulate the economy, and the number of new jobs created in the service sector no longer kept pace with the number of jobs lost in the manufacturing sector. The crime drop, which had been in effect since 1991, leveled off.

## REVISING RUSCHE AND KIRCHHEIMER

Interestingly, throughout this entire time period, as the economy grew or contracted, as crime went up or went down, imprisonment rates continued to grow. These observations raise some interesting dilemmas for the traditional materialist perspective on punishment that stemmed from the Rusche-Kirchheimer perspective, especially regarding the position that links prison growth to unemployment or poor economic conditions.

For instance, from a materialist perspective, the continued expansion of the prison system during the 1990s did not fit the theoretical expectations generated from Rusche and Kirchheimer's arguments. Clearly, from that theoretical perspective, incarceration would be expected to decline as economic circumstances improved. Why weren't these expectations being met?

To some extent, the expected outcome is the result of a rather narrow interpretation of the Rusche-Kirchheimer hypothesis. As you recall, Rusche and Kirchheimer stipulated that each system of production discovers punishments that are appropriate to or fit with the primary emphasis of that system's form of production. In order to make sense of this claim, we must also understand that the American system of production had undergone a dramatic transformation over the previous two and a half decades. In essence, the new service-oriented economic system that dominated the American scene in the 1990s had different characteristics than the old manufacturing economy. These differences might help explain why imprisonment was more heavily relied upon under the new service economy. Thus, we must turn our attention to describing some of these key economic features in order to understand the path taken by the correctional system.

Like any other form of capital, service capital requires a continually expanding marketplace in order to meet the capital accumulation expectations of potential investors and entrepreneurs. In effect, this requires that the demand for a commodity, whether it is service-sector labor or a more traditional commodity used directly by consumers, must also continually increase. The naturally occurring problem for all capitalists is that there is a limit to how much of a commodity people will or can consume, which limits how much of a commodity the capitalist can sell. In turn, consumption is affected by numerous limits, such as the distribution of income. Say, for example, I sell cars that cost $40,000, or at a price that is about what the average American family earns in a year. The price of this car limits its appeal simply because only a small portion of the population can afford to buy one. To expand the number of potential consumers who can purchase my vehicles, I offer them an option to buy the car over time. Even though this option is available, not everyone will use it, and not everyone will qualify for credit because of other financial obligations or because they just don't earn enough annual income. Nevertheless, one way to expand consumption is through credit. As of 2001, 75 percent of U.S. families have assumed some credit. In 2001, the median debt value for U.S. families was $38,800 (Federal Reserve, 2003).

To net a profit, commodities must not only have a market, they must be sold. One of the unique properties or problems of service commodities is that they must be sold on a daily basis (or for a specific contracted period) to generate sustainable income and profits. Thus, the seller of service labor must find buyers for service labor each day, or have a standing contract for its sale. Because a service commodity must be continually replaced to be of any value to its consumers, there is a natural replacement need with a cycle that is much shorter than for commodities such as durable goods. This shorter cycle also increases the potential pool of repeat customers. To take one example, consider the food service sector. Most people eat three times a day, a considerably shorter consumption cycle than for automobiles (five years) or washing machines (ten years). An automobile is "consumed" or purchased once every 5 years, or, on average every 1,825 days, meaning there is only one opportunity in this period, on average, to make an automobile sale to each person. In the same 5 years, a full-service food vendor (breakfast, lunch, and dinner) has the opportunity to make 5,475 potential sales to one customer during the same period (at 3 meals per day). Even if this person eats out only a few times a week, and only one-half of those times at the same location, there would be more than 150 potential sales available to a food service provider over 5 years—*per person*.

From the vantage point of the capitalist, this unique replacement characteristic of service-sector commodities provides both advantages and disadvantages over the ordinary commodity. The advantage of service-sector commodities, as noted, is in the need for relatively frequent replacement in some cases (e.g., lawn care service), or a commodity with a relatively long-term inelastic demand (e.g., food) when compared to the ordinary commodity. The disadvantage for the service-sector commodity is restricted to certain segments of the marketplace that have fluctuating short-term demand. In response, in some service areas, the service-sector provider may enter into flexible labor contracts capable of adjusting to fluctuating demand (e.g., temporary service provision). Nevertheless, such contracts are not always possible, and the service-sector capitalist may have to pay employees even when there is no service to provide.

Given these constraints, what the service-sector capitalist desires is a market for the services she sells that is inelastic in the short term. The mantra of capitalism, however, is to accumulate, and moreso to expand capital accumulation. Thus, the service-sector capitalist desires more than an inelastic market—he desires an expanding marketplace. To be sure, in recent decades, the prison apparatus has provided one such marketplace.

Capitalists have invented a host of businesses that take advantage of the short replacement cycle and long-term inelastic nature of demand that characterizes some service-sector commodities. A number of these businesses sell their commodities to those who run the growing U.S. correctional system. These services include, but are not limited to:

data storage and retrieval; electronic monitoring systems; food services; laundry and clothing services; telecommunication services; Internet services; health-care services; insurance; mailing services; financial services; transportation services; maintenance services; and housing, building, and security (prison guard) services.

In part, the above explanation does not sound plausible for several reasons. First, if we were to follow the empirical literature based on Rusche and Kirchheimer, expanded prison services *could only be offered* in a context where imprisonment was rising, and this would imply—if the Rusche-Kirchheimer hypothesis were correct—a continual increase in unemployment. While the basis for this condition exists given the decline of the manufacturing base in the United States, the opposing expansion of the service sector offsets some, but not all, of the rise in unemployment. Likewise, various governmental policies, such as manipulation of the prime lending rate, also come into play to balance out trends in employment. Second, there are some contradictory conditions that appear necessary to explain the growth of imprisonment in the United States. On the one hand, a certain level of unemployment benefits capitalism by driving down the cost of labor because it creates competition for employment. On the other hand, too much unemployment stifles the ability of the marketplace to expand, reduces consumer demand, and lowers profits.

Consider further that if Rusche and Kirchheimer's advocates were correct that unemployment and imprisonment fluctuate simultaneously, then the marketplace for prison services would not be very secure. Indeed, the demand for prison services would rise and fall as unemployment rose or fell and as various components of the economic and political system adjusted to "correct" the level of employment. In other words, as a marketplace for services—and the assumption being made here is that the prison has become a service marketplace—the prison industry would be volatile and unpredictable if it simply responded to fluctuations in the rate of unemployment. A factor beyond unemployment must be operating to transform the prison into a viable financial investment. One possibility is that there is a mechanism in place that constantly expands the types and numbers of people who are defined as dangerous, which also makes the prison a suitable, growing service market. To be sure, this process is evident in the latter half of the twentieth century (Sheldon,

2000) and has been especially prominent with respect to definitions of dangerousness that employ racial characteristics, as well those associated with drug use (Gordon, 1994).

An alternative explanation, which is likely to operate in conjunction with the first, is that prison-market capitalists, who have an interest in expanding prison service provisions, also play a role in maintaining prison growth. Today, the private prison sector and prison service provision sector is indeed quite large. Like other business sectors, the private prison sector has lobbyists, political action committees (PACs), and industry groups to represent its interests to politicians.

Another plausible explanation that requires amending the hypotheses extracted from Rusche and Kirchheimer's view is that labor market conditions such as unemployment fail to adequately represent the form of economic marginalization to which prison expansion corresponds. The Economic Policy Institute, for example, has detailed one such factor, expanded income inequality, in a study entitled *Pulling Apart*. Average U.S. income inequality grew from the 1970s through the 1990s. By the 1990s, the average income for the top 20 percent of income earners was $137,000, 10 times higher than the average income for the lowest 20 percent of income earners. Income growth for the top 20 percent of families was, on average, approximately $34,000 over this time period (measured in 1997 constant dollars). During the same period, the average income for the bottom 20 percent of families fell by approximately $2,000. In short, aggregate income growth during this period was driven by gains made by the top 20 percent of income earners. As these data indicate, the increase in income produced during this period was not widely shared, and in three-quarters of states, income inequality grew between the 1980s and 1990s. As these figures illustrate, economic marginalization of the lowest wage earners expanded despite a long-term decline in unemployment. The declining incomes for those at the bottom are a result of a loss of well-paying manufacturing jobs, the expansion of low-paying service-sector employment, the decline in the real value of the minimum wage, and the process of globalization, which has pushed the decline in manufacturing by exporting manufacturing jobs to nations with a lower wage basis.

As a simple test of the hypothesized relationship, the upper-income level for the poorest one-fifth of the population in each state (in dollars) and the estimated percentage of the population falling within the poorest one-fifth in each state can be regressed on the change in the rate of imprisonment. Using Gainsborough and Mauer's estimates of the change in imprisonment rates by state for 1991–1998, and controlling for the rate of change in the total UCR crime rate, the upper-income level for the poorest one-fifth of the population by state is a significant predictor ($p = 0.033$; $t = -2.203$) of the change in imprisonment rates. The percentage of those falling into the poorest one-fifth is not significant. This may be due to the fact that this percentage varies little across states (the majority of states [$N = 45$] have between 41 and 49 percent of their population in this category). The results for the negative relationship between the upper income level for the poorest one-fifth of the population and the change in imprisonment, however, lends some evidence favoring the view described above.

### THE PRISON AS INDUSTRY, SOCIAL CONTROL AS COMMODITY

In order to understand more fully what happened to the longstanding association between the labor market and imprisonment during the contemporary period of American capitalism, it is necessary to recast the prison as industry, or at least, as Nils Christie described it, as part of the crime control industry. Understanding the prison as industry also requires that we take into account the fact that the American economy was transformed during the 1970s from a manufacturing to a service basis.

The demise of manufacturing and the rise of the service-sector economy has important implications for the prison as industry view and can serve as the basis for interpreting the association between contemporary trends in imprisonment and economic factors and conditions. To do so, we must also pay attention to the arguments set forth by James O'Connor in his 1973 book, *The Fiscal Crisis of the State*. It was here that O'Connor argued that the state had become part of the accumulation process. In effect, the fiscal crisis experienced by the state was connected to the state's role in stimulating the economy at best, and minimally by enhancing the ability of the capitalist sector to enhance its accumulation potential.

In O'Connor's view, the state can fulfill its role in accumulation either indirectly or directly. The state meets its accumulation function indirectly by guiding the economy in an effort to improve the circumstances for capital accumulation and economic expansion (e.g., the common practice of manipulating the interest rate). The state, however, can also facilitate accumulation directly by spending current reabsorbed wages acquired from taxation (or future reabsorbed wages through debt spending) in ways that transform those wages into payments that expand the available pool of potential surplus value (as surplus value is the source of profit; see Marx, 1974). The privatization of state services, which expanded tremendously during the Reagan administration, provides a useful example of the latter strategy. The importance and impact of the privatization of governmental responsibilities on economic trends should not be overlooked. Through privatization, billions of tax dollars can be redirected to the private sector when the state is forced to purchase rather than provide services. The timing of this effort should also not be overlooked, because the Reagan-initiated privatization movement corresponds with the prolific expansion of the U.S. prison system, as well as the expansion of the entire private prison apparatus.

One of the key features of privatization is that it aids in the transfer of capital from the state to the private sector. In effect, privatization allows the state to expend money it has collected through taxation—which it had previously used to provide governmentally sponsored, nonprofit services—on private, for-profit service providers. Before privatization, the services normally provided by the state were treated as social expenses, and they were viewed as necessary state expenditures that promoted social welfare. Once privatization was implemented, however, the state becomes a "middle man" in the service-provision chain, selecting service providers to replace some of its functions. That is, payments previously made to service workers hired directly by the government (i.e., state workers) are now made to capitalists who absorb part of the previous social expense bill as profit before paying workers to provide contracted services for the state. Evidence of this type of service contact can be found in most U.S. states. In Florida, for example, where this practice is widespread, numerous juvenile detention and rehabilitation programs are operated by private service providers rather than by the state directly.

Under privatization, the capitalist acting as a service provider gets a cut of state social expenses to fulfill the role previously occupied directly by state agents or state employees. This service provision fee, which may be much larger than the salary paid to state employees, diminishes the pool of money the state has available to be spent directly on services. Nevertheless, the private sector, conservative politicians, and social commentators hold out privatization as a more efficient mechanism for service provision (see data above on privatization, pollution, and electricity generation in California).

Indeed, one of the primary legitimation claims made about private-sector service providers is that they are more economically efficient than governmental services, and therefore the private sector would be able to provide services at a lower cost than government, hence reducing the overall tax liability to the public. What was overlooked in this argument was the fact that privatization either depresses wages of workers in affected areas and increases the exploitation of laborers (if we employ an objective definition of exploitation), or it increases unemployment by cutting the number of workers privatized service employers hire to provided a service. Moreover, other important issues are left out of the privatization debate. For example, where criminal justice or other social services are concerned, one important but omitted discussion centers on the legitimacy of allowing private providers to supply services needed to promote social welfare. In addition, no one suggests that the costs of services could be lowered even further if the government placed a limit on the amount of profit capitalists were allowed to extract from service provision agreements that are, after all, designed to benefit the public good. While these types of arguments are of interest to radicals, they must be put aside here to return to the primary question being pursued, namely: How, exactly, does the prison industry fit into this argument?

Before we can fully appreciate the prison as industry view, we must first alter our understanding of the term "industry." In traditional usage, we equate industry with manufacturing or the production of tangible commodities that can be sold in order to transfer value and stimulate capital accumulation. In service industries, however, there are no tangible commodities that embody dead labor values. Rather, what the service sector offers for sale is future or potential labor that provides no direct value in the traditional sense. Service labor, however, may be put to a variety of uses, some of which establish a climate that enhances the ability of capitalists to expand their capital accumulation potential, or which reinforces legitimation and reproduction of the economic system through the operation and expansion of ideological mechanisms. To round out this discussion of prison as industry and its connection to the service sector we must also consider social control as a commodity.

### Social Control as a Commodity

As an industry, the prison is the site of the application of a good deal of service labor; labor that is applied to generate a non-tangible commodity we call social control. It could be argued that without the application of social control, capitalism would be crushed by illegitimate activities. These crimes would include those by both the capitalist and marginal classes. Historically, because social control serves an important function in managing class conflict in capitalist societies, the crimes of the marginal classes have been magnified while the crimes of the powerful have been minimized. Here, however, we must redirect attention to the commodity aspects of social control.

In the form of imprisonment, the commodity we call social control has unique properties to the extent that it accomplishes three conditions required by capitalism: (1) imprisonment is part of the ideological apparatus that reinforces the system of private property rights (especially since most crimes that are punished in the United States are property crimes); (2) in conjunction with criminal labeling processes, imprisonment forces a sector of the working class to whom it is most likely to be applied (a group that consists of the lower and working classes and minorities) into idleness, and, eventually, to become part of the surplus population of unemployable workers. The existence of this portion of the labor market serves to help maintain wages at a minimum level; and (3) imprisonment also provides conditions that expand the marketplace for goods and services sold by the capitalist class, especially when the rate of imprisonment continually expands.

When we conceptualize the prison as industry, we must take account of its ideological and legitimation functions, but we cannot forget that this form of social control plays a role in providing for expanded capital accumulation. In other words, *aside from* its social control, class control, and ideological function, the prison as industry is a site for the consumption of commodities and the service labor provided by the capitalist class.

To be sure, the prison is not an industry in itself, but it is a necessary part of the productive apparatus that has grown up around providing services and commodities used in the social control process. Just as there can be no commodities without consumers, there can be no products specifically targeting social control without social control consumers—in this case, the capitalist state.

This observation raises an obvious but interesting point. In general, the accumulation potential within an industry will be tied to the size of the marketplace it serves, which, in part, is a reflection of the number of consumers, or the amount of product consumed. Naturally, capitalists desire the largest market possible in order to expand the limits of capital accumulation. As noted earlier, it is part of the state's role to provide conditions conducive to capital accumulation. Thus, expanding the prison system simultaneously accomplishes legitimation and accumulation functions the state is required to fulfill under capitalism.

*An Example of the Prison as Industry: Private Corrections*

The idea of prison as industry is nowhere more evident than in the invention of, and movement toward, private correctional facilities. The term "private corrections" covers a diverse array of services the state may purchase to operate prisons and other correctional services (e.g., probation, rehabilitation, drug counseling, etc.). Private correctional facilities specifically involve contracts that provide for the housing of inmates either in state- or privately owned facilities. In more general terms, private correctional services that may be purchased to operate a prison range from security monitoring equipment (and the labor of security monitors) and guards, to portable-module prison cells, maintenance of facilities and inmates (including food, clothing, hygiene products, medical services, etc.,), to the operation or building of entire prisons. Large businesses have stepped forward to occupy this space to participate in the expanded capital market available for providing for the social control of convicted criminals.

In 2002, more than $50 billion was spent on correctional services in the United States. These expenditures included payments for insurance, data storage, telecommunications, health care, printing, transportation, mailing, laundry, clothing, food, security devices, and special housing services. It is difficult to determine the portion of the total correctional bill that was directly paid to the private correctional sector for services. An estimate can be made by reviewing what we know about existing correctional service contract providers.

In 2000, there were thirteen private correctional management firms with active contracts in the United States, which housed more than 120,000 inmates. The largest of these contractors, Corrections Corporation of America (CCA), housed more than 55 percent of the inmates (67,000) in 63 facilities located in 19 states and the District of Columbia in 2005 (http://www.correctionscorp.com/aboutcca.html; Sourcebook of Criminal Justice Statistics, table 6.26). If CCA were treated as an independent correctional system, it would be the fifth-largest correctional system in the United States behind California, Texas, Florida, and New York. In 2003 CCA earned more than $1 billion in revenue, a 12.5 percent increase over 2001 revenue (see CCA's 2003 year-end financial report, http://www.correctionscorp.com). At the same time, CCA expanded its employment by only 1 percent. CCA is large enough to serve as parent corporation to Transcor America Incorporated, a prison transportation service provider. The big business behind CCA was most noticeable when it was added to the New York Stock Exchange in 1994 (ticker symbol CXN). CCA's own calculations of potential profitability based on "man"-day revenue and fixed and variable expenses leaves a profit operating margin of 25.3 percent (see, CCA, 2005: 20), indicating that crime pays private correctional service providers quite well.

As noted above, it is impossible to estimate the exact amount of America's $50 billion private-sector correctional budget. Considering that CCA's piece of the correctional pie is a little more than 2 percent, and that there are many other types of private services—from food to laundry services—that correctional systems purchase, a conservative estimate that 25 to 30 percent (or $12.5 to $15 billion) of prison expenditures are directed toward the private sector does not seem unreasonable.

At this juncture, it is useful to recall O'Connor's argument about the connection between government expenditures and the state's role in providing conditions conducive to the expansion of opportunities for capital accumulation for the capitalist sector. As noted, one means of doing so is to privatize social expenditures so that they are now made to private businesses that carry out service-related tasks previously undertaken by the government. It should be clear from the previous discussion how privatization and growth within the prison sector accomplished these tasks. To round out this discussion, let us turn to an investigation of the growth in potential income generated by the expansion of the prison industry by reviewing growth costs in terms of taxpayer burden.

The taxpayer burden for operating the U.S. correctional system can be measured in several ways. Obviously, tax dollars pay most of the correctional bill. As noted earlier, that bill is so large that the ordinary person has trouble comprehending its enormity. We can make the taxpayer's burden more visible and understandable by translating correctional costs into per capita or per person costs. In 1995, the per capita correctional bill was about $195. The present per capital correctional tax bill is closer to $225.

This doesn't seem like such a large bill, and many might be willing to pay this amount to reduce crime (assuming for the moment that imprisonment reduces crime). Relative to per capita income, per capita prison expenses are a little more than 1 percent of income. But this figure is a misleading indicator of how much the correctional system costs the *average tax payer*. For example if you are the only breadwinner in a family of six, your correctional tax bill is six times $225, or $1,350.

Another way to figure out your cost is to look at the cost per taxpayer rather than the per capita cost. About 12 percent of the U.S. population or 31 million people filed federal tax returns in 2004. State tax requirements increases the number of taxpayers, and we can estimate that there are 50 million such taxpayers. Using this figure, the per-taxpayer costs for the correctional system average around $1,200. The exact amount you pay will vary depending on where you live and your income level. Looked at on a per-taxpayer basis, prison expenses eat up much more of your per capita income: 5.5 percent. And, while even this may not look like a troubling amount, taxes directed toward prisons eat up much more of the tax bill than they once did. Between 1980 and 2000, per capita expenditures on the U.S. prison system rose by $145, or by more than 480 percent in 20 years. In other words, we spent a great deal more on the prison system in 2000 than we did in 1980. And, during this period, prison expenditures increased more rapidly than imprisonment. From 1980 to 2000, the imprisonment rate rose by 243 percent, while the number of inmates incarcerated rose by 318 percent. Relative to the increase in the imprisonment rate, the imprisonment bill rose twice as fast, even tough the prison system was also being privatized to keep down costs. Thus, over time, locking up more people is not simply more costly because we now have larger prison populations. It is also more costly because the costs of doing so rise more quickly than the rate of incarceration. In fact, taxpayer per capita correctional costs grew at such a steady pace that they exceeded the growth of imprisonment, measured by the number of inmates, beginning in 1984. The gap between the two has expanded slowly since.

The correctional tax bill has implications beyond its cost to individual taxpayers. From a materialist perspective, taxes are important for two reasons. First, as O'Connor (1973, 203) argued, "Every important change in the balance of class and political forces is registered in the tax structure." As noted earlier, a key element of the materialist perspective on imprisonment is that imprisonment has become part of the class war in modern America, and, as Ronald Goldfarb (1969) once argued, "prisons are America's poorhouse."

Class warfare is not always directly visible. In earlier times, class warfare was evident in strikes (late-nineteenth, early-twentieth century) or in protests against corporatism (1960s). Often, however, class warfare is hidden within the normal operation of state mechanisms such as the criminal justice system, which primarily focuses on the crimes of the lower classes (Lynch, Michalowki, and Groves, 2000; Reiman, 2003). Class warfare is also evident in various forms of economic inequality. Economic inequality doesn't just happen: it is often the result of specific policies that affect taxation, investments, the business growth cycle, interest rates, and a host of laws that have unequal impact on people from different class positions (Chambliss and Seidman, 1982).

The expansion of economic inequality in America is one measure of both inequality and class conflict. We commonly assume, and are often told by politicians, that there is less economic inequality today than in previous eras. Governmental data, however, indicates that this is not accurate. According to U.S. Census Bureau data on income distribution (the GINI index or index of income concentration), for example, income inequality between the 20 percent of households that receive the lowest income and the 5 percent that receive the greatest share of income has increased substantially—by more than 25 percent—since 1968.

In fact, income inequality is higher now than in the 1940s. In other words, income inequality, and therefore the potential for class conflict, has expanded over the past three decades, at the same time that imprisonment has also been expanding. Keeping this class conflict in check has required the average person to pay more taxes to operate a rapidly expanding prison system that primarily houses poor criminals.

## Conclusion

The discussion of the materialist perspective in this chapter has covered a good deal of ground and a number of different issues, in order to demonstrate why it is necessary to examine explanations for imprisonment that are beyond those ordinarily found in criminological literature. As noted, the majority of criminological explanations of punishment and imprisonment begin with an assumption that crime drives the explanation because, at least on its face, punishment is a response to crime. In the materialist tradition, however, researchers look beyond this apparent connection; as Rusche and Kirchheimer argued, it is necessary to move beyond the assumed connection between crime and punishment if other influences are to be discerned.

Rusche and Kirchheimer argued that each society discovers penal responses that are consistent with that society's system of economic production. They support this contention primarily through the use of historical methods. Beginning in the 1970s, researchers reinterpreted Rusche and Kirchheimer's theoretical arguments so that they could be applied empirically. This lead to the proposition that one of the functions of incarceration was to control the economically marginalized populations produced during the normal course of capitalism. But, as was noted, the relationship between marginalization and imprisonment captured by employment-imprisonment studies applied to industrial capitalism; it appears to have eroded as a useful explanation for imprisonment trends in the United States during more recent decades in which the economy has moved from an industrial to a service basis. To illustrate this point, it was noted that the modified Rusche-Kirchheimer thesis does a poor job of explaining the continued rise in imprisonment seen in the United States during the late 1980s and 1990s, a period of economic expansion tied to the service economy. One example of an alternative explanation has been provided by Michalowski and Carson, who noted that the relationship between unemployment and incarceration trends are conditioned by social structures of accumulation.

This chapter elaborated on how the U.S. economy changed during the 1980s and 1990s, and how these changes could be related to the continued expansion of the American prison system. Important considerations involved deregulation, globalization, and worker productivity. Each of these economic changes expanded economic opportunities for the wealthy, ushering in a period of economic growth and job gains. These gains, however, were class-linked, and at the same time that those with wealth saw their fortunes increase, those at the bottom of the class hierarchy experienced diminishing returns, even though their prospects for employment increased. That is, while visible unemployment declined, the form of employment shifted from manufacturing to service-sector employment, with its lower wages and reduced benefits. While more people were employed, they remained economically marginalized. And, while more people were employed, the incarceration rate continued to rise. This relationship appeared to contradict the Rusche-Kirchheimer model and, most especially, the empirical tests of that model that linked incarceration trends to unemployment levels. But, in the new U.S. economy, employed people were being marginalized by an expansion of the service sector, a contraction of manufacturing, globalization, increased worker productivity, and deregulation. In essence, the simple materialist assumption that the unemployment rate was an appropriate measure of economic marginalization, and not the general assumptions of the Rusche-Kirchheimer view itself, were questionable.

This could be illustrated, for example, by examining the relationship between a different means for measuring marginalization and prison trends, such as the percentage of the population earning incomes that placed them in the lowest income bracket.

In addition, in the new service economy, the prison itself became a service industry, and adapted to the new, open market by expanding the extent of private-sector participation. The interests of private sector capitalists help drive prison expansion through several mechanisms discussed in this chapter. This lead to the private prison sector becoming a multibillion-dollar industry that depended on an expanding marketplace—prisons and prison populations—for its profit. In short, not only did prisons become an important part of the economy, social control was transformed into a commodity.

While this chapter has contributed to extending materialist explanations so that they are relevant to discussions of prison expansion in the United States over the past two decades, it has failed to take other important factors into account. Of particular importance to this view is the relationship between prison growth and race control in the United States (Vogel, 2003). This issue is explored further in the chapters that follow.

## CHAPTER 6

# Prison Effects

## WHO GETS LOCKED UP

THE RATE OF imprisonment in the United States has increased consistently from 1973 through 2000, growing by 920 percent! During that period, the rate of crime rose 42 percent. Thus, over this thirty-year span, as imprisonment increased each and every year, crime was not suppressed; in fact, it was as high in 1991 as it was two decades earlier. A further examination of the relationship between imprisonment and crime rates is found in the next chapter. For now, it is useful to remember that when imprisonment rises, crime sometimes goes down and sometimes up. In other words, in the long run of history measured from 1973 through 2000, a rising rate of imprisonment does not assure citizens of the United States that they are receiving any greater crime control protection.

In response to such a revelation or reading of the data, proponents of the imprisonment binge might propose one of two explanations. The first is that crime would have increased much more than 42 percent if imprisonment had not increased by 920 percent over the past three decades, and several imprisonment proponents have used elaborate statistical models in an effort to prove just such a point (see Clear 1996 for discussion). But we can never know if this statement is true, and this idea can only be accepted on faith. Second, imprisonment proponents will avert our attention away from the long-term association between incarceration and crime to short-term trends, especially those evident in the 1990s. They argue that we must look at periods where the increase in imprisonment had been in effect for some time before we can see benefits. Ignoring twenty years of data that does not fit with their position, however, this argument seems to miss the broader issues involved.

While academics and policy makers will continue to argue about the effectiveness of imprisonment as a crime control strategy, there continues to be a need to examine the impacts of continually raising the rate of incarceration in the United States. We know, for example, there are many more Americans in prison today than in 1973. Thus, in addition to asking how an increased rate of incarceration affects crime, we also need to ask: Who are these Americans who are now locked safely away behind bars? And, how has our imprisonment binge affected the characteristics of the prison population? We examine this issue in the sections that follow.

### Who Is in America's Prisons?

How has the imprisonment binge affected the characteristics of the population of Americans who are locked up in the prison system? If we follow the logic of deterrence and incapacitation arguments, we would hypothesize that the effort to control crime by locking up more criminals *should result* in the incarceration of more *serious offenders,* and that the characteristics of the prison population would change to reflect this emphasis on serious crime. Are the people who have been locked away in America's prisons the most serious criminals in society?

This is a complex question to answer, in part, because it requires acknowledging who is not locked up in prison. As noted earlier, an important criminal element omitted from America's prison system includes white-collar and corporate criminals. Because this group is omitted from prison, we cannot use them to assess whether our nation's imprisonment binge changed the characteristics of inmates housed in prison. We could, however, argue that it would be useful to examine whether there were any long term changes in the level of white collar and corporate crime and the rate at which these offenders were incarcerated. Unfortunately, there is no useful, long-term database on white-collar and corporate crime that details the characteristics of these kinds of criminals or the number of crimes they have committed over the time period we wish to study. Thus, we are largely "stuck" with a focus on the changing characteristics of inmates in American prisons.

Before we can begin that investigation, we must admit that it is difficult to precisely measure the characteristics of prison inmates over the past thirty years because data on the characteristics of prison inmates is not available for the entire period. Further, because the imprisonment binge covers such a long time period, it would be difficult to track the many changes that have occurred in the characteristics of those who are behind bars in America. To make this task more manageable and to reflect more reliable measures of the characteristics of the prison population, the analysis presented below is restricted to more recent years. For some parts of this analysis, the time period is restricted to 1991 through 1997; for other portions, we will begin in 1985. These years were selected due to data limitations, and because these more recent periods mark the greatest growth in America's prison system.

*Offense Type*

One method of examining the characteristics of the prison inmate population is to look at the crimes for which inmates are committed. One reason to examine offense types over time is to determine whether a change in imprisonment philosophy affects the type of inmates who end up in prison.

Previously, it was noted that imprisonment trends in the 1990s were driven by a strong reliance on the assumptions of the social defense or incapactitative model of imprisonment, which is based on the idea that locking up dangerous, repeat offenders will lower the overall rate of criminal offending by removing known criminals from society. Thus, for this model to work as advertised, we would expect to see an increase in the percentage of the prison population that was incarcerated for repeat offending or had a record of serious violent or property crime.

VIOLENT CRIMES. In 1991 violent offenders, or those sent to prison for murder, rape, robbery, kidnapping and assault, composed 46.6 percent of state prison populations in the United States. Over the next six years, under the leadership of policy makers and politicians who endorsed the social defense model, the rate of imprisonment grew by 42 percent, or by an average of 7 percent per year. This rate of growth in the prison population was fairly substantial. During this period of substantial prison growth, the number of inmates incarcerated for violent offenses grew by 41 percent. In other words, the rate of growth of incarceration was slightly greater than the rate of growth in the percentage of inmates sentenced to prison for violent offenses. There was some variation in the change in incarceration by type of crime.

From 1991 through 1997, for instance, the percentage of inmates sent to prison for rape and robbery declined. This decline reflected a similar trend noted in the number of rapes and robberies reported to the police during this time period. The prison proponent could look at these figures further and declare that imprisonment worked. In terms of raw numbers, there were a few more rapists in prisons in 1997 compared to 1991 (27,500 versus 25,500) and quite a few more robbers (152,000 versus 107,800). Over this time period, the number of robberies declined by 189,200, while the number of reported rapes declined by 10,440. It may be plausible that incarcerating an additional 44,200 robbers reduced robberies by 189,200, or by an average of 4.3 robberies per incarcerated robber, or that the additional 2,000 incarcerated rapists prevented 10,440 rapes, or 5.2 rapes per offender. Some of these differences might be attributed to an incapacitation effect, and the remainder to a deterrent effect, or vice versa. From a cost-benefit perspective, if we assume that it costs $25,000 annually to house an inmate in prison, we can ask: Are the 4.3 robberies suppressed by the $25,000 spent to incarcerate an inmate equivalent? Could we reduce robberies by 4.3 by spending less than $25,000 in a different way?

During the same period, the percentage of inmates sent to prison for murder, manslaughter, and assault increased, even though the number of these crimes reported to police fell. From 1991 through 1997, the number of inmates sentenced for homicide increased by 48,600, while the number sentenced for assault increased by 41,500. At the same time, the number of murders and non-negligent homicides reported to police fell by 6,490 (from 24,700 to 18,210), while the number of assaults fell by 69,540 (from 1,092,740 to 1,023,200). For the incarceration proponent, this means that locking up 48,600 murderers prevented 6,490 murders, or only 0.13 homicides for each murderer incarcerated. This seems plausible since murderers are harder to deter than other offenders. For assaults, locking up an additional 41,500 people prevented 69,540 assaults, or 1.7 per added inmate. In sum, locking up more offenders for homicide and assault had a minimal impact on these offenses. Again, we can also approach the reduction in crime from a cost-benefit perspective. How much should be spent to reduce the number of assaults by 1.7, or the number of homicides by 0.13? Is the price tag for a prison sentence ($25,000) too high? To suppress one homicide, 7.7 homicide offenders would need to be incarcerated at a cost of $192,000 per homicide. If we could lock up offenders and eliminate all homicides in this way (e.g., all 18,210 that occurred in 1997), we would somehow need to identify 7.7 times as many potential homicide offenders to incarcerate. This would mean locking up more than 420,000 potential homicide offenders at a cost of more than $3.5 billion a year.

Taken together, these data indicate that while the overall percentage of the prison population incarcerated for violent crime remained relatively stable from 1991 through 1997, there was some variation in the percentage of offenders sentenced for specific violent crimes. These data also indicate that the impact of incarceration varies by the type of violent crime. Why is it, we might ask, that incarceration has such widely different effects by the type of crime? Why were robberies reduced by 4.3 offenses per added inmate, rapes by 5.2, assaults by 1.7, and homicides by only 0.13 offenses per added inmate? Homicide is a fairly stable crime with small variations from year to year. This crime, which is often seen as a crime of passion and circumstances, does not appear to respond to incarceration. Assaults are similar to homicides in the sense that they are greatly affected by situational characteristics and passions. Why should they decrease by so much more than homicides, yet still be reduced by a rather slim margin? It is unlikely, for example, that those who commit assault are more likely than those who commit homicide to consider the consequences of their actions, or that they decide to stop before the event turns into a homicide because of the punishment. And why should robbers, who would be more likely to have planned their actions, be less likely to be affected by increased punishment than those who commit rapes? This fact would appear to contradict the logic of deterrence theory. The problem is that neither deterrence theory nor social defense theory is useful for explaining *why* different kinds of offenders might react differently to rising rates of punishment. Thus, while the outcomes noted appear consistent with deterrence and social defense arguments, we cannot use these views to predict why the effect of punishment varies across different groups of violent offenders. And, because we cannot do this, we are unsure how much we should raise the number or rate of people incarcerated for each of these offenses to obtain a substantial reduction in crime. In addition, let us not forget that here we have concentrated on a period where raising the rate of incarceration appeared to lower crime, and that for the period between 1973 and 1999 this outcome occurred only half the time. This means that there are a number of other points in time for which we could compare crime and imprisonment data that would not seem to support deterrence or incapacitation arguments at all, where the relationship between the number of each type of offender incarcerated would appear to have very different effects on crime reductions (or increases) for each offense type.

Let us also remember that to this point we have only examined the relationship between crime and imprisonment for violent crimes. Let us now turn our attention to other offenses to see how the deterrence and social defense views fair.

PROPERTY CRIMES. From 1991 through 1997, there was a decline in the percentage of the prison population incarcerated for major property crimes (burglary, larceny, motor vehicle theft, arson, and stolen property), from 24.4 percent in 1991 to 21.5 percent in 1997. The number of these crimes reported to police also fell during this time period. In other words, while there were more people in prison for property crimes in 1997 compared to 1991, the percentage of the prison population represented by property offenders declined, and the number of property crimes was also reduced. These data indicate that the emphasis on locking up more criminals did not lead to a greater representation of major property offenders among the prison population. To be sure, numerically, there were more property offenders locked up in 1997 compared to 1991; but the percent of offenders they represented declined. Let us examine what happened to the relationship between crime and imprisonment for property offenses.

In 1991, there were 142,100 property offenders (burglary, larceny, motor vehicle theft) in prison in the United States, and 179,900 by 1997. In 1991, there were 12,961,100 property offenses reported to police; in 1997, there were 11,558,500. In sum, in 1997, there were 37,800 more offenders locked up in state prisons for property offenses than in 1991, while there were 1,402,600 fewer property offenses reported to police, or roughly 37.1 fewer property crimes per added inmate. More specifically, there were 24,600 more burglars behind bars and 696,700 fewer burglaries reported, or an average of 28.3 fewer burglaries per added burglar.

For larceny-thefts, the comparable figures are 398,400 fewer crimes and 9,400 more incarcerated larceny-theft offenders, or 42.3 fewer crimes per added larcenist. For motor vehicle thefts there were an added 3,800 offenders, 307,500 fewer motor vehicle thefts, or 80.9 fewer motor vehicle thefts per incarcerated motor vehicle theft offender. Few of these reductions seem plausible since it would imply that the average offender incarcerated for any one of these offenses committed an extraordinarily large number of offenses (social defense) or dissuaded an unusually large number of other potential offenders (deterrence). Logically, the larger deterrent effect seen for property crimes compared to violent crime make sense since property offenders might be easier to deter through imprisonment. This finding would indicate that if prisons are providing social control or deterrence, they do so for crimes of lesser seriousness (property crimes) rather than violent crimes. To be sure, it could easily be argued that property offenders are more likely than violent crime offenders to consider the costs and rewards of crime. This outcome is problematic, however, given the seriousness of imprisonment as a response to crime, and our expectations concerning those crimes imprisonment should be the most effective at controlling.

The imprisonment proponent would cheerfully report these data to us, and note that sending more people to prison for major property offenses, even if they were not incarcerated in the same proportions in 1991 and 1997, appeared to affect crime. In response, we might ask why the differences are so great across individual property offenses. Consider, for example, that the number of larcenies suppressed per incarcerated larceny offender is well below the number of auto thefts suppressed per incarcerated motor vehicle offender. We might expect the reverse relationship since the payoff of a larceny-theft is small compared to the payoff from a motor vehicle theft, while the price of imprisonment is high compared to the economic gain of a larceny versus an auto theft. We might also suggest to the prison proponent that other factors may have affected the level of these crimes, such as a rising employment rate and greater access to less expensive home-security and anti–auto theft devices. And we would be remiss in our argument if we did not also point out that during other periods where incarceration rose, these crimes went up, meaning that the relationships we are examining may just be aberrations, especially since the prison proponent cannot offer specific arguments as to why imprisonment should affect different types of offenders differently, or in the manner noted in these data.

We should not lose sight of the other issue these data present. In particular, the changes in the characteristics of the United States prison population appear to contradict the policy emphasis of the social defense model—incarcerating more criminals did not result in a greater representation of serious violent or property crime offenders among inmates. To be sure, the number of these offenders increased; but at the same time, their proportional representation among inmates declined. These observations about the difference between the number and proportion of different types of offenders incarcerated in prison leads to the following question: if our growing prison system wasn't incarcerating a significantly larger population of serious violent and property offenders, then who was it incarcerating?

DRUG AND PUBLIC ORDER OFFENDERS. In sum, the growth of imprisonment from 1991 through 1997 did not result in greater representation of serious violent and property offenders among the prison population if we measure representation proportionally. To be sure, numerically, there were indeed more serious offenders behind bars in 1997 than in 1991. Yet, the decline in the proportion of violent and property offenders in prison means that the representation of some kind of "other" kind of criminal increased during this period.

Proponents of the social defense model would be expected to argue that these facts do not necessarily prove that prisons are not protecting society. Surely, if we lock up more criminals, society has a greater degree of protection. This argument cannot be dismissed out of hand, and it is likely that some degree of protection occurred simply from locking up more serious violent and property offenders, even if the percentage of the prison population made up of these offenders did not increase. To be fair in our representation of this view, we reviewed data examining the changes in the prison population and crime over time for specific offenses. While the crimes we examined declined as the number of inmates imprisoned rose, we also discovered that there was no guidance offered by deterrence or social defense theory that might predict the specific patterns of increases in punishment and the decreases in crime that were observed for the time period examined. Further, it should be noted once again that the crime suppression effect noted for this specific time period is not evident for other time periods during which incarceration rose. Data speaking to this issue will be reviewed later in this chapter. At this point, we must still answer one question: if prisons were locking up more inmates, and the proportional representation of serious inmates remained the same or declined, what crimes were now more prevalent among those for which inmates were being incarcerated? The partial answer to this question is that there was an increase in the proportional representation of drug and public order offenders.

From 1991 through 1997, the number of inmates incarcerated in state prisons for drug offenses rose significantly, from 155,000 to 222,100, or by 67,100. To place this increase in perspective, consider that for this same time period, the number of property offenders incarcerated expanded by 30 percent while the number of incarcerated drug offenders grew by 43 percent.

Another interesting fact about the increase in drug-related offenses relates to the race and ethnicity of incarcerated offenders. Approximately 57 percent of drug offenders incarcerated in state prisons were black, while 19 percent were Hispanic, and 23 percent were white. These figures, which will be reviewed later in this chapter in greater detail, point toward the conclusion that Marc Mauer calls the "race to incarcerate," and what Austin and Irwin call the "imprisonment binge," which have focused not only on lesser offenses, such as drug offenses, but also involves a distinct racial and ethnic bias.

The social defense argument, as we now well know, is based on the idea that expanding the use of imprisonment for serious offenses reduced crime. Thus, we expect that when placed into practice, an expansion of imprisonment results in locking up more offenders, provides the public with a greater degree of protection, and results in a crime reduction because serious offenders have been targeted. This expectation should apply to drug offenders. Thus as the proportion of drug offenders within the prison population rises, we would expect that the increase is reflected by a substantial expansion of the proportion of drug offenders incarcerated for more serious drug crimes, especially drug trafficking. However, when we break down the increase in the incarceration of drug offenders we find that from 1991 through 1997, the percentage of the prison population incarcerated for drug trafficking declined from

13.3 percent to 11.3 percent. Again, while there were more drug traffickers in prison in 1997 than in 1991, they made up a smaller percentage of the total prison population and a smaller percentage of convicted drug offenders.

Violent, property, and drug trafficking offenders committed the kinds of serious crimes we would expect our booming prison system to incapacitate in an effort to protect citizens from crime. The fact that the overall percentage of these three classes of offenders as a percentage of the total prison population declined implies that our growing prison system was being used to control some other group of less serious offenders. Who exactly were these other less serious offenders?

The dramatic expansion in drug offenders incarcerated from 1991 through 1997 was related to an increase in the percentage of the prison population incarcerated for drug possession (from 7.6 percent to 8.8 percent). Thus, one group that our growing prison system controlled "much better" were drug users, and not the group we expected to be targeted more forcefully through an increase in imprisonment, drug traffickers. In addition, we would be remiss if we did not point out that "as the proportion of prison admissions for drug crimes have increased, so have the proportions of nonwhites being sent to prison" (Austin and Irwin, 2003, 29). It is commonly assumed by many that such a relationship reflects actual drug use and offending patterns. Later in this chapter, data that contradicts this widely held assumption will be presented. For now, it is sufficient to point out that the expansion of imprisonment that funneled more drug offenders into American prisons also served as a mechanism for incarcerating a larger proportion of the minority population.

Other offenders were also more prevalent in prisons in 1997 compared to 1991. During this period, the percentage of the prison population incarcerated for "other offenses" (including traffic offenses, DWI/DUI, drunkenness, vagrancy, nonsupport, unlawful assembly, vice and rioting, obstruction, and weapons violations), among many other public order offenses, also increased. Though the increase was not substantial in terms of percent growth—offenders in these categories made up 3.4 percent of the prison population in 1991 compared to 4.3 percent by 1997—the expanded number of such inmates rivaled and even surpassed the increase in the number of offenders locked up for homicides, robberies, rapes, assaults, and all property crimes for this period. Indeed, by

1997, there were 58,700 more public order offenders in America's prisons—10,000 more than the number of added murderers; 15,000 more than the number of offenders convicted of assaults; 20,000 more than for property crimes. A proportion of these public order offenders were there as third-time felons, and their violations included third-strike "crimes" as lowly as vagrancy. Again, we must acknowledge that some of the offenders locked up by the sweeping imprisonment movement did include serious public order offenders who were incarcerated for weapons offenses. But we must also recognize that it was more likely that the liberty of much more minor criminal offenders were targeted by our imprisonment binge (Austin and Irwin, 2003).

In sum, evidence concerning the percentages of violent, property, drug, and public order offenders indicates that one of the trends in imprisonment associated with the social defense movement involved expanded incarceration of less serious offenders as a proportion of the prison population, as well as a contraction of more serious offenders measured proportional to the prison population. The expanding control exerted by imprisonment drew in more serious offenders numerically; at the same time, however, it drew in many more less serious offenders.

REPEAT OFFENDERS. As noted on several occasions, the expansion of imprisonment generated by a reliance on social defense philosophy should protect the public from crime. One way this might happen in that the increase in imprisonment leads to enhanced incarceration of violent criminals as a percentage of the prison population. That is, we expect new prison space to be devoted to locking up a greater number of violent offenders relative to other offenders. We discovered that this did not occur. Likewise, we made a similar argument about serious property crime. We also discovered that while the number of serious property criminals increased, their representation as a proportion of the prison population declined. Finally, we examined shifts in the percentage of the prison population incarcerated for drug trafficking, and found that this also declined. Thus, the last hope that the expanded use of imprisonment is tied to the social defense approach, and that social defense accomplished its mission, is that the percentage of inmates incarcerated for repeat offenses grew. In other words, if imprisonment has been expanded, and the goal of that expansion is greater public protection, we would hope that the increase in incarceration focused on offenders who were more likely than others to have a history of recidivism or repeat offending.

The data for state prisons in the United States indicates that this trend also did not emerge for the time period under investigation. From 1991 through 1997, in fact, we witnessed the opposite trend: the percentage of the prison population with no prior criminal sentence increased from 19.3 percent to 24.1 percent. These data clearly indicate that the expanded use of imprisonment was not being directed toward controlling the most serious, repeat offenders who might be a threat to the public. It also indicates the expanding prison system during this period was, in part, driven by drawing in or including offenders who previously were more likely to be excluded from prison populations. This phenomena, which criminologists refer to as "net widening," becomes a problem to the extent that expanding the population eligible for incarceration may not be the best mechanism to control crime, nor the best use of a rather costly resources such as imprisonment.

The trends in inmate characteristics reviewed above tell only part of the story of how the expanded use of imprisonment changed the focus of imprisonment in the United States. The movement to lock up more criminals should have produced lower rates of crime by incarcerating a greater number of serious property and violent crime offenders, and offenders who were committed to crime as a way of life (those with prior criminal records). We expect that a focus on these offenders would increase the proportion of the prison population made up of serious and repeat violent and property crime offenders. As the data indicate, this trend did not emerge, which calls into question, at minimum, the implementation of the social defense incarceration machine that has been set into motion in the United States. These facts also lead us to the possibility that this movement had other goals as well. These goals are evident in changing trends for other inmate characteristics.

The objection that can be raised to the foregoing discussion is that the expanded use of imprisonment protects society by locking up less serious offenders before they can become more serious offenders, and that this practice deters other criminals or alters the future behavior of those who have been incarcerated. The recidivism literature, however, would contradict this claim (Flanagan, 1982; Gendreau, Goggin, Cullen, 1999; Smith, Goggin, Gendreau, 2002); this claim would also be refuted by research that discovers that prisons can act as "schools" for teaching criminal techniques.

Nevertheless, the discussion above does not completely eliminate the claim that locking up a larger proportion of less serious offenders reduces crime. It should be noted, however, that these data refer only to the period in the 1990s when crime was declining at a rapid rate. As noted in preceding chapters, data from other time periods do not support the contention that prison expansion reduces the level of crime. Before a conclusion can be reached, data from different time periods and regions must also be considered.

### RACE AND IMPRISONMENT: THE DRUG EFFECT

The data presented above about offense seriousness, type of offense, and repeat offending point toward the conclusion that America's imprisonment binge had much less to do with controlling major crimes than advertised. In addition, the purported goals of America's prison expansion movement is called into question and delegitimized because of its apparent connection to enhanced racial control. This statement requires some explanation.

Currently, approximately two-thirds of the state prison population in the United States is black or Hispanic. The casual observer might conclude that the large proportion of minorities represented in state prisons is a simple function that reflects the differential participation of various racial and ethnic groups in criminal activity (Beckett and Western, 2001). To be sure, the casual observer's conclusion is supported by the images of crime to which they are exposed by the media. But this conclusion is far from the truth. The errors contained in this view can be examined by inspecting the data generated by various self-report studies. These studies are useful for establishing the approximate ratio of behaviors across different racial and ethnic groups, even though the result may not reflect the exact extent of a behavior within any of the specific groups because of the limitations of self-report data and methods. Nevertheless, self-report studies indicate that there appears to be two to three times as much crime self-reported by African-Americans compared to whites. This data would seem to justify the higher concentration of African-Americans in the U.S. prison system. This would, however, be an inappropriate conclusion reached by failing to take into account the percentage of the population that is composed of whites and African-Americans. Because this is an important point, a brief example is offered to clarify this claim (for extended discussion, see Lynch, 2002).

African-Americans constitute about 12 percent of the American population, while approximately 75 percent of the population is white. Thus, for every 100 Americans, 75 are white, and 12 are African-American. This means that there are 6 times as many whites as African Americans among every 100 Americans. To understand the meaning of this population ratio with respect to crime, consider the following example. For the purposes of this example, let us assume that out of the 75 whites in our population of 100, 15 are criminal offenders. (Any number of white criminals can be used as long as it can be tripled without exceeding 100). Next, we calculate a rate of white offending per 100 whites ($15 / 75 = x / 100$; $1500 = 75x$; $x = 20$), which comes to $20 / 100$. As noted, self-report studies indicate that the rate of offending among African-Americans is 2 to 3 times higher than among whites. So, let us assume the more extreme case and set the African-American rate of offending 3 times higher than the white level of offending, or at 60 per 100.

So far, what we have created is a representation of crime by racial groups that reflects what is known about the distribution of crime by race. But, to determine if African-Americans are overrepresented in prison, we need to consider that the rates we have calculated are misleading because they *overrepresent* the contribution of African-Americans *to the total number of crimes being committed*. In other words, the image of crime we derive by knowing that the rate of self-reporting of crime is three times higher among African-Americans compared to whites does not accurately represent to the extent to which whites and African-Americans contribute to the *total level of crime* in the United States. This is true because the rate calculations we made above contain a less than obvious error. The rate calculations set the African-American and white population so that they consist of the same number of individuals: 100. But, in the real world, there are six times as many whites as African-Americans. Thus, to know how many actual crimes are committed by these two groups, we would need to either have six times as many whites as African-Americans, or one-sixth as many African-Americans as whites, represented in our example.

To correct for this error, let us multiply the white population by 6. For each group, we assume a constant rate of offending derived from the above example, 20 per 100. To discover the number of crimes committed by the white population, we multiply the rate per 100 (which is 20) by 6, the number of groups of 100 whites. Doing so, we discover that the white population committed 120 crimes. If there are 600 whites, and the African-American population is one-sixth that size, there would be 100 African-Americans. From the calculation above, their rate of offending is 60 crimes per 100 African-Americans. Thus, in a population of 700 people where 600 are white and 100 are African-America, there will be 180 crimes. Two-thirds of those crimes or 120 crimes will be committed by whites. One third of the crimes will be committed by African-Americans. In other words, *when self-reported race-based rates of offending are adjusted by the population's racial composition, we discover that whites committed twice as much crime as African-Americans.* The standardized self-reported rates, which assumed that the African-American and white populations consisted of the same number of individuals, however, inverted this reality.

This observation is important to the current discussion because it makes us wonder why there are more African Americans in prison than whites since whites committed twice as much of the total crime. The answer is that there might be more African-Americans in prison if the crimes they commit are much more serious than the crimes whites commit. Or, this situation could arise due to racial biases that operate throughout the criminal justice process, beginning with differential patrol and arrest patterns in African-American and white communities. These issues need to be examined further.

Above, we discovered that one of the changes that affected the characteristics of the prison population from 1991 through 1997 was an increase in the proportion of incarcerated drug offenders. A significant proportion of those admitted to prison during this period were minority drug offenders (Mauer, 1999). This result is consistent with widely held stereotypes about drug use. Thus, it makes sense to examine drug-use patterns across racial and ethnic groups to ascertain whether generally held public opinions about drug-use patterns and prison trends for drug-use offenders fit with more accurate estimates of drug use by various racial and ethnic groups. For the purposes of this example, consider the data collected by the U.S. Department of Health and Human Services as reported in the National Household Survey on Drug Abuse: Population Estimates, 1998, which provides information on drug use by various racial and ethnic groups. These data are displayed in table 6.1.

Table 6.1 indicates that self-reported use of drugs is higher for whites than for blacks or Hispanics for all drugs with the exception of heroin. To further illustrate the disparity in use of drugs by race and ethnicity, table 6.2 displays the number of drug users by race and ethnicity per 100 people in the population, taking account of the approximate national percentage of the population that falls into each racial and ethnic group. For purposes of this table, the population percentages for each group were set as follows: white = 72 percent; black = 13 percent; Hispanic = 8 percent.

As table 6.2 demonstrates, the racial and ethnic population adjusted drug use reported by whites is, for each and every category of drug use, between 3 (heroin) to 15 times higher (inhalants) when compared to population adjusted reported black drug use, and between 1.4 (heroin) to 23 times higher (LSD) when compared to population adjusted drug use reported by Hispanics. As an example of the relationship between race/ethnicity and drug use, consider that: (1) for every 100 U.S. citizens, 32 report having used marijuana. Of these users, 81 percent (N = 26) are white; (2) for every 100 citizens, 9.7 report using cocaine. Of these users, 82 percent (N = 8) are white; (3) for every 100 citizens, 7.8 report using LSD. Of these users, 90 percent (N = 7) are white; (4) the only exception to this pattern of extraordinarily high drug use by whites is for heroin, where only 52 percent of reported users are white (N = 1).

Readers may be surprised to discover what those who study drug-use patterns have long known—that whites are responsible for more drug use in the United States than minorities. But no one should really be surprised that whites make up the majority of drug users for one simple reason: whites make up a larger percentage of the population than blacks or Hispanics. For example, there are approximate six whites for every black in the United States, and nine whites for every Hispanic. For these groups to exceed white drug use, the number of drug users among blacks and Hispanic population would have to be more than six and nine times higher, respectively, than drug use among whites. As tables 6.1 and 6.2 indicate, this is not the case.

TABLE 6.1
*Drug Use by Type of Drug and Race of Respondents, 1998*

| | Percent Reporting Drug Use, Ever | | |
| --- | --- | --- | --- |
| | White | Black | Hispanic |
| Alcohol | 85.2 | 71.7 | 70.8 |
| Marijuana | 35.5 | 30.2 | 23.2 |
| Cocaine* | 11.4 | 8.5 | 8.9 |
| Inhalants | 6.6 | 2.2 | 4.1 |
| Hallucinogens | 11.5 | 4.8 | 5.3 |
| Psychotherapeutics | 10.3 | 6.6 | 6.3 |
| Stimulants | 5.0 | 2.9 | 2.6 |
| Tranquillizers | 3.9 | 2.9 | 2.4 |
| PCP | 3.9 | 2.8 | 2.0 |
| LSD | 9.2 | 4.0 | 4.1 |
| Heroin | 1.0 | 1.9 | 0.7 |

*Includes both powdered and crack cocaine.

To illustrate this point further, let us assume that the percentage of people incarcerated for cocaine related violations reflects the average racial and ethnic breakdowns noted by Harrison and Beck (2003) in their study of the nation's incarcerated drug offender population. Out of 100 offenders incarcerated for cocaine use, this would mean there were 57 blacks, 19 Hispanics, and 23 whites (1 person is in the "other" racial or ethnic category). How does the breakdown of offenders in prison reflect actual drug-use patterns? We can make this assessment by referring to table 6.2, which indicates that for every 100 Americans, 8 reported users of cocaine are white, 1 is black, and 1 is Hispanic.[1] Added together, there are 10 self-reported cocaine users for every 100 Americans. Taking these reports as representative of actual drug-use patterns, we can multiply these numbers to derive the expected number of whites, blacks, and Hispanics that ought to be found in a prison population of 100 cocaine users *if* incarceration were an exact reflection of actual self-reported drug use. The calculation is simple because all we need to do is multiply our 10 drug users by 10 to create a population of 100 users. Doing so, we

TABLE 6.2

*Drug Use by Type of Drug and Race of Respondents, Population Adjusted, and Per 100 Citizens, 1998*

| | Number of Users by Race/Ethnicity Per 100 Citizens | | |
| --- | --- | --- | --- |
| | White | Black | Hispanic |
| Alcohol | 61 | 9 | 6 |
| Marijuana | 26 | 4 | 2 |
| Cocaine★ | 8 | 1 | 0.7 |
| Inhalants | 5 | 0.3 | 0.3 |
| Hallucinogens | 8 | 0.6 | 0.4 |
| Psychotherapeutics | 7 | 1 | 0.5 |
| Stimulants | 4 | 0.4 | 0.2 |
| Tranquillizers | 3 | 0.4 | 0.2 |
| PCP | 3 | 0.4 | 0.2 |
| LSD | 7 | 0.5 | 0.3 |
| Heroin | 1 | 0.3 | 0.6 |

★Includes both powdered and crack cocaine.

find that our population of 100 cocaine users *should* contain 80 whites, 10 blacks, and 10 Hispanics. These figures can now be compared to the number of cocaine users who are incarcerated for cocaine crimes. When this comparison is made, we find that there are 10 black users but 57 blacks incarcerated, 10 Hispanic users but 19 Hispanics incarcerated, and 80 white users but only 23 whites incarcerated. In other words, there are 47 more blacks, 9 more Hispanics, and 57 fewer whites incarcerated than would be expected from self-reported drug use data *if* incarceration reflected reported drug-use patterns. Unless there is a uniform reporting bias linked to race or ethnicity, or blacks and Hispanics possess much larger quantities of cocaine than whites, we can assume that these data are somewhat representative of the proportion of drug users from each race and ethnic group who should end up in prison. Thus, what these data indicate is that our system of detecting, arresting and convicting drug offenders is not very good at finding white cocaine users. In fact, only about 29 percent of reported white cocaine users are represented in the prison population. In contrast, our system of detecting, arresting, and convicting minority drug users seems very efficient, representing 5.7 times as many black cocaine users as expected, and 1.9 times as many Hispanic cocaine users as expected. In fact, using these data, we can estimate that if incarceration outcomes were an exact reflection of drug arrests, that police would need to arrest 5.7 times the number of blacks they were expected to discover, 1.9 times as many Hispanics as they would be expected to discover, and only about one-quarter of the white cocaine users they would be expected to discover (if discovery were proportional to self-reported use). But, this is an unlikely cause of the racial differences found in prison populations incarcerated for drug crimes. Approximately 60 percent of arrests for drug use involve white defendants. Thus, while the police indeed arrest whites at a lower rate than expected, the reduced rate of apprehension by police is not so severe as to account for the observed racial differences evident in prison populations. Indeed, the remaining steps in the criminal justice process contribute significantly to the wide-ranging racial and ethnic disparity found at the stage of incarceration (see Miller, 1998). Some of the difference may be due to legitimate factors, such as the seriousness of the offense. It is unlikely, however, that black or Hispanic defendants possess the large quantities of drugs that would produce such disparate results. Rather, unequal laws, such as those that apply specifically to crack-cocaine, may be the culprit, as studies indicate (Meierhoefer, 1992). In addition, as tables 6.1 and 6.2 illustrate, whites are more likely to be involved in serious drug use compared to African-Americans and Hispanics.

The results presented above may not be completely accurate to the extent that the data collected and reported by the U.S. Department of Health and Human Services is flawed. Even if we doubt the accuracy of these data, the flaws in this study would have to be *extraordinarily large* to erase the reported racial/ethnic differences noted. While this study may contain some methodological limitations, it is doubtful that these limitations are severe enough to produce results that would be wholly inconsistent with actual drug-use patterns, or inconsistent enough to overreport white and underreport black and Hispanic drug use in proportions large enough to erase the biases that seem evident in the incarceration of minorities for drug offenses.

The data in tables 6.1 and 6.2 provide a useful comparison to arrest and imprisonment data on race and drugs. In the year 2000, for example, nearly 53 percent of federal prison inmates serving sentences for drug crimes were white, a figure far below the reported drug-use patterns reported in tables 6.1 and 6.2. Blacks, in contrast, made up nearly 46 percent of federal inmates incarcerated for drug crimes, a figure far in excess of the percentage of the U.S. population of drug users that are black. Also, consider that nearly 64 percent of those arrested for drug crimes in the United States are white (1999 data), and we can begin to understand the complicated processing mechanism that lands a larger proportion of minorities in prison for drug use. That is, minorities are more likely to be arrested for drug use compared to their actual drug use. Once arrested, they are more likely to be charged and prosecuted. And, once charged and prosecuted, they are more likely to be convicted and sentenced to prison. At each stage of process, race-related difference, which individually may be small, adds up to a rather large end result (Mauer, 1999).

The race-related drug-crime-imprisonment effects noted above are not a simple function of an increasing incarceration rate. We should recognize that numerous other laws also affect the frequency with which blacks are incarcerated for drug crime. The war on drugs, for example, has also taken a greater toll on black Americans. In a study conducted by the Federal Judiciary Center, Meierhoefer (1992) estimated that mandatory minimums for crack-cocaine offenses (a drug that is the same chemically as powdered cocaine) increased black-white sentence lengths differences. The new mandatory crack minimums pushed differences in black-white sentence lengths from 11 percent prior to passage of these laws to 49 percent afterward. In the long run, this means that the number of blacks in prison for crack offenses will increase more substantially than the number of whites even if the two populations were sentenced at the same rates because the black offenders received longer sentences. As indicated earlier, we know that blacks are sentenced to prison for cocaine-related offenses at a substantially higher rate than whites, which only exacerbates the overrepresentation of blacks in our growing prison system.

As noted earlier, America's imprisonment binge has been greatly affected by the number of people incarcerated for drug offenses. The impact of expanded incarceration for drug offenses has a differential impact by race. Between 1990 and 2000, for example, the increase in drug incarcerations expanded the incarcerated black drug offender population by 27 percent, while the white incarcerated drug offender population grew by 15 percent (Harrison and Beck, 2003). While the incarcerated drug offender population for both races was on the rise during this period, the increase for blacks was nearly twice the rate of increase for whites. In part, this difference is explained by sentencing patterns: 33 percent of white defendants convicted of a drug violation in state courts were sent to prison in 1998, compared to 51 percent of black defendants (Durose and Langan, 2001).

### THE PERSISTENCE OF RACE EFFECTS

Race differences are seen across a broad spectrum of correctional system data (Beckett and Western, 2001; Jacobs and Carmichael, 2001; Pettit and Western, 2004; Smith, 2004; Yates and Fording, 2005). These data, when combined with studies of the prevalence of crime across racial groups, and other data on criminal justice processing, indicate that more blacks end up in prison because of various racial biases, many of which have become institutionalized and hidden in the criminal justice system (Austin and Allen, 2000; Lynch and Patterson, 1991, 1996). As an example of the persistence and consistency of racial bias in imprisonment, consider the data presented in table 6.3 taken from the *Sourcebook of Criminal Justice Statistics* (table 6.32, 511, 2000), showing the rate of sentenced prisoners per 100,000 United States residents by race and age.

This table indicates that for each age group, with the exception of the fifty-five and older category, the black rate of incarceration is approximately seven to nine times higher than the white rate of incarceration, while the Hispanic rate of incarceration is two to three times higher than the white rate of incarceration. These race-related differences might be acceptable *if* they were a reflection of actual offending rate differences across racial groups. There are several reasons, however, to suspect that this is not the case, as the examples above illustrated.

To further illustrate the degree of bias represented by these data, we can compare them to evidence from victimization data. The National Crime Victim Survey conducted through the U.S. Department of Justice, Bureau of Justice Statistics, collects data from crime victims concerning their victimization experiences using a household survey.

TABLE 6.3

*Incarceration Rate Per 100,000 By Race and Age, for Males in State and Federal Prisons, 2000*

| Age Group | Race/ Ethnicity of Inmates Sentenced to Prison | | | |
|---|---|---|---|---|
| | All | White | Black | Hispanic |
| 18–19 | 785 | 302 | 2,679 | 1,058 |
| 20–24 | 2,045 | 866 | 7,276 | 2,503 |
| 25–29 | 2,520 | 1,108 | 9,749 | 2,890 |
| 30–34 | 2,355 | 1,219 | 8,690 | 2,740 |
| 35–39 | 1,889 | 995 | 7,511 | 2,134 |
| 40–44 | 1,316 | 697 | 4,995 | 2,088 |
| 45–54 | 707 | 428 | 2,699 | 1,144 |
| 55 + | 164 | 112 | 540 | 401 |
| Total | 904 | 449 | 3,457 | 1,220 |

As part of this survey, data on the perceived race of offenders are collected from crime victim for acts of personal violence where victims and offenders had direct contact (rape, robbery, and assault). Victims of these crimes report that the race of the offender is white 63 percent of the time and black 24 percent of the time. While percent white and black varies by the type of crime, these are all serious offenses, and offense seriousness cannot explain the race differentials that result in criminal justice processing biases or differences in rates of imprisonment across racial groups (see Lynch 2002).

The data on drug-race and age-race differences in incarceration and offending indicate that blacks are much more likely to be incarcerated than would be indicated by their rates of offending. Over time, as Scott Christianson pointed out in his article, "Our Black Prisons," the prison population in the United States has become increasingly concentrated with minority offenders, a position that has been supported by a number of other studies (Mauer, 1999). The trend of incarcerating a larger number of minorities, and a persistent shift in the racial and ethnic compositions of American prisons, has been accelerated during the prison boom (Austin and Irwin, 2003). Increasingly, our prison system has become a more and more visible mechanism of race control.

As further evidence of the race effect of the imprisonment binge, consider that in 1985, 3 percent of the U.S. population was under some form of correctional control (housed in jails or prison, or on probation or parole). By 1997, this figure increased to 5 percent, and is now around 8 percent. Between 1985 and 1997, the percentage of the U.S. black population under correctional control increased from 5.3 to 9 percent. Measured as a percent increase, the black population under correctional control expanded by 109 percent from 1985 through 1997. During the same time period, the percentage increase for whites was 84 percent. By 1997, the ratio of blacks to whites incarcerated was nearly 7 to 1 in terms of rate ratios (4,850 blacks and 705 whites per 100,000 blacks were under correctional control).

The imprisonment binge has had numerous consequences for the black community. One neglected impact is on the ability of blacks to vote, which is often restricted by a felony conviction or imprisonment. This became a national issue during the 2000 presidential elections in Florida. News reports suggest that in Florida numerous black voters were denied voting privileges due to prior felony convictions (some of those denied did not, in reality, have felony convictions). To be sure, there are laws in many states that deny convicted felons the right to vote, and Fellner and Mauer (1998) estimated that 13 percent of all black adults are excluded from voting due to criminal convictions. Further, this rate of voting disenfranchisement for black males is seven times the national average. The voice of these 1.4 million (black) people probably would have made the difference in the last presidential election, even if only a small number of them had voted in important states such as Florida. Moreover, the fact that criminal justice processing biases examined above contribute to differential voter disenfranchisement is a serious concern in a democracy.

Consider also that many other life chances are restricted by a felony conviction or incarceration, such as the ability of the affected person to gain employment, and the racial and ethnic biases that seem to adhere in criminal justice processes (Miller, 1996; Pettit and Western, 2004). A study published by the Bureau of Justice Statistics (Bonczar and Beck, 1997) estimated that at then applicable rates of incarceration, *a newborn black male had a one-in-four likelihood of imprisonment during their lifetime.* Compare this to the one-in-twenty-three chance that a white male newborn has of ending up in prison, and we can begin to understand imprisonment's differential effects on the life course of people of different racial backgrounds in the United States. Again, these differences become more disturbing when we consider that they may be the result of racial biases in criminal justice processes.

With these facts in mind, it can be suggested that the recent growth of the U.S. prison system is part of the modern history of race control and segregation that has come to characterize American society (Massey and Denton, 1993). Our prison system, in other words, not only reflects the degree of racial segregation seen in society at large, but has become part of the mechanism that supports and produces racial segregation. The larger the prison system has become, the larger the percentage of the black population segregated in prisons has also become. As the percentage of the black population that is incarcerated increases, the probability that blacks, who now are more likely to bear the stigma associated with the ex-con label, will have fewer opportunities to advance economically also has expanded, locking them into communities that have higher rates of ex-offenders and a lower chance of attracting the revitalizing economic opportunities (for discussion, see Rose and Clear, 1998; Clear, Rose, and Ryder, 2001; Clear and Rose, 1999; Clear, 2003). Prisons, in effect, have become a part of the now vicious circle of segregation, community decay, and disinvestment that has come to characterized modern American minority communities (Hagan, 1997).

### Prisons: A Class Act

Each year, the Bureau of Justice Statistics (BJS) publishes statistics about the characteristics of prison populations. As part of this survey, BJS published a more extensive census of prison inmates that used to include various personal characteristics of prison inmates, such as income in the year prior to arrest, the inmate's occupation at time of arrest, and educational achievement. These data were useful for discerning the social class of inmates. While BJS still published this prison census, it now excludes information on income and occupation necessary for making inmate social class determinations. Currently, the only useful information that remains for making a class assessment is level of educational attainment.

In 2002, 88 percent of inmates in state prisons in the United States had a high school education or less. Fourteen percent had an eight grade education or less, while 29 percent had some high school, and 45 percent had some sort of high school diploma (GED or an actual high school diploma). Taken together, 89 percent of inmates had a high school education or less. These figures are well below the educational attainment of the general U.S. population, where about 41 percent of the population fall into the same educational categories.

Furthermore, consider that from 1991 through 2000, the percentage of inmates with college degrees declined somewhat, at the same time that an increasing number of white-collar and corporate crime scandals were being uncovered in America.

While it is true that white-collar and corporate offenders, if convicted and sentenced to imprisonment, are very likely to serve their sentences in federal prisons and therefore are not included in these data, educational data for the federal prison system do not show any substantial increase in the percentage of inmates with college degrees.

Available evidence suggests that America's imprisonment binge has concentrated its efforts on lower-class criminals. When coupled with the observation that America's imprisonment binge has also concentrated on less serious crimes, and that the expansion of imprisonment has not been employed to incarcerate a substantial segment of white-collar and corporate criminals, we, like Jeffrey Reiman (2003), can conclude that "the rich get richer while the poor get prison."

PRISON TRENDS AND GENDER

While not a major focus of this work, I would be remiss if I failed to note the gendered effects of imprisonment. Did the growth of U.S. prisons affect the incarceration rates for men and women in similar ways? The answer to this question is complex and would require extensive analysis to address completely. Nevertheless, a few general observations can be used to depict the overall trends and differences. These trends indicate that the imprisonment binge had a disproportionate impact on women compared to men, and on African-American women in particular,

From the initiation of the imprisonment binge in 1973 through 2004, the rate of incarceration for men (men imprisoned per 100,000 population) grew from 96 to 486, or by more than 400 percent. During the same period, the imprisonment rate for women expanded by 966 percent, from 6 per 100,000 to 64 per 100,000. Overall, the percentage of the prison population composed of women also increased from 2.7 percent to 6.7 percent. Most striking, perhaps, is that the number of women in U.S. prisons grew from 6,004 in 1973 to over 85,000 by 2004.

Although women continue to make up a small proportion of the U.S. prison population, the evidence suggests that prison expansion had an unequal gender impact. Thus, the imprisonment binge not only maintained a focus on the lower class, expanded the proportion of the prison population composed of African-Americans and Hispanics, but also entailed a significant increase in the representation of women in U.S. prisons.

The racial and ethnic differences evident for male prison populations are also evident in the female prison population. Harrison and Beck (2006) note that in 2004 black females were incarcerated in U.S. prisons and jails at a rate of 359 per 100,000, compared to a rate of 143 for Hispanic women and 81 for white females. The extent of racial and ethnic disparity is lower for female compared to male inmates, but is nevertheless problematic (for further data comparing incarceration differences by gender, race, and ethnicity see Bonczar, 2003). To put the race–gender link into further context, consider Bonczar's (2003) estimate that the number of black women ever incarcerated in the United States (231,000 or 1.7 percent of black women) exceeds the number of white women ever incarcerated (225,000 or 0.3 percent of white women). This is surprising given that the number of white females far exceeds the size of the black female population.

In terms of offense type, about one-half of male inmates are incarcerated for violent crimes, while only one-third of women are incarcerated for those offenses (Harrison and Beck, 2006). Female inmates were much more likely to be incarcerated for lesser offenses than males. For example, while one in five male inmates were serving time for drug offenses in 2002, the comparable figure for females was one out of three (Harrison and Beck, 2006).

Overall, similar factors affected the rise in female and male imprisonment rates in the United States. For both groups, the increase is linked to a rise in drug-related incarceration, and for both there is evidence of racial and ethnic disparity. Thus, several of the general observations made about the imprisonment binge apply to both female and male imprisonment trends. Analyzing the exact differences between these two trends is beyond the scope of this investigation. But it appears, at least on the surface, that the imprisonment binge, while having similar effects across gender groups, also has a gender-specific content that caused female imprisonment rates to rise more quickly than men's rates. Future research is needed to sort out and address the race and gender linked dynamics these data suggest.

### CONCLUSION

In sum, this chapter has demonstrated that the growth of America's prison system has not resulted in the types of shifts in the inmate population that one would expect to result from a greater reliance on social defense incapacitation strategies. While there are more serious and repeat violent and property offenders in prison today compared to thirty, twenty, or even ten years earlier, the percentage of the prison population represented by these serious offenders has declined. At the same time, the percentage of the prison population that is composed of less serious offenders has risen; so, too, has the representation of minorities and the poor. In this sense, America's imprisonment binge can be seen as being a form of class and race control, and not as the simple crime control strategy we assume.

## CHAPTER 7

# The Imprisonment Binge and Crime

THIS CHAPTER EXAMINES the association between crime and imprisonment in the United States since 1973. One of the interesting features of this period was that the number of people imprisoned and the rate of imprisonment both showed a persistent annual increase. This circumstance establishes conditions required for a "natural" experiment assessing the impact of imprisonment on crime to the extent that one of the key elements, incarceration, was constantly increased. Following the logic of both the deterrence and incapacitation approaches, there should be a persistent decrease in crime, *if incarceration is an effective crime control strategy* and no other factors affect the level of crime in society. Here, it is not necessary to determine whether it is incapacitation or deterrence that affects crime. Rather, the concern is whether an increase in incarceration produces the desired result—a decline in crime. A number of different strategies were employed to address this issue.

## CRIME AND IMPRISONMENT CHANGE RATIOS

One way to assess the association between imprisonment and crime is to calculate change ratios. Change ratios can be employed to determine the relationship between changes in crime and imprisonment.

The numerator in the change ratio calculated here is the percent change in the number of index crimes (those crimes that make up the Federal Bureau of Investigation's "crimes index": murder, rape, robbery, assault, larceny-theft, motor vehicle theft, burglary, and arson) known to police per 100,000 citizens. The denominator in the change ratio will be the *lagged* percent change in the number of inmates in prison.[1] The denominator is lagged one year on the assumption that the deterrent or incapacitative effect of incarceration does not have an immediate effect on crime, but rather a future impact on offending. While a one-year lag may not be the most appropriate choice (Greenberg, 2001b), prior research has employed this lag (Cantor and Land, 2001; Cantor and Land, 1985). In addition, the lag effect is theoretically logical since incarcerated felony offenders have sentences of at least one year. The average sentence, however, is longer than one year, meaning that the long term incapacitative effect should last for several years. While the impact of incarceration through incapacitation should be immediate, the impact of the deterrent effect is likely to be lagged, especially in terms of its impact on other potential offenders. Moreover, since there is a time delay between arrest, conviction, and sentencing that may take several months, and we are examining the crime suppression effects of imprisonment rather than arrest, the one-year lag seems appropriate. Furthermore, if prisons deter, the effects of imprisonment are not constrained to contemporaneous effects, but can be expected to persist over an extended period. This would be especially true with respect to the United States, where the population has been widely exposed to news stories about the growth of the prison system.

The change ratio will yield either a positive or negative outcome. During the time period examined, the change in imprisonment *was always positive* because imprisonment expanded each year. Theoretically, this expansion should cause the crime rate to decline. Thus, to provide evidence of a deterrent or incapacitative effect, the change ratio would need to be negative. However, it is also plausible that raising the rate of imprisonment fails to lower the rate of offending, disconfirming the expectations of this argument, in which case the ratio will produce a positive outcome.

I will call the negative crime-imprisonment ratios *crime suppression effects* or CSEs because an increase in the level of imprisonment suppressed the level of crime in the following year. Thus, a CSE outcome supports incapacitation or deterrence hypotheses. It is also possible for the crime-imprisonment change ratio to be positive. A positive crime-imprisonment change ratio indicates that crime increased following an increase in the rate of incarceration. I call these positive outcomes *crime enhancement effects,* or CEEs, because crime rises along with the level of punishment. When the crime-punishment ratio is characterized as CEE, this contradicts deterrence and incapacitation assumptions.

For the purposes of this analysis, aggregated data on crime and imprisonment trends for all fifty states for the years 1973 through 2004 were employed. Because a lagged effect is employed there are thirty-one change ratios that can be calculated for this time period.

For the period under investigation, there were fourteen instances of CSE and seventeen CEEs. This outcome is not statistically different, meaning that during this period of America's imprisonment binge, an increase in incarceration is no more likely to suppress crime than it is to enhance crime. In other words, we are not able to predict with any accuracy whether the rate of crime will fall or rise following an increase in incarceration. The lack of a significant association between the change in imprisonment and crime for this time period indicates that the factors that cause crime to rise and fall exist independently of the assumed association between crime and imprisonment.

The utility of calculating CSE and CEE ratios is to illustrate how much crime is either suppressed (CSE) or enhanced (CEE) in relationship to a 1 percent increase in imprisonment. For example, table 7.1 indicates a CSE effect of -0.32 for the 1975 rate of imprisonment on the 1976 rate of crime (because of the lagged effect imprisonment is hypothesized to have on criminal offending). Because the CSE and CEE are percent change ratios, the ratio calculates how much crime declined (CSE) or fell (CEE) relative to a 1 percent rise in imprisonment. Thus, the CSE -0.32 indicates that on average, crime was suppressed by 3.2 percent in 1976. From table 7.1, we see that the largest annual average CSE was -1.58 percent (1998 imprisonment on 1999 crime), the smallest CSE was -0.1 (1994 on 1995 crime), and the mean crime suppression effect was -0.48. In sum, for the period under investigation, for years where a rise in imprisonment led to a decline in crime, on average a 1 percent rise in imprisonment produced a 0.48 percent decline in crime, which indicates a deterrent or incapacitative effect. But this result is only a summary of CSEs. To get a complete picture of the effect of imprisonment on crime, we must also consider the crime enhancement effects (CEEs).

Table 7.1 indicates that the largest crime enhancement effect was 8.95 (imprisonment change, 1978–1979, on 1980 crime), while the smallest crime enhancement effect was 0.02 (the imprisonment change, 1979–1980, on 1981 crime). The mean CEE was 1.37, which was 0.89 percent greater than the mean crime suppression effect. In short, on average, in individual years, crime tended to rise more than it declined as imprisonment increased.

TABLE 7.1

*Crime Suppression and Enhancement Effects of Incarceration Changes, on Crime Changes, 1973–2003*

| Year | % Change Imprisonment | % Change Crime* | CSE Effect | CEE Effect |
|------|------|------|------|------|
| 1973 | 3.2 | 17.2 | — | 5.38 |
| 1974 | 7.0 | 10.1 | — | 1.44 |
| 1975 | 10.1 | 0.5 | — | 0.05 |
| 1976 | 9.2 | -3.2 | -0.35 | — |
| 1977 | 8.6 | 2.0 | — | 0.23 |
| 1978 | 3.1 | 9.3 | — | 3.00 |
| 1979 | 2.4 | 9.5 | — | 8.95 |
| 1980 | 4.8 | 0.1 | — | 0.02 |
| 1981 | 12.0 | -3.4 | -0.28 | — |
| 1982 | 11.8 | -6.7 | -0.57 | — |
| 1983 | 6.0 | -1.9 | -0.32 | — |
| 1984 | 5.7 | 4.6 | — | 0.81 |
| 1985 | 8.4 | 6.3 | — | 0.75 |
| 1986 | 8.6 | 2.3 | — | 0.27 |
| 1987 | 7.4 | 3.1 | — | 0.42 |
| 1988 | 7.7 | 2.4 | — | 0.31 |
| 1989 | 12.8 | 1.6 | — | 0.13 |
| 1990 | 8.7 | 2.7 | — | 0.31 |
| 1991 | 6.7 | -2.9 | -0.48 | — |
| 1992 | 7.1 | -2.0 | -0.28 | — |
| 1993 | 10.1 | -1.1 | -0.11 | — |
| 1994 | 9.1 | -0.9 | -0.10 | — |
| 1995 | 6.7 | -2.7 | -0.41 | — |
| 1996 | 4.9 | -2.2 | -0.45 | — |
| 1997 | 5.0 | -5.4 | -1.08 | — |
| 1998 | 4.3 | -6.8 | -1.58 | — |
| 1999 | 4.7 | -0.2 | -0.09 | — |
| 2000 | 2.1 | 2.3 | — | 1.10 |
| 2001 | 1.1 | 0.1 | — | 0.09 |
| 2002 | 2.6 | 0.4 | — | 0.15 |

*(continued)*

TABLE 7.1 *(continued)*

| Year | % Change Imprisonment | % Change Crime★ | CSE Effect | CEE Effect |
|------|------|------|------|------|
| 2003 | 2.0 | -1.1 | -0.55 | — |
| 2004 | 1.8 | — | — | — |
| ★★Sum | | | -6.65 | 23.33 |
| N | | | 14 | 17 |
| Mean | | | -0.48 | 1.37 |

★ Because a lag was included, the percent change in crime for any listed year is the change for the next year (e.g., the percent change in crime listed for 1973 is the change in crime between 1973 and 1974, while the imprisonment change is from 1972 to 1973).

★★ Excludes 2004.

The CSE and CEE scores can also be summed to calculate the mass effect of each for this time period. The mass crime suppression effect was -6.65, while the mass of the crime enhancement effect was 23.33. In sum, these figures indicate that the mass CEE effect outweiged the mass CSE over this time period.

Another important observation is that there were seventeen CEEs and fourteen CSEs for this time period. That is, over this period where imprisonment was continually rising, crime was more likely to rise (the number of CEEs) than fall (the number of CSEs).

So far, the data above do not support the idea that a rise in imprisonment is related to a decline in crime. It is quite possible, however, that a CEE or CSE outcome is related to the magnitude of the change in imprisonment rate. Deterrence or incapacitation theorists might argue that while a CEE is slightly more likely than a CSE for this time period, the likelihood of each is related to the magnitude of the change in imprisonment. This proposition can be easily assessed by adding imprisonment changes for each effect together, and dividing by the number for years for which each effect is present. Following this procedure, the average change in imprisonment was 7.11 percent for CSE years and 6.14 percent for CEE years. While the average change in imprisonment is indeed greater in CSE years, the difference is less than 1 percent. The difference in magnitudes in imprisonment change, however, cannot explain why crime rose or fell since, in theory, expanding imprisonment should cause crime to fall—the magnitude should make little difference since imprisonment is always expanding during this time period. Furthermore, the 0.97 percent difference in imprisonment across CSE and CEE years does not appear large enough to explain the larger difference noted in crime between that same period (the mean of which is 1.85 percent; or the difference between the average CSE effect of -0.48 and the average CEE effect of 1.37).

Given this result, however, is it plausible that larger changes in imprisonment are more likely to lead to a CSE. This can be assessed by dividing the data into two groups: one above the mean imprisonment change and the other below the mean change (6.8 percent). For the 16 years in which the mean change in imprisonment was less than 6.8 percent, there were 8 CEE effects and 8 CSE effects. Thus, for below mean changes, either outcome was equally likely. For the fifteen years above the mean imprisonment change, there were nine CEE effects and six CSE effects. This finding also fails to support deterrence and incapacitative arguments. Taken together, these findings indicate that higher or lower than average changes in imprisonment do not predict the direction of the change in crime. Moreover, and contrary to expectations, a larger than average change in imprisonment is more likely to be associated with an *increase* in crime. There are some submerged trends in these general trends that bear some comment. Because the number of submerged trends are derived from very few cases in each category, it is difficult to rely on these trends to any substantial degree.

What is the specific effect of a change in imprisonment that was below the mean? For the 8 CEE years, the average CEE effect was 5.4. For the remaining 8 years where CSE effects were seen, the average CSE was -2.9. Thus, lower than average changes in imprisonment were no more likely to suppress or enhance crime. However, the average CEE effect is much larger than the average CSE effect, indicating that when imprisonment rose less than the mean, crime was not more likely to increase substantially.

For the 15 years in which the imprisonment change was above the mean, the average annual CEE effect was 3.74 (N = 9), while the annual average CSE effect was—2.88 (N = 6). Thus, higher than average changes in imprisonment were slightly more likely to produce a CEE than a CSE, while the average CEE for these years was larger than the average CSE. These submerged trends indicate that there are clearly tradeoffs to raising the rate of incarceration. However, neither submerged trend supports the idea that imprisonment consistently reduces crime.

To summarize, the following findings that contradict deterrence and incapacitation arguments are drawn from the relationships in table 7.1: (1) the rise in incarceration by itself for the time period under investigation was slightly more likely to produce a CEE rather than a CSE effect; (2) an above-average rise in imprisonment for this period (by more than 6.8 percent) was more likely to produce a CEE than a CSE effect; (3) a rise in incarceration less than the mean for this period was no more likely to produces a CEE than a CSE, although the average CEE in these cases exceeds the average CSE.

In sum, the long-term trend in imprisonment does not, by itself, appear to cause a reduction in crime. Indeed, over the period examined, where imprisonment rose continually, crime was more likely to rise than fall even when the magnitude of the change in imprisonment is considered. These data contradict the expectations of deterrence and incapacitative theories.

Despite this evidence, policy experts who have isolated the crime and imprisonment trends from the 1990s have used these data to support the expansion of imprisonment. The next section examines whether the continuation in the rising trend in imprisonment from 1991 through 2000 can lower crime significantly, and how long this process might take. In conjunction with that analysis, I also examine the costs of this policy.

Before moving to this forecast, however, let me briefly consider the chance association between incarceration and crime over the past thirty years. For example, as noted earlier in this book, materialists have often argued that there is an association between economic processes and trends observable in a society's rate of criminal offending or its justice processes. If we were to examine the relationship between, for instance, unemployment and crime for the time period 1973 through 1999, what would we see? The result is that there is a chance association between changes in the annual unemployment rate and the crime rate for this period: half of the time crime goes up or down when unemployment goes up or down. The other half of the time, there appears to be no relationship between crime and unemployment, so that a rising unemployment rate may coexist with a declining crime rate, or a declining unemployment rate may coexist with a rising rate of crime. While the unemployment-crime relationship does not produce a significant outcome, we should recognize that changes in the unemployment rate are as useful for predicting changes in crime as are changes in the imprisonment rate. In other words, neither position is extremely useful from a policy perspective, and neither one should be relied upon alone to determine whether crime might rise or fall.

### FORECASTING THE DEMISE OF CRIME

Forecasting is tricky work. When forecasting, it is assumed that the previous trend will continue into the future. Sometimes, this assumption is justifiable, and sometimes not. For the purposes of the present analysis, the assumption is that the relationship between crime and imprisonment in the future will be represented by the relationship that existed between crime and imprisonment during the 1990s. This is a restrictive assumption to the extent that for much of this period, imprisonment was rising (in fact, imprisonment, as we already know, rose every year in the 1990s) while crime was falling (this is true for eight of the ten years during the 1990s). From the longer-term trend analysis presented above based on table 7.1, the restrictiveness of this assumption is that it intentionally exaggerates the deterrent or incapacitative effects of imprisonment on crime. We are not using this forecast to discuss in any direct way the ability of imprisonment to act as a deterrent, or its incapacitative effect. Rather, we will employ these data to discuss how big the prison system in the United States would have to grow to lower crime substantially if we also assume that imprisonment lowers the level of crime. This limitation, while bothersome, will nevertheless help illustrate how much imprisonment must be expanded and at what financial cost if imprisonment were a successful crime control strategy. Before proceeding, we should also recognize that the forecast shown below is restrictive to the extent that any other "shocks" that might disturb the relationship between the crime and imprisonment rate are omitted. These omitted factors include a wide variety of causes criminologists have determined affect rates of criminal offending.

During the 1990s, the imprisonment rate grew by an average of 5.4 percent per year. And while the imprisonment rate grew, the crime rate fell by an average of 3.6 percent per year. Again, it bears mention that the data from the 1990s are an aberration to the extent that they are inconsistent with data on crime and imprisonment over the full thirty-year period during which the United States has experimented with the impact of raising incarceration on crime (see table 7.1). Nevertheless, since most proponents of imprisonment as a solution to crime use the 1990s as their example, it seems fitting to use data from this time period to forecast the impact of imprisonment on crime into the future.

In 1999, there were 1,304,074 inmates in American prisons. The rate of imprisonment was 476 per 100,000 citizens, while the rate of crime was 4,266.8 per 100,000 citizens. Taking these figures as the starting point, a forecast can be made that observes how increasing the rate of incarceration by an average of 5.4 percent per year affects the rate of crime, which is predicted to decline by 3.4 percent per year. How far into the future do we have to raise the rate of imprisonment, by how much overall, and at what cost, to get an appreciably lower rate of criminal offending?

The annual crime and imprisonment rate forecasts contained in table 7.2 illustrate that it would take a very long time for increases in imprisonment that characterized the big prison system found in the United States during the 1990s to reduce crime substantially. Consider, for instance, that between 1999 and 2012, the rate of imprisonment would increase by nearly 100 percent, while the rate of crime would decline by approximately 39 percent. Given the average rate of growth and the average decline in crime from the 1990s, it would take until the year 2018 to reduce crime to one-half its 1999 level. Further, a 75 percent reduction in crime would take until the year 2036, at which point the rate of imprisonment would have increased by more than 600 percent!

Looked at another way, we can see that in order to reduce crime to one-half its 1999 level, the United States would require an increase in the rate of imprisonment to 1,295 inmates per 100,000, or an increase of 351 inmates per 100,000 citizens over 1999 levels. A 75 percent reduction in crime requires an incarceration rate of 3,339 per 100,000 citizens,

Table 7.2

*Forecast of Crime and Imprisonment Rates from
1990s Trends★*

| | Rate Per 100,000 Population | |
|---|---|---|
| Year | Imprisonment | Crime |
| 1999 | 476 | 4,266.8 |
| 2000 | 502 | 4,109.4 |
| 2001 | 529 | 3,957.8 |
| 2002 | 558 | 3,811.8 |
| 2003 | 588 | 3,671.1 |
| . | | |
| . | | |
| 2010 | 850 | 2,821.5 |
| 2011 | 896 | 2,717.4 |
| 2012 | 944 | 2,617.1 |
| . | | |
| 2018 | 1,295 | 2,088.5 |
| . | | |
| 2020 | 1,439 | 1,937.2 |
| 2021 | 1,517 | 1,865.7 |
| 2022 | 1,599 | 1,769.9 |
| . | | |
| . | | |
| 2036 | 3,339 | 1,044.6 |

★ This forecast assumes a direct relationship between increasing the rate of incarceration and the crime rate predicted by the trends in crime and imprisonment from the
1990s, when the annual average change in the imprisonment rate was 5.4 percent, and the average annual decline
in crime was 3.6 percent. To simplify this table, not all
years are presented, and where years are omitted, a dot is
placed in the table for the reader's convenience.

or by more than 2,900 inmates per 100,000, which would add more inmates than were incarcerated in 1999 to the system.

Based on this forecast, and assuming a constant population (or no
population growth), the actual number of people the United States would
need to imprison to achieve crime reduction would be enormous. For

example, to obtain a crime reduction of 50 percent by 2018, the United States would be required to incarcerate 3.5 million inmates. To achieve a 75 percent reduction in crime by 2036, the United States would have to incarcerate over 7 million inmates. If our prison system is big now, the idea that it should be seven times larger appears ridiculous.

What is left out of this picture so far is the costs associated with using imprisonment to control crime. Forecasting correctional costs forward from 1999, the United States would be required to spend $122 billion per year on the correctional systems in 2018, and $315 billion per year by 2036. And these figures are not adjusted for inflation, which would increase the overall costs dramatically. Nor do they include the necessary adjustment for the loans and bonds that would be required to build a prison system to house seven million inmates by 2036. Consider, for instance, that adjusting projected 2036 prison costs by inflation alone (5 percent per year) would mean that the cost of the correctional system to the average U.S. household would add $8,000 to the tax bill. Loan and bond costs would double the expected per-household tax liability. And even these dire predictions do not necessarily represent the true costs involved in expanding the prison system.

Consider that catching so many more criminals will require more police officers and more court personnel from judges to bailiffs, more district attorneys and public defen;ders, more police stations, more jails to hold defendants awaiting trial, more court buildings, more buses to transport criminals, and so on. The cost of making the prison system bigger, in other words, extends well beyond the simple costs of more prison space, or the money needed to pay for an inmate's upkeep. Adding more prisoners to the system requires that the entire system expand. If the system were to become two, three, four, or seven times bigger than it is now, the costs of attempting to reduce crime through increasing the rate of incarceration become prohibitive.

### IMPRISONMENT RATES, CRIME RATES, AND REGION, 1999

The aggregate analysis of the trend in crime and imprisonment undertaken above may not be the kind of data that is convincing to some people. Some readers may be thinking that we need to look at what happens at smaller levels of aggregation to see the impact of a rising rate of incarceration on crime (e.g., Greenberg, 2001b). Thus, even if it makes sense theoretically to examine the assumption that an increasing rate of imprisonment lowers crime over time across the entire United States, it is possible to examine this relationship in other ways. One reason we might choose a different method of analysis or a different unit of aggregation has to do with the kind of assumptions we make about the relationship between crime and imprisonment. For example, if we assume that rational offenders are deterred from crime by higher rates of incarceration, then it makes sense to see if this assumption holds true when we examine areas that have different levels of incarceration. This can be accomplished by looking at the relationship between crime and imprisonment across various geographic levels.

It also makes sense to look at the relationship between crime and imprisonment as it relates to concepts like rationality at the geographic level because the idea of rationality itself is not time dependent. Furthermore, there is no reason to assume that rationality is differentially distributed in a population based upon people's location or residence. In fact, if rationality were dependent on time or geography, or was unevenly distributed among the population for other reasons, it could be argued that this fact alone would negate the ability of punishment to act as a deterrent. In other words, if we were to posit that rationality were conditioned by some additional factor(s), then the strength of this argument would be substantially weakened. In fact, if such additional conditions held, we could not assume that an enhanced rate of punishment would necessarily reduce crime without controlling for these additional conditions. If, for example, we found that higher rates of imprisonment only reduced crime when there was also a decline in some other factor like unemployment, then we would be unable to conclude that increasing the rate of imprisonment by itself would reduce crime.

Previously, the assumption that the level of imprisonment and crime were related was examined over time using the period 1973–2004. This period was employed because it resembled a natural experiment to the extent that imprisonment rose consistently. Given this fact, we would expect to find a consistent decline in crime. As noted, there is no consistent relationship between imprisonment and crime for that time period. It is still possible, however, that such a relationship exists, and that the existence of this relationship was masked by the kind of data that was employed. To address this possibility, we now turn our attention to an analysis of the relationship between crime and imprisonment at a lower level by focusing on smaller aggregations of states for the year 1999.

For the geographic analysis, imprisonment data will be measured as a rate of incarcerated people per 100,000 population for each state. Crime rate data are measured per 1,000 people and is rounded to the nearest one-tenth. States will be grouped into four regions—northeastern, midwestern, southern, and western—following procedures typically employed to make these distinctions (see table 7.3). Simple analyses will be employed to illustrate the relationship between crime and imprisonment across states and within regions.

The year 1999 was chosen for this analysis for several reasons. First, the sample of years 1992–1999 were marked by a persistent increase in imprisonment and a persistent decrease in crime. From these years, 1999 was chosen at random. Second, it would seem that a geographic relationship between crime and imprisonment should be more likely during a time period where there was a persistent relationship between a rising imprisonment rate and a reduction in crime than during other periods. Such a relationship might not be evident at the geographic level, however, if the aggregated U.S. trend was substantially affected by trends found within one region.

Table 7.4 contains the data on imprisonment and crime rates by state and region. It also contains information about the number of black and white inmates incarcerated in each state, the ratio of black to white inmates (R-Ratio), the ratio of blacks to whites in the general population (P-Ratio), and the black/white prison ratio divided by the black/white population ratio (RR/PR). The meaning of these data will be explored later in this chapter. For now, it is noted that:

(1) An R-Ratio of 1 means that an equivalent number of blacks and whites are incarcerated within a state's prison system. An R-Ratio greater than 1 indicates that more blacks than whites were incarcerated in a given state. In contrast, an R-Ratio of less than 1 means that more whites than blacks were incarcerated in a given state.

(2) The P-Ratio is a general population measure of the ratio of blacks to whites in each state. The P-Ratio indicates the number of blacks for one white in the general population within each

state. For example, a P-Ratio of 0.10 means there are ten times as many whites in the population as blacks, or 1 black for every 10 whites. A P-Ratio of 0.50, would indicate that there is 1 black for every two whites in the population.

(3)  The RR/PR ratio can be interpreted as an index of racial representation. This ratio expresses the extent to which blacks are overrepresented within a state prison system compared to their representation in the general population of each state. The RR/PR ratio is derived by dividing the R-Ratio by the P-Ratio. The RR/PR ratio is interpreted in the same way as the R-Ratio. An RR/PR ratio of 1.00 indicates that the ratio of blacks imprisoned within a state is equal to the ratio of blacks to whites found in the general population. RR/PR ratios in excess of 1 indicate that the ratio of blacks to whites in a state's prison system exceeds the ratio of blacks to whites in the general population. RR/PR ratios in excess of 3 likely indicates the existence of fairly extensive institutionalized discrimination.

### Imprisonment and Crime Rates, 1999

Let us first summarize the information about crime and imprisonment rates found in table 7.4, omitting the Washington DC area as an outlier. The highest rates of imprisonment for 1999 were found in Louisiana (776 per 100,000) and Texas (762 per 100,000). Two additional states, Oklahoma and Mississippi, have imprisonment rates in the mid-600s. Four more states have rates in the 500s. Seven of the eight states with the highest rates of incarceration (the exception is Nevada) are located in the south.

The state with the lowest rate of incarceration was Minnesota, where 125 inmates per 100,000 population were imprisoned. Minnesota's rate of incarceration was 6.2 times lower than the rate of incarceration found in Louisiana, the state with the highest rate of imprisonment. In addition to Minnesota, 6 other states had incarceration rates lower than 200 per 100,000. Four of these states were in the northeast.

The mean rate of imprisonment across all states was 381 per 100,000 population. Regionally, mean imprisonment rates per 100,000 vary greatly: northeast, 274; midwest, 319; west, 361; south, 508. It is evident from these regional data that the mean imprisonment rate for the United States is influenced by the high mean rates found across southern states,

TABLE 7.3
*States by Region*

| | |
|---|---|
| Northeastern: | Connecticut, Maine, Massachusetts, New Hampshire, New Jersey, New York, Pennsylvania, Rhode Island, Vermont |
| Midwestern: | Illinois, Indiana, Iowa, Kansas, Michigan, Minnesota, Missouri, Nebraska, North Dakota, Ohio, South Dakota, Wisconsin |
| Southern: | Alabama, Arkansas, Delaware, Florida, Georgia, Kentucky, Louisiana, Maryland, Mississippi, North Carolina, Oklahoma, South Carolina, Tennessee, Texas, Virginia, West Virginia |
| Western: | Alaska, Arizona, California, Colorado, Hawaii, Idaho, Montana, New Mexico, Nevada, Oregon, Utah, Washington, Wyoming |

where only two states, North Carolina and Kentucky, have imprisonment rates below 400. Taken together, these data illustrate that there is significant variation in the use of imprisonment across states and regions within the United States.

There is also significant variation in the level of crime per 1,000 citizens across states and regions. The lowest crime rates, 22.8 per 1,000, are seen in New Hampshire and Nevada. The highest crime rate was found in Florida (62.1 per 1,000 population). Regionally, crime rates were lowest in the northeast (31.1), followed by the midwest (37.4), south (42.8), and west (44.0).

Having summarized the general findings in these state-based data, it is appropriate to investigate the relationship between the level of imprisonment and crime across states. Recall that the deterrence and incapacitation arguments suggest that criminals are either deterred or prevented from committing crime by the level of incarceration. Thus, we would expect that states with the highest levels of incarceration would have the lowest levels of crime. This hypothesis can be tested in a simple manner by performing a test of statistical correlation between the rates of imprisonment and crime across states. The deterrence-incapacitation hypothesis would be rejected if the correlation between the rate of imprisonment and crime were positive, because this indicates that states with higher levels of imprisonment also have higher levels of crime.

The Pearson's R correlation between imprisonment and crime rates for 50 U.S. states in 1999 is .455, and, moreover, this relationship is statistically significant ($p = .001$). The correlation indicates that the

TABLE 7.4

Imprisonment Rates (Per 100,000), and Crime Rates (Per 1,000) in 1999, and Number and Ratio of Black and White Inmates and Population by State and Region in 1997

| | | | Prison Population | | | | |
| | Imprisonment | Crime | White | Black | R-Ratio | P-Ratio | RR/PR |
|---|---|---|---|---|---|---|---|
| NORTHEAST | 274 | 31.1 | 65,661 | 88,803 | 1.35 | 0.16 | 10.0 |
| Connecticut | 397 | 33.9 | 4,630 | 8,059 | 1.75 | 0.11 | 15.8 |
| Maine | 133 | 28.8 | 1,469 | 58 | 0.04 | 0.005 | 7.9 |
| Massachusetts | 266 | 32.6 | 5,590 | 3,448 | 0.62 | 0.07 | 8.8 |
| New Hampshire | 187 | 22.8 | 2,019 | 120 | 0.06 | 0.007 | 8.5 |
| New Jersey | 384 | 34.0 | 7,316 | 18,572 | 2.54 | 0.18 | 14.1 |
| New York | 400 | 32.8 | 29,665 | 37,488 | 1.26 | 0.23 | 5.5 |
| Pennsylvania | 305 | 31.1 | 11,632 | 19,847 | 1.71 | 0.11 | 15.5 |
| Rhode Island | 193 | 35.8 | 2,157 | 1,175 | 0.35 | 0.05 | 10.9 |
| Vermont | 198 | 28.2 | 1,193 | 36 | 0.03 | 0.005 | 6.0 |
| MIDWEST | 319 | 37.4 | 97,802 | 111,674 | 1.14 | 0.07 | 11.7 |
| Illinois | 368 | 45.1 | 9,995 | 26,522 | 2.65 | 0.19 | 14.0 |
| Indiana | 324 | 37.7 | 10,132 | 7,707 | 0.76 | 0.09 | 8.5 |
| Iowa | 252 | 32.2 | 4,800 | 1,696 | 0.35 | 0.02 | 17.7 |

*(continued)*

TABLE 7.4 *(continued)*

| | Imprisonment | Crime | Prison Population | | R-Ratio | P-Ratio | RR/PR |
| | | | White | Black | | | |
|---|---|---|---|---|---|---|---|
| Kansas | 321 | 44.4 | 4,608 | 3,028 | 0.66 | 0.06 | 11.0 |
| Michigan | 472 | 43.2 | 18,482 | 24,936 | 1.35 | 0.17 | 7.9 |
| Minnesota | 125 | 36.0 | 2,559 | 1,964 | 0.77 | 0.03 | 25.6 |
| Missouri | 477 | 45.8 | 12,917 | 10,968 | 0.85 | 0.13 | 6.5 |
| Nebraska | 217 | 41.1 | 2,237 | 1,008 | 0.45 | 0.04 | 11.3 |
| North Dakota | 137 | 23.9 | 611 | 20 | 0.03 | 0.007 | 7.0 |
| Ohio | 417 | 40.0 | 21,846 | 25,938 | 1.19 | 0.13 | 9.1 |
| South Dakota | 339 | 26.4 | 1,705 | 99 | 0.06 | 0.007 | 8.2 |
| Wisconsin | 375 | 33.0 | 7,910 | 7,788 | 0.99 | 0.06 | 16.4 |
| SOUTH | 503 | 42.8 | 165,008 | 273,605 | 1.66 | 0.28 | 6.8 |
| Alabama | 549 | 44.1 | 7,615 | 14,594 | 1.92 | 0.36 | 5.3 |
| Arkansas | 443 | 40.4 | 4,448 | 5,543 | 1.25 | 0.20 | 6.3 |
| Delaware | 493 | 48.4 | 1,942 | 3,481 | 1.79 | 0.24 | 7.5 |
| DOC★ | 1343 | 80.7 | 91 | 9,096 | ★★★ | 1.87 | 53.5 |
| Florida | 456 | 62.1 | 27,445 | 35,721 | 1.30 | 0.19 | 6.9 |

*(continued)*

TABLE 7.4 *(continued)*

| | | | Prison Population | | | | |
|---|---|---|---|---|---|---|---|
| | Imprisonment | Crime | White | Black | R-Ratio | P-Ratio | RR/PR |
| Georgia | 532 | 51.5 | 11,983 | 24,392 | 2.04 | 0.41 | 5.0 |
| Kentucky | 385 | 28.8 | 8,976 | 5,586 | 0.62 | 0.08 | 7.8 |
| Louisiana | 776 | 57.5 | 6,852 | 22,360 | 3.26 | 0.49 | 6.7 |
| Maryland | 427 | 49.2 | 4,998 | 17,196 | 3.44 | 0.41 | 8.4 |
| Mississippi | 626 | 42.7 | 3,560 | 10,663 | 3.00 | 0.58 | 5.2 |
| North Carolina | 345 | 51.8 | 10,044 | 20,418 | 2.03 | 0.29 | 7.0 |
| Oklahoma | 662 | 46.8 | 11,188 | 7097 | 0.63 | 0.09 | 7.1 |
| South Carolina | 543 | 53.2 | 6,282 | 14,762 | 2.35 | 0.43 | 5.5 |
| Tennessee | 408 | 46.9 | 8,114 | 8,437 | 1.04 | 0.20 | 5.2 |
| Texas | 762 | 50.3 | 39,697 | 63,883 | 1.61 | 0.15 | 10.7 |
| Virginia | 447 | 33.7 | 9,221 | 18,970 | 2.06 | 0.26 | 7.9 |
| West Virginia | 196 | 27.2 | 2,643 | 502 | 0.19 | 0.03 | 6.3 |
| WESTERN | 361 | 44.0 | 11,2440 | 63,440 | 0.56 | 0.04 | 6.4 |
| Alaska | 374 | 43.6 | 1,895 | 600 | 0.32 | 0.05 | 6.1 |

*(continued)*

TABLE 7.4 *(continued)*

| | Imprisonment | Crime | Prison Population | | R-Ratio | P-Ratio | RR/PR |
| | | | White | Black | | | |
|---|---|---|---|---|---|---|---|
| Arizona | 495 | 59.0 | 18,686 | 3,523 | 0.19 | 0.04 | 4.8 |
| California | 481 | 38.1 | 46,957 | 48,331 | 1.03 | 0.10 | 10.3 |
| Colorado | 383 | 40.6 | 9,562 | 3320 | 0.35 | 0.05 | 6.9 |
| Hawaii | 320 | 48.4 | 1,063 | 232 | 0.22 | 0.09 | 2.4 |
| Idaho | 385 | 31.5 | 3,165 | 65 | 0.02 | 0.006 | 3.4 |
| Montana | 335 | 40.7 | 2,058 | 35 | 0.02 | 0.004 | 4.2 |
| Nevada | 509 | 22.8 | 5,048 | 2,407 | 0.48 | 0.09 | 5.3 |
| New Mexico | 270 | 59.6 | 3,892 | 545 | 0.14 | 0.03 | 4.7 |
| Oregon | 293 | 50.0 | 5,839 | 1,010 | 0.17 | 0.02 | 8.7 |
| Utah | 245 | 49.8 | 3,709 | 328 | 0.09 | 0.009 | 9.8 |
| Washington | 251 | 52.6 | 9,376 | 2,962 | 0.32 | 0.04 | 7.9 |
| Wyoming | 355 | 34.5 | 1,190 | 82 | 0.07 | 0.009 | 7.7 |

*Totals and means for south exclude D.C.

**Regional data in italics are means.

relationship between imprisonment rates and crime is the reverse of the outcome predicted by the deterrence or incapacitation arguments, while the test of significance indicates that the relationship is nonrandom. This finding leads to the rejection of deterrence and incapacitative arguments, and supports the findings yielded by the earlier time-series data. Taken together, both the cross-sectional and time-series outcomes reject the theoretical idea that higher rates of imprisonment are associated with lower rates of offending. Indeed, the cross-sectional data suggests just the opposite: high rates of imprisonment are found in places with high rates of crime. Regionally, the exception to this general relationship is found among the western states, where higher rates of imprisonment are indeed associated with lower rates of criminal offending. There is not much in this finding to suggest that the relationship found in the western states holds out hope for those supporting deterrence or incapacitation arguments since a similar relationship is not evident in the south, where the rate of imprisonment is significantly higher (the rate of incarceration in the south is nearly 40 percent higher than the rate of incarceration across western states). One would expect that if the deterrence or incapacitation argument had validity, the regions and states with the highest rates of incarceration would have the lowest rates of crime. This would be true *unless* there was reason to believe that some other factor related to these theories also varied by state or region. For example, theoretically, deterrence works because rational actors calculate the costs and rewards of punishments. The increased rate at which offenders were sent to prison in the South is a significant cost. As noted, the south's rate of imprisonment was nearly 40 percent higher than in western states; it is also 58 percent higher than the average rate of imprisonment in the midwest, and nearly 84 percent higher than in the northeast. Likewise the correlation between crime and imprisonment in the south is positive, meaning that crime rates and imprisonment rates fluctuate in the same direction (not in opposite directions as predicted by deterrence or incapacitation arguments). But, the crux of the problem is how to explain these regional differences in light of deterrence assumptions concerning the rationality of offenders. Could it be that people who live in western states are more rational than people who live in northeastern, midwestern, and southern states? Such an argument hardly seems plausible.

## BACK TO PRISONS, RACE, AND SEGREGATION

In their book, *American Apartheid: Segregation and the Making of the Underclass,* Douglas Massey and Nancy Denton (1993) state that

> No group in the history of the United States has ever experienced the sustained high level of residential segregation that has been imposed on blacks in large American cities for the past fifty years. This extreme racial isolation did not just happen; it was manufactured by whites through a series of self-conscious actions and *purposeful institutional arrangements* that continue today. Not only is the depth of black segregation unprecedented and utterly unique compared with that of other groups, but it shows little sign of change with the passage of time or improvements in socioeconomic status (2; emphasis added).

As an introduction to the present discussion of prisons, race, and segregation, Massey and Denton's comments are of extreme importance because they admit what many Americans would deny: the deep-seated and widespread nature of institutionalized racism in America. To be sure, other have written very important books on race (e.g., Myrdal, 1944; West, 1994; Carnoy, 1994; Pinkney1984). Some have also examined issues such as segregation (Hacker, 1995), while others (e.g., Miller, 1996; Mauer, 1999) specifically discuss race, crime, and imprisonment. The issue of racial segregation, however, is not one that has been adequately addressed with respect to America's prison system.

For the present discussion, Massey and Denton's comments and orientation toward racial segregation are important for at least three reasons. First, their analysis demonstrates that race continues to matter in modern America (West, 1994). Second, that it matters much more than might be suspected, and has far reaching implications. And third, that the races are still segregated in America, and that the degree of racial separation measured by residential segregation is much worse today than sixty or seventy years earlier.

Why is racial segregation so important? The reason has to do with the many effects of segregation, which Massey and Denton summarize as follows:

If policymakers, scholars, and the public have been reluctant to acknowledge segregation's persistence, they have likewise been blind
to its consequences for American blacks. Residential segregation is
not a neutral fact; it systematically undermines the social and economic well-being of blacks in the United States. Because of racial
segregation, a significant share of black America is condemned to
experience a social environment where poverty and joblessness are
the norm, where a majority of children are born out of wedlock,
where most families are on welfare, where educational failure pre-
vails, and where social and physical deterioration abound. Through
prolonged exposure to such an environment, black chances for social
and economic success are drastically reduced (1993: 2).

In short, not only is there a high level of unacknowledged segregation
in America, but because of its widespread nature and our unwillingness
to recognize its existence, a diverse array of negative consequences befall
black communities and individuals.

Why begin a discussion of race and prisons with reference to Massey
and Denton's comments concerning forms of residential or spatial segregation that are prevalent in the "free world" across a variety of communities found in the United States? Because these comments not only
apply to communities, but to prisons as well, which have also become
sites of racial segregation. Massey and Denton's orientation also helps us
to better understand one of the neglected roles prisons play in American
society, and how they also contribute to detrimental life conditions for
American blacks and their communities, a point support by the research
of Todd Clear and Dina Rose.

More specifically, and to be very clear on this point, if Massey and
Denton's argument is accepted and applied to the U.S. prison system,
it helps explain why the racial composition of American prisons is so
heavily slanted: because our big prison system has become part of the
"purposeful institutional arraignments" that help fortify racial segregation. Consider, for the moment, the evidence presented in table 7.4 concerning the prison racial ratio as compared to the racial ratio of the free
population for each state (RR/PR ratio). These ratios illustrate the extensive degree of racial segregation prisons help foster. To be sure, different states incarcerate blacks at different rates, and in different proportions

relative to the representation of the black population within a given state. With the exception of six states (Arizona, Hawaii, Idaho, Montana, New Mexico, and Georgia), all other states incarcerate blacks at a rate that is more than five times higher than the proportion of a given state's population that is black relative to whites. This ratio thus provides evidence of an extensive and pervasive form of racial segregation—one that involves the institution of the prison.

At one extreme is the District of Columbia with its RR/PR ratio of 540.3. This ratio indicates that in the District of Columbia blacks are 540 times more prevalent in prison than in the general population. While this is certainly the most extreme case, 44 states have RR/PR ratios in excess of 5; 37 have RR/PR ratios of 6 or more; and 12 have ratios of 10 of more. Thus, prisons certainly appear to be places where there is an excessive concentration of the black population.

As a physical location (that comprises a social space in which punishment is applied), prisons have become a very visible component of "purposeful institutional arrangements" that facilitate racial segregation. Consider for the moment that there are more young black men in America's prisons than on American college campuses (Mauer, 1999). This fact helps place the degree of racial segregation in America, and the prison's role in racial segregation, into a broader context.

To further explore the context of prisons and race, an investigation of the correlation between the general population's black–white ratio and the use of imprisonment across states is also relevant. Across states, the Pearson R correlation between population racial composition and the rate of imprisonment is .526, which is statistically significant (p < .000). This relationship demonstrates that the higher the black population within a state, the more likely that state is to have a high rate of incarceration. A number of studies support this finding (Yates, 1997; Beckett and Western, 2001; Jacobs and Carmichael, 2001; Smith, 2004; Pettit and Western, 2004; Ruddell, 2005; Yates and Fording, 2005).

Several explanations of this relationship are plausible. First, since the average African-American has a significantly lower class status (measured by wealth, income, and education) than the average white, states with high African-American populations may have a significant number of poorer citizens. Following the logic of numerous theories of crime (e.g., see Vold, Bernard, and Snipes, 2002, for review), it is reasonable to assume that these states may also harbor conditions conducive to crime, and that given high concentrations of African-Americans, they are likely to be more adversely affected than whites. This explanation is useful to the extent that it seems logical. And, while a greater percentage of the African-American community is likely to suffer from poverty conditions compared to whites, a larger overall percentage of the poor are white. Thus, states with small African-American populations but high white poverty rates (e.g., West Virginia) would also be expected to have elevated rates of incarceration.

This proposition can be assessed by regressing the crime rate and the black-white population ratio against the rate of imprisonment. If the relationship between racial composition across states and imprisonment rates is mediated by the crime rate, then the relationship between racial composition and imprisonment would disappear or become extremely attenuated once we control for crime in a multiple regression format. Likewise, if the relationships between racial composition and imprisonment were conditioned by poverty rates, then adding poverty rates as a control variable should remove or lessen the relationship between racial composition and imprisonment rates. When crime rates, state racial composition and poverty rates are regressed against cross state imprisonment rates, the following results emerge. The adjusted R square for the equation is 49.0 percent, meaning that these three variables alone account for close to one half of the variation in rates of incarceration across states. Further, the relationship between state racial composition (the black-white ratio) and imprisonment is positive and statistically significant ($p < .000$; $b = 532.13$). Likewise, the relationship between poverty and imprisonment is positive, though not quite statistically significant ($p = .052$; $b = 10.68$). The relationship between the crime rate and the imprisonment rate is positive, but statistically insignificant ($p = .157$; $b = 2.35$). Although this is an incomplete test of the relationship between imprisonment rates and racial composition, this analysis indicates that of the included variables, racial composition has the strongest impact on the level of incarceration, and, further, that this relationship exists independently of the level of crime or poverty. Moreover, any relationship between crime rates and imprisonment rates (the Pearson R for state crime and imprisonment rates is .613, and is significant at $p = .000$) is removed once racial composition is controlled for in the analysis.

It is no accident that prisons contain more young black males than American colleges and universities, or that prisons have become more important in the lives of young black men than colleges. And, this is not because African-American males are responsible for a large percentage of the U.S. crime rate. Indeed, while blacks are overrepresented among criminal populations, whites commit the majority of crime in the United States (Lynch, 2002, 2000b). As an institution, prisons and colleges contribute to the maintenance of segregation in American society. The underrepresentation of black men in American colleges—which can also be associated with the poor primary and secondary schools black youth attend and lack adequate financial resources; the failure to motivate and connect with these youth; the failure to connect black youth to social and economic institutions that ensure success; the high failure (dropout) rates found in primarily black schools—guarantees that black Americans will not be equipped to compete in the job market. Their inability to compete in the economic marketplace helps lock them into impoverished lifestyles and diminishes the odds that they will achieve sufficient financial success to "escape" segregated communities. The overrepresentation of blacks in prison, well in excess of their contribution to America's crime problem, in itself becomes a form of segregation. At the same time, high imprisonment rates for blacks add detrimental labels that frustrates black Americans efforts to advance economically. In short, it can be said that the social and physical distribution of young black men in prisons and colleges and universities (which could be described as part of the geography of young black men) reflects broader forms of institutionalized racism prevalent in American society.

It would, of course, be incorrect to attribute the forms of discrimination and racial segregation blacks face as being the result of their elevated chances of imprisonment alone. Clearly, many other factors contribute to the social, economic, political, and physical isolation of blacks in American society (Massey and Denton, 1993). To be sure, the prison itself may appear to be little more than a site where we can see the outcome of the various racial biases incorporated into criminal justice processes. But, the prison is not simply the culmination and reflection of broader or more general institutionalized biases; it also aids in maintaining attitudes and stereotypes about crime and criminals that legitimize institutionalized and individualized racial biases (Reiman, 2003) while contributing directly to the physical segregation of "the races" in America. For example, the "ex-con" label and "record" bestowed upon individuals who have been incarcerated diminishes the likelihood that they will find future employment. This formal label, which has numerous informal social control effects, continues the punishment of the offender unlucky enough to have been caught, prosecuted, found guilty, and sentenced, over the remainder of that individual's life. Because institutionalized police procedures focus more on events in minority communities, the likelihood that black law violators will be caught, prosecuted, and convicted is greater than for whites.

The experience of being in prison, and the ex-con label, dramatically alters the lives of those who have been incarcerated, and generally not in a positive manner. The ex-con is often socially and economically isolated from the mainstream, either driving them further into deviant lifestyles, embedding them into criminal careers, or attaching them to a life that vacillates quite easily between crime and conformity. Thus, rather than deter or rehabilitate the offender, the prison is more likely to establish a more persistent pattern of offending. For those who doubt that this is the case, all one needs to do is consider the high rate of recidivism among the former-inmate population.

It is necessary to understand the race-linked nature of the effects of imprisonment. Blacks and Hispanics comprise about 70 percent of the prison population in the United States, meaning that minorities are the majority within America's prisons. They are not in prison because they are society's worst criminals, as is illustrated by the substantial literature that focuses on notable financial and violent crimes committed by white corporate executives (e.g., Reiman, 2003; Simon and Eitzen, 2000; Friedrichs, 2004; Burns and Lynch, 2004; Lynch and Michalowski, 2006).

While minorities comprise the majority of the prison population in the United States, consider also that compared to other groups, a rather sizeable proportion of the black population is or has been in prison (Mauer, 1999), or has a substantial lifetime likelihood of being imprisoned (Bonczar and Beck, 1997; Pettit and Western, 2004). Table 7.5 shows the lifetime likelihood of imprisonment by race at different ages as estimated by Bureau of Justice Statisticians, Thomas Bonczar and Allen Beck. As table 7.5 illustrates, black males are more likely than white males in every age group to be incarcerated. It should be noted that the diminishing race ratio that results with increased age is, in part, due to the fact that the population of blacks available for incarceration diminishes more rapidly than the population of white available for incarceration due to an increase in the number of blacks incarcerated, as well as reduced participation in crime that is attributable to the aging process, and differentials in race related mortality rates.

Let us examine the race ratios found in table 7.5 more closely. These ratios indicate how much more likely a black male is than a white male of the same age to be incarcerated. The sizeable imprisonment chance difference for black males compared to white males at birth (6.48) indicates that blacks are substantially more likely (nearly 6.5 times more likely) than whites *to have their life course altered* by a serious form of criminal justice intervention. This finding indicates that criminologists who study the life course need to make a more extensive effort to study how race shapes life course (see Lynch, 1996 for discussion).

Consider also that through age 20, the race ratio remains above 6, and that that it is not until the age of 45 that the ratio declines significantly (to 2.63). Thus, it is not surprising that the detrimental effects of imprisonment fall most heavily on black offenders, and, equally if not more importantly, on black communities (Clear, 1994), and most importantly, on young black males. While the institution of imprisonment is not the only cause of these effects (Massey and Denton, 1993; see also, Hacker, 1995), it certainly contributes to, and intensifies the kinds of problems black Americans encounter everyday, especially for individuals who have been incarcerated.

Finally, it is instructive to examine one last table illustrating the relationship between race and imprisonment in the United States. This table also depicts changes in the racial composition of American prisons since 1980.

In 1980, the black–white imprisonment rate ratio was 6.6, meaning that given equivalent sized base populations, blacks were 6.6 times more likely to be in prison than whites. This level of racial disparity in incarceration is at least twice the estimated offending difference between whites and blacks in the United States (Lynch and Schuck, 2003; Lynch, 2002, 2000). The peak race related imprisonment difference occurred in 1996, when blacks were 8.4 times as likely to be imprisoned compared to whites. Since 1996, the rate in racial differences has slowly declined,

TABLE 7.5

*Lifetime Chance of Imprisonment by Age and Race for Males*★

| Age★★ | White Male | Black Male | Race Ratio★★★ |
|-------|-----------|-----------|---------------|
| Birth | 4.4 | 28.5 | 6.48 |
| 20 | 4.1 | 25.3 | 6.17 |
| 25 | 3.0 | 17.3 | 5.77 |
| 30 | 2.1 | 10.8 | 5.14 |
| 35 | 1.5 | 6.5 | 4.33 |
| 40 | 1.1 | 3.6 | 3.27 |
| 45 | 0.8 | 2.1 | 2.63 |

★ Adapted from Bonczar and Allen, 1997.

★★ Age related estimates are the likelihood of imprisonment for each age for those not already incarcerated.

★★★ The race ratio was derived by dividing the percentage of black males likely to be incarcerated at each age by the percentage of white males likely to be incarcerated at each age.

and by 2003, had reached a magnitude of 7.3, still significantly higher than in 1980.

Overall, the imprisonment rate for white offenders increased by 177 percent from 1980 through 2003 while the black imprisonment rate increased by 207 percent. The good news, for black Americans at least, is that since 1996, the increase in imprisonment has slowed for blacks and accelerated for whites. For this period, the increase in the incarceration rate for blacks was 10 percent, while for whites, the increase was 26 percent. Whatever its cause(s), the escalated rate at which whites were being imprisoned in recent years has not—and cannot—make up for the longer term pattern or history of racial bias these data illustrate.

CONCLUSION

This chapter has covered a good deal of terrain, and each element describe herein showed flaws in the argument that increasing the rate of imprisonment reduces crime, or that imprisonment is primarily about controlling crime. As you recall, data on crime suppression effects (CSE) and crime enhancement effects (see table 7.1) illustrated that the idea

TABLE 7.6

*Rate of Imprisonment Per 100,000 Population, by Race and Ethnicity, Various Years, 1980–2003*

|      | White | Black | Hispanic | B/W Ratio | M/W Ratio |
|------|-------|-------|----------|-----------|-----------|
| 2003 | 465   | 3405  | 1231     | 7.3       | 10.0      |
| 2002 | 450   | 3535  | 1177     | 7.9       | 10.5      |
| 2000 | 449   | 3457  | 1220     | 7.7       | 10.4      |
| 1999 | 417   | 3408  | 1335     | 8.2       | 11.4      |
| 1997 | 386   | 3209  | 1273     | 8.3       | 11.6      |
| 1996 | 370   | 3098  | 1278     | 8.4       | 11.9      |
| 1992 | 372   | 2678  |          | 7.2       |           |
| 1991 | 352   | 2523  |          | 7.2       |           |
| 1990 | 339   | 2376  |          | 7.0       |           |
| 1989 | 317   | 2200  |          | 6.9       |           |
| 1985 | 246   | 1559  |          | 6.4       |           |
| 1980 | 168   | 1111  |          | 6.6       |           |

1. Complied from various Bureau of Justice Statistics annual reports on prisoners in the United States.

2. Data on Hispanic inmates is unavailable for the entire period under investigation.

3. B/W ratio is the black–white ratio, which is derived by dividing the black rate of imprisonment by the white rate of imprisonment.

4. M/W ratio is the minority-white ratio, derived by adding the black/white imprisonment rate ratio and the Hispanic/white imprisonment rate ratio.

that raising imprisonment consistently since 1973 does not produce a persistent pattern in the rise and fall of crime. Indeed, despite smaller periods within this era where a rise in imprisonment appeared to reduce crime, the overall effect of imprisonment on crime for the entire period 1973 through 2004—which was noted contained a natural experiment where the imprisonment rate in the United States rose each and every year—was one of crime enhancement. The effect discovered here may be similar to the "brutalization hypothesis" researchers have discovered with respect to the use of capital punishment: namely, that the use of executions seems to increase rather than decrease the homicide rate (see Cochran, Chamlin, and Seth, 1994).

Despite these results, this chapter also examined the issue of how large the U.S. prison system would need to become to suppress crime significantly. Following the lead of researchers who have focused solely on data from the 1990s, when a rising rate of incarceration appears to lower the rate of criminal offending, imprisonment and crime rates were forecast forward to determine levels of each if the path taken in the 1990s continued. This analysis indicated that significant reductions (one-half the level of crime in 1999) in crime would not occur until 2018. To do so, the rate of imprisonment, however, had to increase an additional 176 percent above its 1999 level, which translated into an extraordinarily large and expensive prison system.

This chapter also examined cross sectional data on imprisonment and crime. Here, too, the data indicated that the relationship that exists between the two is more fancy than fact. It was demonstrated that states with high rates of incarceration had high rates of crime and not the low rates deterrence or incapacitation theory would predict.

In examining these data, we returned to reexamine the relationship between race and imprisonment in the United States. State-level data indicated that imprisonment was highest in states that had large African-American populations, and that the size of a state's African-American population was a better predictor of incarceration rates than crime rates, or conditions that may cause crime such as poverty.

In the next chapter, one final issue will be examined before a general summary of this book is presented. That chapter focuses on the problems presented by a massive prison system in an era where energy resources are being depleted and oil is becoming more scarce. This chapter is included to illustrate an additional problem with America's large prison system that policy makers need to address.

CHAPTER 8

# The End of Oil and the
# Future of American Prisons?

THIS CHAPTER EXAMINES operating and reforming
America's large prison system within the context of two interrelated
problems: the decline of the fossil fuel or "the end of oil," and global
warming.[1] Researchers who take an extreme view on the end of oil
are concerned that a worse-case scenario will develop unless societies
immediately begin to overhaul energy production, produce non–fossil
fuel energy alternatives, and teach people to live on less by promot-
ing sustainable growth as both an economic development strategy and
consumptive value system. Some, for example, have suggested that the
end of oil will correspond with the end of industrial society (Duncan,
2005). The majority of end-of-oil researchers share a pessimistic view
that the kinds of rapid technological change needed to avert disaster cannot emerge quickly enough to alleviate the fossil-fuel shortage or global
warming. Yet there are signs of hope, such as the 100 plus mile per gallon
hybrids researchers have recently developed (Kristof 2006).

It should be noted that the pessimistic attitudes of many end-of-
oil researchers stems from the impact of *emerging fossil fuel–based energy alternatives* on the global environment. The end of oil literature is
not simply about estimating when and if oil supplies will decline and
threaten the world's energy supply—it is also about the level of pollution and global warming,[2] and whether alternative fossil-fuel sources
(not fossil-fuel alternatives) can solve this problem. For example, there
may be enough oil available in oil sands or shale to operate a fossil-fuel
economy well beyond the middle of this century. But at what cost to
human and environmental health? Thus, questions about the end of
oil must also be addressed with environmental effects in mind. Human

societies cannot continue to employ fossil fuels without dire environmental consequences.

End-of-oil researchers are also not all of one mind. Like any other area of research, some believe that the issue is extremely urgent, while others argue that the sense of urgency is a gross exaggeration (e.g., see Michael C. Lynch's position, http://www.hubbertpeak.com/Lynch, or that taken by the George W. Bush White House). This latter group rejects the end of oil as plausible, and at worst sees future energy needs being met by alternative fossil-fuel technologies (e.g., coal, shale- and sand-based oil, natural gas). This view also dismisses the related problems of pollution and global warming as irrelevant and overblown.

The middle ground is occupied by a more optimistic group (e.g., Vaiteeswarah, 2003), which believes that scientific ingenuity will save us from the end of oil, produce an alternative energy system that will spur economic growth (Lovins et al., 2005), and that energy innovations will push the end-of-oil scenario further into the future, allowing more time to develop an alternative energy infrastructure. This group is optimistic about fossil-fuel alternatives such as shale and sand oils, and typically fails to address related environmental issues such as the impact of fossil-fuel alternatives on global warming.

Despite this controversy, even the world's largest oil companies recognize the problems presented by the dwindling world supply of oil. John Browne, CEO of the world's second-largest energy company, BP, argues that it is necessary to develop non–fossil fuel energy alternatives. The emerging consensus among oil companies is depicted in the following excerpt from a letter to the public published by Chevron chairman and CEO, David J. O' Reilly:

> Energy will be one of the defining issues of this century. One thing is clear: the era of easy oil is over. What we do now will determine how well we meet the energy needs of the entire world in this century and beyond. Demand is soaring like never before . . . some say that in twenty years the world will consume forty percent more oil than it does today. . . . We can wait until a crisis forces us to do something. Or we can commit to working together, and start by asking the tough questions: How do we meet the energy needs of the developing world and those of the industrialized nations? What role

will renewables and alternative energies play? How do we accelerate our conservation efforts? Whatever actions we take, we must look not just to the next year, but to the next 50 years.

Each view outlined above lays out a different scenario for energy in the twenty-first century. Regardless of which view is consulted, however, there is concern that some type of energy alternative will be required during the twenty-first century.

This chapter represents an effort to examine the imprisonment binge in the United States in relation to the energy issues outlined above. How can criminal justice systems be redesigned to use less energy and produce less pollution? How can these goals and those of doing justice be aligned?

These kinds of questions are alien to criminal justice researchers to the extent that theories of punishment and justice, or social policies on justice, are typically developed in an intellectual vacuum where social, economic, and even environmental concerns are omitted from consideration. Given the energy and pollution issues facing the world, however, criminal justice and penal policy can no longer be made in such a vacuum. Indeed, it is time to recognize that energy and pollution issues are among the most important factors impinging on continued growth of criminal justice and prison systems.

Peak oil, non–fossil fuel alternatives, and global warming are issues on which government leaders must step up and provide direction, and which must be incorporated into a more sensible and realistic approach to crime and justice in the United States. The direction must come from all levels of government, and include revising everything from the economy to social services, as well as educating and resocializing the public. As a criminologist, I contend that one issue to which these observations ought to be applied is the American system of imprisonment (and also to the way in which policing is practiced in the United States, a significant issue that is not the subject of this book).

This chapter is designed to sensitize criminal justice researchers, policy makers, and the public to the ways in which a declining oil supply will affect the mission of the criminal justice system, the need to consider energy resources when forging future criminal justice policies, and, especially, the wisdom of continuing to expand a large prison system that does not accomplish the mission of reducing crime. It is possible that the end of oil may occur later than predicted and that new, less- or non-polluting energy sources will be discovered and made widely available. But we cannot sit back and hope that this scenario emerges, for if it does not, American institutions, such as the prison system, will be burdened with a tremendous challenge.

The tendency of U.S. criminal justice policy makers to expand the criminal justice system and continue building prisons must be considered against a potential future energy crisis and the demands for increased energy criminal justice expansion poses. Devising criminal justice alternatives may require rethinking the philosophical basis of criminal justice in the United States, which is currently based on enlarging criminal justice functions to enhance the deterrent and incapacitiative effects of criminal responses. As the early chapters illustrate, these goals are not being met.

Before turning to a discussion of how the American correctional system might be reformed to respond to changing energy conditions, further background information is presented.

## DEPENDING ON OIL

Colin Campbell[3] (2001:1), a leading peak-oil researcher, noted, "The fundamental driver of the 20th Century's economic prosperity has been an abundant supply of cheap oil." Expanding on this point, Jeremy Rifkin (2002) suggests that in the near future, energy production and consumption will become the primary determinants of twenty-first-century economic development. These views reflect widespread agreement among geologists, physicists, large-scale financial planners, and even oil companies that the world is running out of oil. To make matters worse, there is no viable (by which I mean, readily available, widespread, large-scale, easily converted, non–global warming, low-pollution) energy alternative in sight. And, like everything else, America's prison system is dependent on a source of energy. Furthermore, because the U.S. prison system is the largest in the world, it consumes a great deal of energy.

If peak-oil researchers are correct, and action is not taken, the end of oil will disrupt world economies (e.g., cause widespread inflation, depressions, increased poverty, enhanced between class disparities in wealth), and the cost of operating social institutions like prisons will expand. Ordinary criminal justice functions will become a challenge to operate in an oil-depleted world. These observations suggest that criminal justice researchers and policy planners must become aware of warnings about the potential for a coming energy crisis, and that they must act now to reorganize criminal justice practices and procedures to be on the safe side. Absent significant reform, social control institutions in America could one day come to a grinding halt, *assuming the dire forecasts of peak-oil researchers are correct.*

### THE DECLINING AVAILABILITY OF OIL

As noted, there are various views concerning the scope of the problem presented by peak oil. The Society for Peak Oil Study, among others, lays out the most extreme case. Of particular concern is transforming the world's current fossil-fuel economy in the face of scientific evidence that world oil production is near its peak.

The phrase "peak oil" refers to the point when one-half of the world's oil reserve will have been used up or depleted. "So what?" you may be thinking. "There is still one-half of the oil reserve left. It has taken more than a century to use the first half. When the oil peak is reached, there should be another one hundred years of oil remaining." The problem is that the half remaining after the peak is reached will be insufficient to support world energy needs beyond the middle of the twenty-first century because of increased rates of energy use.

The idea of a peak in oil production was initiated by geologist M. King Hubbert, who in 1956 employed U.S. oil consumption, production, and reserve data to predict the U.S. oil crisis in the 1970s. King's predictions (known as "Hubbert's Peak" or "Hubbert's Curve") presented at the meetings of the American Petroleum Institute were widely known to those in the oil industry. This study was greeted with much skepticism. Many believed that the supply of oil under the earth's crust was rather limitless and not easily depleted. As a result, Hubbert's predictions were largely ignored. Oil production evidence from the United States, however, indicated that Hubbert's Peak indeed occurred, probably in 1971 (Heinberg, 2003). Despite this evidence, U.S. oil executives and policy makers continued to downplay the significance of a peak oil crisis, and did little to prepare for the era where oil supplies would dwindle. This began to change in the early 1990s, when a number of studies on peak oil were published or presented at conferences and made available on the Internet.

Hubbert's paper accurately predicted the 1970s U.S. oil crisis, which many believed was artificial and created by oil companies to enhance profits. Once the mid-1970s oil crisis passed and Congress provided the oil industry with substantial tax incentives that would maintain low gas and oil prices, concern over oil shortages disappeared from the public agenda. Since then, a number of analyses have applied the assumptions behind Hubbert's Peak to world oil-reserve data, resulting in numerous recent publications on the world's declining oil reserve (Campbell, 2003, 1998; Campbell and Laherrere, 1998; Deffeyes, 2001; Goodstein, 2004; Heinberg, 2003; Roberts, 2004). Based on these analyses, the world oil-production peak is expected sometime within the next decade (as early as 2006 and as late as 2020; see figure 8.1). Once that peak is reached, there will be between twenty-five to forty years of oil remaining at current levels of oil consumption (the end-of-oil estimate depends on estimates for population growth, the rate of emergence and use of energy alternatives, and economic expansion that individual models employed by different researchers; Goodstein, 2004). Whatever date is affixed to the world oil peak, these predictions indicate that a potentially large energy crisis looms in the near future. As indicated below, the peak-oil phenomenon is particularly relevant to the United States.

## THE UNITED STATES, OIL, AND OIL DEPENDENCE

The United States is the world's leading consumer of oil, meaning it is also likely to be the nation that suffers extraordinary hardships from the declining availability of oil. Unfortunately, U.S. policy makers have done little to plan for the challenges presented by a declining world oil supply. Especially problematic are U.S. energy policies laid out under the George W. Bush administration and the willingness of current national energy policy agents to tradeoff air pollution increases and increased threats to public health for an energy policy that expands U.S. reliance on "dirty" fossil fuels such as coal. And, because U.S. energy policy has not been adequately addressed nor problematized by national energy policy agents, policy makers in other national, state, and local agencies have been slow to address the need to develop alternative energy resources and how the decline of oil will impact the ability of social institutions to carry out their assigned duties.

Although less than 5 percent of the world's population resides within the United States, its residents consume 25 percent all oil produced in the world annually, with oil consumption exceeding the population ratio by a factor of 5. Further, U.S. oil consumption has risen over the past forty years, with an increasingly larger percentage supplied by foreign nations, especially since the early 1970s, when the United States reached its peak in domestic oil supply (Duncan, 2005).[4]

Few if any major policy initiatives in the United States address this problem. Furthermore, the policies that have been instituted, such as the opening of the Arctic National Wildlife Refuge (ANWR) to oil exploration, are shortsighted responses that will add only a few years to the domestic oil reserve at current use levels.[5] The expansion of natural gas supplies is another misguided policy.[6]

### Synthesis: The Implications of Peak Oil

To be sure, the information presented above paints a dramatic picture of the future of oil. New discoveries may emerge that will forestall the end of oil or provide viable alternative energy options; nevertheless, the end of oil is possible,[7] and a failure to recognize this possibility could lead to social problems that are difficult to address if the most serious scenarios are not considered. With oil prices rising and the oil peak nearing, the time is now to devise alterative criminal justice policies that fit the new energy era that is rumbling toward us.

Taken together, the criminal justice apparatus operated at the local, state, and federal levels in the United States is massive. This system was built without regard to energy consumption during an era where energy supply, consumption, and costs, and the environmental impact of consuming vast amounts of energy, were not part of criminal justice planning. The relationship between energy availability, energy costs, and criminal justice policy can no longer be ignored, and will come to shape criminal justice policy. Alternatives to our mass system of incarceration, the tendency to over-criminalize and thereby expand the need for policing, and the extensive reliance on fossil-fuelled patrol vehicles to carry out police work are some of the areas that can be reassessed and redesigned.

The coming energy crisis will have dramatic effects on the way social institutions are organized, from their architecture to the missions they

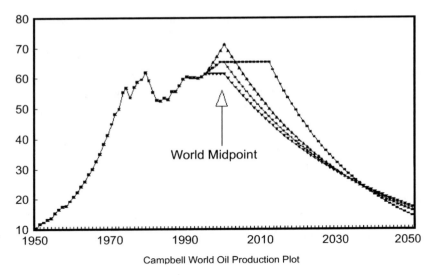

8.1. Peak-Oil Estimates, Four Models for World Oil Production, http://www.hubbertpeak.com/summary.htm

pursue. It is necessary for criminal justice planners and policy makers to familiarize themselves with energy- and oil-crisis issues, and to institute policies that reduce reliance on old fossil fuel criminal justice technologies.

### Punishing with Less Fossil Fuel

Assume for the moment that criminal justice policy makers fail to change the course of the American system of imprisonment, and that the development of alternative energy sources lags. By the time the peak oil crisis affects the generation of electricity—a commodity widely used to secure U.S. prisons—there may be several million inmates behind bars. With rolling brownouts and rising energy costs, how would the U.S. maintain its big system of imprisonment? How would it ensure that the public would be safe? Truthfully, it is unlikely that it could. Would this, perhaps, result in states across the nation releasing millions of inmates who have been locked away in institutions that are ineffective mechanisms for changing behavior? Given current developments in U.S. energy policy, and the speed with which an alternative energy infrastructure is proceeding, this is one possibility. Of course, this outcome can be averted if criminal justice policy makers, law makers, and criminal justice administrators join together *NOW* and put policies in place that will stave off this possibility.

To change the prison system is not extraordinarily difficult. What will be difficult is to change the opinions of the public and lawmakers, and to convince them that such changes are needed. Lawmakers and the public need to be taught to recognize that our country must institute a correctional system based on offender reform rather than deterrence and incapacitation (Cullen and Gilbert, 1982; Clear, 1996), and that we ought to adopt correctional models found in nations with small, effective prison systems to deal with crime reduction, escalating prison size and costs, looming energy supply problems, and global warming. There is a need, in other words, to unite criminal justice policy and philosophy with green theories and practices (e.g., see Frank and Lynch, 1992; Lynch and Stretesky, 2003; South, 1998; South and Beirne, 1998; Berine and South, 2006).

To be sure, changing the prison system so that it can be smaller will require adopting a new philosophy of punishment. The data reviewed in previous chapters indicates that the U.S. prison system is not effective especially given its extraordinary size. What we must keep in mind when considering prison reform is that the majority are sent back into society, not reformed by being locked away. As noted in an early chapter, about 70 percent of former inmates return to crime after their release from prison. Clearly, this fact indicates that the current strategy behind punishment is not effectively correcting their behavior. To be sure, these inmates are being punished, but at what cost? These costs are difficult to calculate because they involve estimating wasted energy, global warming effects, wasted resources employed to incarcerated inmates who are not affected by imprisonment, and the continued costs of crime, as well as many intangible effects on the lives of individuals who are incarcerated and their families (Clear, 1996).

Reducing the size of the prison population will also require changing laws and policing practices; for economic, energy, and environmental reasons, the police department of the future can no longer afford to be built around large, centralized police stations and the police cruiser. Thus, while the remainder of this chapter examines prisons and energy resources, I recognize that reforming prisons alone is an insufficient reform, and that the entire criminal justice apparatus needs to be revised consistent with energy and environmental conservation concerns.

IMPRISONMENT AND THE OIL CRISIS

The American prison system was designed solely with reference to assumptions about crime control that failed to take energy consumption issues into consideration. Consistent with the U.S. consumer cultural orientation, the American prison system has experienced continual expansion over the past thirty years and become a behemoth that is now the world's largest. America's environmentally outdated correctional system of isolated, high-capacity prisons presents numerous challenges in an era where the energy needed to operate and secure those facilities will become more limited and costly.

Financially, the rising price of fossil fuels will increase a variety of prison system costs. An endless array of everyday commodities found in prisons are made using oil (e.g., safety glass, detergents, linoleum, plastic products, clothing, fertilizers, pesticides, ink, cameras, clothing, etc.). The prices and supply of these widely used commodities, as well as the supply and price of food, will increase as oil becomes less available.[8]

The large spaces enclosed within prison walls will present a financial burden in terms of increased heating and cooling expenses as the availability of fossil fuels declines. There are two options: plan for the use of alternative heating and cooling sources or, as some will undoubtedly argue, turn off prison heating and cooling systems. The latter response is unrealistic in both humanitarian and prison security terms. Unheated inmates in prison systems in cold climates can be expected to die; hot and agitated inmates are more likely to act aggressively, or perhaps riot. In addition, the lack of heating and cooling would pose a burden to staff and make recruiting correctional personnel even more difficult.

Transportation costs to large, out-of-the-way prisons that characterize the American prison will also rise. In addition, since tarred roadways are constructed from oil and rock, repairing them will become more costly. Road-repair funds are likely to be concentrated where they are most needed—in urban areas—leaving rural roads leading to prisons in disrepair, which will drive up vehicle repair costs, and, in extreme cases, may become a security issue.

Taken together, the future of rising heating, cooling, transportation, food, clothing, and security costs associated with the declining supply of fossil fuels will make prison operation costs rise exponentially in a fossil-fuel-driven prison system. Likewise, the security of the prison system is likely to be compromised by reoccurring oil shortages and power outages that will accompany the era of oil's decline (a relevant example involves the effect of deregulation of electricity in California discussed previously).

To accommodate to this future, the American prison system must be redesigned now. All traditional prison building should be placed on hold, and certainly no large prisons should be built—these are simply a waste of tax dollars given the future of oil (not to mention that they are wasteful with respect to the stated goal of reducing crime). Prison building emphasis needs to be shifted to replacing fossil-fuel facilities. Small prisons that can supply their own energy needs through solar and geothermal energy must replace the large prison of the fossil-fuel era. In addition, these prisons should be placed in relative proximity to or within urban areas to reduce transportation costs.

Building new, environmentally sound and energy efficient prisons is only one step. The bigger issue will become reducing the size of the American prison population. Consider, for example, that less than one-half of prison inmates are serving time for violent offenses, or that the largest proportion of growth in the prison population over the past decade is due to a rising rate of incarcerating drug offenders (Austin and Irwin, 2000), and it becomes easy to imagine how laws can be reformed to reduce the size of the American prison population.

## SMALLER, LOCALIZED, ENVIRONMENTALLY FRIENDLY CORRECTIONAL FACILITIES

To accommodate the difficulties of energy provision in a non-fossil-fuel era and to become environmentally sound, the behemoth U.S. prisons must be dismantled. Instead of large, centralized prisons that involve long-distance transportation of inmates, smaller, local prisons or reform centers (call them what you like) should be encouraged or even mandated. Small local prisons can address a number of energy and ecological issues, and substantially reduce fossil fuel energy consumption through environmentally friendly, energy-conscious design. Depending on their geographic location, small prisons can derive energy using passive and active solar energy technology to convert sunlight into heating and cooling, and solar photovoltaic cells to convert sunlight into electricity. Another option is geothermal heating and cooling systems, which reduce heating and cooling energy costs by 30 to 60 percent. In some locations, wind-powered electrical generators would also be feasible alternatives. These alternative energy sources would meet the energy needs of small prisons, drastically reduce or eliminate the need for fossil-fuel-generated electricity, and perhaps even yield a surplus of energy that could be sold to utilities or channeled to local power grids to provide free energy for street lights—another crime reduction tool.

Building America's smaller prison system will entail some expense. The free energy these prisons will employ, however, and the reduced stress on the environment, will offset construction costs against reduced future energy expenses, as well as intangible costs such as being able to lock up criminal offenders in secure locations that will not be compromised by energy shortages. A number of alternative energy systems are already in use in various criminal justice functions in the United States and elsewhere (see table 8.1, detailing alternative energy use in the criminal justice system, and some cost-savings estimates, at the end of this chapter).

## TRANSITIONING TO THE NON-FOSSIL-FUEL PRISON

Above, it was suggested that one way to dismantle America massive fossil-fueled prison is to place a moratorium on prison building, and to encourage the transformation to small, local prisons that are more energy efficient and environmentally friendly. To accomplish this goal, and to lower the total U.S. prison population, laws will also need to be rewritten. To help reduce the rate of reoffending, these new prisons must be built around rehabilitative philosophies. But, to be successful, the building of an alternative, smaller prison system requires other forms of encouragement as well. Below, one such alternative is outlined. The assumption behind this alternative is based on a model of small prisons operated at the county level.

Criminals are discovered at the local level, yet they are often retained for incarceration in state facilities. Within each state, county and other local law enforcement officials make decisions that determine the kinds and number of offenders that will be discovered and prosecuted. Local policies, therefore, can have a tremendous impact on state correctional resources. And, because local authorities in, for instance, counties, institute different or unique procedures, each county has a differential impact on the state prison load. Thus, in order to engineer a smaller prison system, it is necessary to devise a plan that affects local-level decision making concerning the enforcement of laws, and the selection of the kinds and numbers of offenders who will end up incarcerated. To do so, it may be effective to offer local authorities incentives. What incentive can counties be given to reduce the number of inmates sent to state prison?

A useful, long-term example is found in the Minnesota Community Correctional Act of 1973. With one of the lowest imprisonment rates per 100,000 citizens in the nation (125 per 100,000), Minnesota sets an excellent example of how the correctional population can be reduced while saving money, energy, and keeping crime to a minimum.

First, Minnesota recognizes that imprisonment is a "necessary" option for "violent, predatory or unmanageable" offenders. At the same time, however, Minnesota also recognizes that these offenders are in the minority, and that a significant portion of offenders can be treated in the community (see "Minnesota Department of Corrections Sentencing to Service Program Review/Assessment Report," January, 2003, http://www.doc.state.mn.us/publications/pdf/stsreviewassessment2003.pdf).

Second, participation in community corrections programs is a voluntary decision made by each county. Counties are persuaded to participate through the use of financial incentives. The objective is to get counties to operate community correctional programs that divert offenders from terms of incarceration in state prisons. To do so, a mechanism for distributing state correctional funds to counties has been enacted that produced the resources counties need to operate community correctional programs (see, for example, Minnesota State Laws, 2004, section 401.1, http://www.revisor.leg.state.mn.us/stats/401/10.html). Other financial incentives may also stem from operating community correctional programs. For example, Minnesota's Sentencing to Service (STS) programs operated by counties yield three dollars in benefits for each dollar invested in the program through the service work performed by program participants (offenders). In addition, with respect to STS programs, "Counties may operate their own programs with the state providing matching funds or counties may contract with the state to provide STS services. In return for state matching funds, it is expected that up to one-half of the work completed by a county crew will be on projects for

state agencies" (http://www.doc.state.mn.us/ publications/pdf/stsrevie-
wassessment2003.pdf).

Community correctional programs not only return money to counties, they can provide needed local services and create employment. More
importantly, it is in the best interest of communities to design programs
that will result in offender rehabilitation. For example, some programs in
Minnesota require enrollment in offender appropriate educational programs, job-training programs, or employment as a condition for participation. In Washington County, more than 75 percent of offenders were
employed or enrolled in educational training courses (see Washington
County Annual Performance Report for 2005, Community Corrections,
http://www.co.washington.mn.us/client_files/documents/adm/Per-
fMeas-2005/ADM-PM-05-CmmCrrctns.pdf).

To be sure, creating an appropriate funding formula that accomplishes the goals of decentralization is complex, though an example that
has been used can be located in Minnesota law (Minnesota Statutes 2004,
401.10). In addition to incentives that force decentralization, policy makers must be sure to include incentives that require localized facilities to
employ alternative energy sourses (perhaps even requiring that facilities generate excessive power that can be used by other state offices and
agencies in the county as a return on the state's investment).

The benefits of a decentralized system of incarceration extend beyond energy consumption and supply, and should not be overlooked.
Smaller institutions are more conducive to establishing programs useful for rehabilitation. Community-based prison centers also facilitate rehabilitation by maintaining offender-community ties and interactions.
Smaller institutions save resources and energy. They can also be used, as
in the example from Minnesota, to provide labor for local projects in
ways that a centralized prison system cannot. Smaller prisons are also tied
to local communities, and give communities a stake in their success, a
stake that is missing in the big prison system model that currently domi-
nates in the United States.

## CONCLUSION

This chapter offers a glimpse at an issue that will come to have a
large impact on American society and its criminal justice processes: the
coming oil crisis. This idea is introduced to facilitate consideration of

how the American criminal justice system will meet the challenge of an oil-deficient future. In addition to offering some preliminary ideas concerning how the criminal justice can be reorganized and redesigned in an energy-efficient manner, this analysis has also drawn attention to related key issues. First, there is the concern of figuring out the fit between various philosophies of doing justice and energy-efficient policies. Energy efficiency may require that philosophies of justice are shifted away from the current preoccupation with incapacitation and deterrence, which have served to create a large, energy-inefficient system of justice that also offers little evidence of its effectiveness as a crime control strategy (e.g., Clear, 1994; Rose and Clear, 1998; Austin and Irwin, 2003; Welch, 2004b).

It is always a bad idea to attempt to predict the future—one is sure to be wrong on some if not many accounts. The decline of the oil era, however, looms large on the horizon. The folly is to think that it will not emerge, and that it is not necessary to plan the path for a new criminal justice and correctional system that takes energy consumption into account.

Today, the United States imports 60 percent of its oil from foreign nations, having already reached its own oil peak in the early 1970s. The U.S. fossil-fuel economy and social organization is, with each passing year, becoming more dependent on the supply of oil from foreign nations. More extensive drilling within U.S. boundaries will not solve that problem because oil is running out worldwide, while world energy demands are increasing annually. The George W. Bush White House has denied the possibility that we may run out of oil, and has placed greater emphasis on fossil fuel as energy sources.[9] According to available science, this is a grand mistake. At the national level, energy policy is headed in the wrong direction. This does not mean that state and local criminal justice planners and researchers must follow this policy blindly, or close their eyes and hope that the inevitable energy crisis does not occur. It is in our best interest to recognize the end of the oil era, and to plan for a new, energy-efficient criminal justice system now.

On the basis of scientific evidence, it is clear that the world's remaining oil reserve will be seriously threatened or depleted by mid-century if current levels of oil use are not curtailed. Not only must we begin to reform basis economic production, we must also begin to redesign basic

TABLE 8.1
*Alternative Energy Examples in the Criminal Justice System*

This table contains examples of alternative energy policies instituted in various locations that provide energy for operating prisons and policing. In the United States, these policies have been instituted in an ad hoc manner, and not as the basis of a larger energy reform effort. Currently, the exceptions to this statement would include the Tennessee prison system.

*Prison*

Michigan: The Michigan Department of Corrections contracted for energy efficient building modifications to two medium-security facilities, the Muskegon and Marquette prisons. The contract covered installation of simple energy efficient technology, including replacing and adding insulation, converting lighting, replacing old thermostats with energy efficient controls, installing heat recovery systems, and heating and cooling zone controls. The seven-year cost savings, after expenses, amounted to $495,916 for the two facilities. Energy savings were estimated in cost terms and not in energy quantities. (1993) (http://www.michigan.gov/documents/state_of_MI_correctional_facility_case_study_01–0026_121538_7.pdf).

Utah: An extensive renovation occurred at the Utah State Prison at Bluffdale, which included installation of wind-power generators and geothermal energy. First-year estimates indicate energy savings of 40 percent on electricity and 60 percent on natural gas. First-year financial savings were guaranteed by contractors at $409,832. This large facility houses 4,300 inmates, demonstrating that energy efficient technology can be put to use to provide energy for large facilities. (August, 2003) (http://www.geothermal-biz.com/docs/utah.pdf).

Tennessee: The energy-efficiency projects entered into by the state of Tennessee for its prison system yielded $1.9 million in savings for 1998 alone. Projects have included both low (e.g., insulation) and high technology (e.g., geothermal energy) energy solutions (http://www.rebuild.org/attachments/partnerupdates/Janfeb2003pu.pdf).

England: Her Majesty's Prison Service (HMPS) has instituted numerous practices designed to enhance environmental quality for citizens and lower the costs of imprisonment. For example, fifty-two institutions have met reduced carbon dioxide emission (a global warming gas) standards set in 2002. Between 2000 and 2003, HMPS has invested over 4 million pounds on energy improvements. The costs of these improvements are expected to be recouped from energy savings within three years. Energy-efficient projects have included simple and advanced applications (e.g., solar, wind, and geothermal power). These projects are considered to be system wide policies (http://www.swea.co.uk/prisons.htm).

Sweden: In 1999, Swedish prison officials began installation of a limited-use solar heating system at two prisons, generating significant annual savings estimated to cover the costs of the installation within eight years. Additional benefits were obtained from lowered carbon dioxide production (http://www.caddet.org/infostore/display.php?id=18926).

*(continued)*

TABLE 8.1 *(continued)*

*Policing*

Individual police departments have engaged in a number of efforts to employ alternative energy sources. Recently (July, 2004), for example, the police department in Westport, Rhode Island, tested Toyota's hybrid vehicle, the Prius, for suitability as a police vehicle (http://www.eastbayri.com/story/282301604225817.php). Hybrid vehicles have also become the vehicle of choice for University Police at the North Illinois University (http://www.niu.edu/PubAffairs/RELEASES/2004/june/hybrid.shtml).

A solar police station has been built in Vallejo, California (August, 2002). The station house uses photovoltaic cells that convert solar rays into electricity. The system is capable of producing more electrical power than the station consumes. The system cost $295,000, and is estimated to produce between $15,000 to $18,000 per year in excess electricity (http://www.spgsolar.com/press_vallejo_pd_pr1.html).

New York State police turned to solar power to operate Adirondacks radio transmission towers in 1998 (http://www.awesomesonsolar.com/PV.html). To reduce its impact on the environment, the Bend City, Oregon, police decided to buy 10 percent of its energy needs from a company that provides renewable energy using wind power generators. This small effort has an environmental impact equivalent to eliminating the use of thirteen patrol cars for a year (http://www.pacificpower.net/Article/Article38518.html). The Anaheim, California, city government installed photovoltaic solar converters on its main and eastern police stations as part of a citywide effort to reduce energy use, lower levels of air pollution, and save on expenses (http://www.powerlight.com/case-studies/state/anaheim.shtml).

social institutions to accommodate to a future where oil is costly and scarce. Energy intensive criminal justice practices must be altered, and a new energy-efficient model of criminal justice must be implemented. Without such a model, the United States faces the possibility of a serious ripple-effect crisis, as oil shortages affect the ability of the criminal justice system to perform its assigned duties.

The longer the need for energy related criminal justice reform is ignored, the more likely it becomes that the criminal justice system will be inadequately prepared to provide for public safety in the future. A decade from now, our criminal justice system will either be redesigned to function efficiently using alternative energy sources, or it will become the victim of our unwillingness to take the necessary steps toward reform now, and become increasingly susceptible to the insecurity of the world oil market.

## CHAPTER 9

# A Consuming Culture

THE HISTORY OF the American prison system is an effort to perfect the use of the penal apparatus the Quakers introduced in Philadelphia meant for the reform of the criminal offender. America, more so than another other nation, has relied upon the prison as a means of responding to criminals, and has expanded this apparatus far beyond the level found in other nations. But, throughout its history, especially in the modern era, the U.S. prison system has not lived up to the lofty ideals of the Quakers.

In the United States, the prison began as a means of reform, and was later adopted to fulfill other functions that included deterrence and incapacitation. Along the way, the American prison served industry as a center of profit-making activity under the influence of the Auburn model and later during the industrial prison era of the early 1900s (Barnes and Teeters, 1945). Perhaps one reason the American prison system is so big is that it lacks a clear, consistent, and appropriate purpose. It has been used to meet the goals of several different philosophies, and it has been used to meet some of these goals despite the fact that existing evidence suggests that it has been unable to fulfill the functions specified by those philosophies, especially with respect to deterrence and incapacitation. While the American prison system is certainly much larger than the prison systems found in other nations, it nevertheless does not appear big enough to deter or incapacitate a significant portion of the criminal population.

The problem may be that prisons fail to address the causes of crime. Indeed, the data on the relationship between imprisonment and crime reviewed here suggests as much, since the two trends are rarely found to exist together in the expected direction, at the predicted magnitude, or in any persistent manner. We will return to this idea below.

The failure of the American prison system means three things. First, there is no simple connection between crime and punishment. Second, the absence of this simple connection means that the problem of crime cannot be solved simply by manipulating the level of imprisonment. Third, the failures of the American system of imprisonment makes alternative explanations for its expansion appear more legitimate and, perhaps, logical (e.g., models of economy or race control). These alternatives only become clear when the assumed relationship between crime and imprisonment is discarded, and the economic-, class-, and race–control dimensions of the American system of imprisonment are revealed.

The American prison system is, and may be, troubled by other issues as well. To be sure, as discussed in the previous chapter, policy makers must begin to take energy issues into account when determining prison policy. The massive prison apparatus currently in use in the United States cannot be sustained in the future if predictions of an energy strapped future come to pass.

## CONSPICUOUS CONSUMPTION

One must also consider that the American prison system is the sign of a society that has taken conspicuous consumption, which Veblen (1899) identified as a cultural characteristic of American society, to an extreme. In simple terms, conspicuous consumption involves the purchase of expensive commodities and services in an effort to create public displays of both wealth and social status. In Veblen's analysis, examples of conspicuous consumption often involved "extravagant" or unnecessary purchases of commodities and services in ways that communicated one's social status to others. Veblen described this as a cultural rather than a personal tendency, meaning that it had widespread origins and effects, and that the effort to communicate status through this mechanism was widely understood and especially relevant in capitalist cultures. Thus, conspicuous consumption can be seen as being motivated by cultural and economic structures. Since Veblen viewed conspicuous consumption as a societal feature, this idea has applications beyond the analysis of the consumption patterns of individuals. Indeed, if Veblen was correct, social institutions might also participate in and contribute to reinforcing patterns of conspicuous consumption. Interpreted in this way, it is possible to view the massive expansion of U.S. prisons as an institutional example of conspicuous consumption.

America's behemoth prison system requires an extraordinarily large capital outlay. In addition, this outlay can be considered conspicuous to the extent that prison expenditures are highly visible, produce large prison buildings, consume extensive physical space, secure the world's largest prison population, and generate other forms of communication, such as news stories, that may contribute to spreading images of the system's excessive consumption and grandeur. These images and messages are not only visible to the American public, but to people in other nations. For example, from its very beginning, the unique American approach to crime that constituted the prison system was investigated and copied by a number of other nations. Moreover, even in the contemporary world, America's prison system is held out as an example for criminal justice policy in other nations.

Hidden beneath the most visible signs of conspicuous consumption that the American prisons system stands for, are the costs related to human lives caught up in the system in ways described by, among others, Todd Clear, Francis Cullen, John Irwin, and James Austin. Indeed, the consumption of human lives by the prison system would appear to be the most forceful image of conspicuous consumption a society could make: only a culture rich in labor power can afford to engage in the consumption of human lives. The meaning of this form of consumption is, furthermore, enhanced by the use of the death penalty in the United States. This form of consumption is especially relevant when U.S. and European criminal justice processes are compared, since no other Western, industrialized nation uses the death penalty or consumes its citizens in this manner.

To be sure, American culture is driven by consumption. As noted earlier, though the population of the United States makes up less than 5 percent of the world's population, Americans consume 25 percent of the world's annual production of oil. With respect to prisons, the United States consumes more resources, more services, more physical space, and, relative to the size of its population, many more lives in terms of incarceration and death. In this sense, America's big prison system is simply another symptom of the tendency to desire and consume vast quantities, as the examples in the introduction to this book illustrated.

Another important feature of conspicuous consumption as described by Veblen includes the tendency to consume irrationally. As has been demonstrated throughout this book, the American prison system is an irrational response to crime to the extent that it fails to control or reduce crime. Thus, on this account, building, maintaining, and expanding America's big prison system also fits within Veblen's view of conspicuous consumption.

## IRRATIONAL CONSUMPTION

Whether or not the U.S. prison system is a form of conspicuous consumption, America citizens and policy makers must come to grips with the facts about American prisons. Consider the following facts that have been reviewed throughout this book. For example, the United States has the world's largest prison system, which, if it was an effective mechanism for controlling crime, would have reduced the crime rate to a fraction of its current level. As we have seen, the massive expansion of prisons that has been underway unimpeded since 1973 has led to only a minor reduction in crime over the long run. Indeed, the trends in crime and punishment for this time period do not correspond well, and one would be hard pressed to conclude—moreover, I will go as far as to say that given the evidence, one would be wrong to conclude—that increases in the use of imprisonment in the United States had lead to a crime reduction. The temporal relationship between the rate of incarceration and crime fails to provide evidence that greater use of prisons deters or incapacitates offenders in ways that reduce the overall rate of offending. This is true when the long-run trend is considered. Short-term trends sometimes show a deterrent or incapacitative effect; however, we need to be skeptical of this effect because it is not evident over any significant period of time. Furthermore, the ability of imprisonment to reduce crime is not seen in cross-state or cross-regional analysis either. To be sure, some research shows evidence of this effect. But sometimes showing this effect is not sufficient evidence from a scientific perspective. Indeed, if those who found such effects were honest, they would have to admit that the majority of studies and the long-term trend for the United States indicate that expanding prisons as a means of controlling crime is a waste of time and effort—it is not only conspicuous consumption, it is irrational consumption of resources.

Researchers and policy makers, however, do not often admit such a possibility when they discuss proposals for growing the American prison system. This may have to do with the fact that they would have to explain why our nation has produced such a big prison system if it fails in its mission of crime control. To do so might require looking at some ugly options. As other studies and data presented in earlier chapters suggest, America's prison system is part of the class- and race-control structure that has been built in American society. American prisons overwhelmingly house the poor and racial minorities. This is not, as was illustrated earlier, because they pose the greatest threat to American society in terms of financial loses, threats to our personal or national security, or in terms of the level of violence these populations commit. Clearly, the various crimes of the upper-class person with money, power, and status—white-collar crime, environmental crimes, corporate crimes, governmental crimes, and crimes against foreign nations—are much more costly on these accounts than ordinary street crimes. Yet these are precisely the people who are not found in American's prisons.

### RETHINKING CRIME AND PUNISHMENT

In our society, punishment is widespread. But so too is crime. Historically, this was not always the case. In previous eras of U.S. history, lower rates of crime and lower rates of imprisonment and punishment coexisted. The changing nature of crime and punishment in the United States may be due to changes in the nature of the social and economic structure. It has also been demonstrated that low rates of incarceration do not themselves produce high rates of crime. This was demonstrated by examining cross-cultural, time series, and cross-state data. In addition, previous chapters also demonstrated that high rates of incarceration do not produce low rates of offending.

Faced with these facts, we are left with a problem. That problem, stated simply, is the identification of the causes of crime, and how to generate public policies that address those causes.

In various literatures—from sociology, criminology, economics, public policy, biology, psychology—a wide variety of answers to the question "what causes crime?" have been offered. The search for the answer to this question has consumed the lives of many scholars, and has filled libraries with prospective answers. To keep the current discussion manageable, I will address only a few relevant facts and factors (several factors I omit are discussed by Reiman, 2003).

First, the majority of crime that is committed in the United States involves the illegal acquisition of property, engaging in activities to acquire money to use for other illegal purposes, or efforts to obtain money to acquire legitimate property, which is a sign of wealth and status. This characteristic of crime in the United States is especially true if we include among the crimes we are examining the offenses of white-collar, corporate, environmental, and even some governmental criminals. But, without including these crimes, the majority of street crime or ordinary criminal offenses still involve efforts to acquire property and money, either directly or indirectly.

Second, we must consider that modern American society, more so than other modern nations, promotes the idea that the successful individual is one who acquires and accumulates property and economic resources.

Third, we must also keep in mind that while our society stresses achievements that are tied to economic success, our economic system is designed in a way that excludes a broad segment of the population from obtaining the kinds of success the system promotes (Ryan, 1982). For example, only 10 percent of the U.S. population earns more than $75,000, a figure many would target as an appropriate salary. At the same time, more than one-half of the population earns less than $42,000 a year, and a substantial proportion of those people earn substandard, minimum-wage, or poverty-level wages. In a society that promotes economic success, such extensive inequality is bound to produce social problems. Many studies link poverty and inequality to the probability of engaging in crime (Messner and Rosenfeld, 2001).

Fourth, over time, it has become increasingly harder to succeed in American society (Frank and Cook, 1996). This can be illustrated by examining the growth in inequality in income and wealth that has characterized American society over the past three decades. For the average person, success has become more difficult as the U.S. economy was transformed from an industrial to a service economy. But the struggle for success has been more forcefully felt by those at the lower end of the economic spectrum, where a life course of intergenerational poverty has become more widespread.

Fifth, the study of crime trends in the United States offers important information about the causes of crime. This trend tends to oscillate, which discounts pure psychological or biological explanations of crime.

For crime trends to be expressions of psychological states or biological factors alone, there would have to be massive, short term shifts in both, which is unlikely. Crime-trend analysis, however, indicates that the oscillation in crime is more closely linked to cultural and economic changes and conditions. Other factors may be important as well, such as exposure to environmental toxins that affect behavior. These exposure patterns change over time, and have geographic dimensions that are connected to urban locations and the race and class characteristics of communities (Stretesky and Lynch, 2001, 2003, 2004; Lynch, 2004).

There are a number of other details that might be considered here as well to flesh out this argument further (see Lynch and Michalowski, 2006). Each of these considerations point in the same direction as those briefly examined above. Taken together, these views lead to the conclusion that the mechanism for reducing crime lies beyond punishment and may actually be found in redesigning the system of rewards or achievement that has come to define America's cultural and economic systems.

To be sure, reform of this magnitude is not easy. One option is to alter the cultural meanings attached to success. This could be accomplished by attaching the idea of success to a host of social goals that would be promoted as desirable and useful. These could include jobs in public service or volunteerism. Whatever path is chosen, it must make a break from our cultural obsession with wealth and property as the primary measures of success.

Economically, reducing crime requires creating more extensive access to well-paying jobs and redistributing the way we remunerate people for the jobs they perform. It also requires a substantial reorientation in our economic goals from infinite expansion to sustainable development or even zero growth. To be sure, growth has become the ultimate measure of economic performance in the United States. But growth brings with it success for few and problems for many, including increased pollution, global warming, and the decline of natural ecosystems. Oftentimes, we have become so attached to growth that we overlook these negative outcomes and justify growth and accumulation as natural human tendencies. The anthropological literature, however, indicates that growth and accumulation are not natural states of human nature. Indeed, the human race has lived out the majority of its existence in sustainable or zero development societies that promote social equity and where achievement was not tied to the ability to accumulate material possessions (Sahlin, 1972).

The kinds of policies that would engender the changes outlined above have not been implemented in the United States, and certainly have not been entertained as a crime control strategy. To be sure, these are ambitious goals that would benefit a greater number of people than they would disadvantage, which is the mark of utilitarian social philosophy used in other areas of U.S. policy. But America is an ambitious nation. These are by no means surefire solutions to the problem of crime. We have, however, lived too long with a punitive approach to crime that does not work. It is time to terminate America's big prison experiment and look elsewhere for the solutions to the problem of crime.

## CONCLUDING COMMENTS

The American prison system is the oldest and biggest in the world. It challenges our nation on a daily basis. This system of punishment is in need of a drastic overhaul. It is costly, and it fails to meet its mission. Its existence fools the American public into thinking that politicians are doing something about crime when, in effect, by failing to reform the prison system, those politicians are doing nothing at all about crime.

Prisons don't need to be bigger, to house more inmates, to expand. What is needed is an effective crime response. The history of the past three decades in the United States has proven beyond a shadow of a doubt that prison expansion is not the way to control crime. We must admit that our national prison policy has been wrong, and that prisons are not an effective crime control strategy. The problem of crime is much more complex than the simple crime-punishment assumptions America embraces.

It is easy enough to display the various forms of evidence that support this view and which have made up the contents of this book. It is quite another, however, to have the courage and conviction to act on these data and to reform a system that has dominated the American response to crime for more than two centuries, and which over the past three decades, more than in any other era, has become the symbol of America's failing crime control efforts.

# Notes

## Chapter 2    Prisons, Crime, and Other Related Matters

1. Interestingly, there is little research that compares punitiveness across cultures (e.g., Newman, 1980). Much of the existing research on that topic employs

Table E.N. 1

*Average Sentence Length in Months for Six Crimes*

(Burglary (1), Motor Vehicle Theft (2), Robbery (3), Assault (4), Rape (5), Homicide (6), and the average sentence length for these offenses in each nation (7)) for Eight Nations (Percentage of U.S. Sentence Length in Parentheses).

|              | 1      | 2      | 3     | 4     | 5     | 6     | 7     |
| ------------ | ------ | ------ | ----- | ----- | ----- | ----- | ----- |
| U.S.         | 35.0   | 20.7   | 76.4  | 40.4  | 115.9 | 250.0 | 96.6  |
| England      | 19.3   | 8.3    | 40.0  | 14.0  | 76.5  | 179.9 | 56.3  |
|              | (55)   | (40)   | (52)  | (35)  | (66)  | (72)  | (58)  |
| Australia    | 34.3   | 27.9   | 72.0  | 36.2  | 82.8  | 178.3 | 71.8  |
|              | (98)   | (135)  | (94)  | (90)  | (72)  | (71)  | (74)  |
| Canada       | 9.0    | 1.6    | 24.2  | 5.0   | 106.6 | 120.8 | 44.5  |
|              | (26)   | (8)    | (31)  | (12)  | (92)  | (48)  | (46)  |
| Netherlands  | 12.7   | 8.5    | 12.4  | 5.0   | 17.4  | 100.4 | 26.1  |
|              | (36)   | (41)   | (16)  | (12)  | (15)  | (40)  | (27)  |
| Scotland     | 8      | 5.4    | 29.6  | 17.2  | 81.4  | 191.6 | 55.5  |
|              | (23)   | (26)   | (39)  | (43)  | (70)  | (77)  | (58)  |
| Sweden       | 8.2    | 4.0    | 29.8  | 5.4   | 36.9  | 94.5  | 29.8  |
|              | (23)   | (19)   | (39)  | (13)  | (32)  | (38)  | (31)  |
| Switzerland  | 19.1   | 9.4    | 35.6  | 11.7  | 49.7  | 96.6  | 37.0  |
|              | (55)   | (45)   | (47)  | (29)  | (43)  | (39)  | (38)  |
| Average      | 18.2   | 10.7   | 40    | 16.2  | 70.9  | 151.5 |       |
|              | (52)   | (51)   | (52)  | (40)  | (61)  | (61)  |       |

This table was adapted from: Farrington, David P., Patrick Langan, and Michael Tonry, 2004, "Cross National Studies in Crime and Justice," Bureau of Justice Statistics, NCJ 200988, Washington, DC: U.S. Department of Justice, http://www.ojp.usdoj.gov/bjs/pub/ pdf/cnscj.pdf. Data for England/Wales, Canada, Netherlands, Scotland, and Switzerland are from 1999. Data for U.S., Australia, and Sweden are from 1996. Percentage scores are rounded to nearest whole number.

questionnaires, and uses questionnaire responses to develop measures of crime seriousness as perceived by respondents. For the purposes of this book, a better measure of punitiveness is sentence length or time served in prison, which measures actual penal severity imposed by governments rather that the perceived punitiveness of citizens. While cross-national sentence length data are limited, the few studies of this issue (Farrington, 2000; Farrington, Langan, and Tonry, 2004; J. Lynch, 1993, 1988) supports the contention that U.S. sentence lengths are significantly longer than those found in other nations. Average sentence lengths for eight nations and six crime types are found in table E.N. 1.

This table clearly indicates two important points. First, average sentence lengths in the United States tend to be longer than in other nations. Because sentence lengths for only a limited number of nations have been examined, there may indeed be nations where the average prison sentence is longer than in the United States. However, average sentence lengths for crime are significantly longer in the United States than in other nations. The one exception to this generalization is noted for the criminal sentences in Australia. For three of the seven crimes, however, Australian sentence lengths are less than two-thirds of those found in the United States. For motor vehicle theft, Australian sentences are quite severe, exceeding U.S. penalty lengths by an average of 7.2 months.

Second, the average sentence lengths and sentence trends displayed in this table illustrate that U.S. sentence lengths are significantly longer than those in other nations. This finding challenges popular public opinion in the United States that prison sentences are not severe enough. Clearly, in comparison to other nations, U.S. sentence lengths are long, and the average sentence length in other nations is between 40 and 61 percent shorter than in the United States. We can conclude from these data, though the data are limited, that the U.S. sentencing system is very punitive.

## Chapter 4    Raising Questions About America's Big Prison System

1. The Durkheimian position on crime and punishment has a number of interesting ramifications and implications, and has influenced both the development of theories of crime (e.g., anomie, social disorganization, social control theory) and punishment (e.g., stability of punishment hypothesis). There is, however, one assumption contained within Durkheim that is most difficult to explain, and upon which much of his discussion of crime and punishment is hinged. That assumption has to do with the "average" or "acceptable" level of crime in a society.

Durkheim posited that crime was normal, and that the normality of crime could be proven by it widespread existence. In this view, all "healthy" societies had crime. These crimes helped mark the social boundary of acceptable and unacceptable behavior. For Durkheim, a healthy society also had a given level of crime, or what he referred to as the average level of crime. For Durkheim, this average level of crime could be determined by measuring the amount of crime normally found in a society. While Durkheim is clear on these definitional matters, he is not at all clear on the empirical aspects of this issue.

For example, how is the normal or average amount of crime in a society measured? Clearly, to obtain an average, this measure must be taken over a series of years. But, how many years are needed to determine this average? If the time period is short, and crime is rising or falling, does this imply that a society in this condition is normal? Because crime within a given nation may not be stable, average, or normal over any shorter period of time, should the measurement of crime be an average across similar countries? Or should the measure be made across a diverse array of nations to discover the social average?

It would appear from the procedures employed by Durkheim that his preference was to mix measurements across nations over a short period of time, and from this, derive the general rule or average. In part, Durkheim's point was that an acceptable or average level of crime was not a fabrication, but a fact that could be ascertained using scientific study.

For Durkheim, measuring crime was important because it could tell us something about the general health of a society. The societies that had too much or too little crime were in some way "unhealthy." So, too, was the society in which the rate of crime changed rapidly, either by expansion or contraction. Rapid changes in the rate of crime indicated that the social order had shifted, and that people were either now overly constrained (rapidly contracting rate of crime) or too unrestrained (rapidly rising rate of crime) by norms and values. It has generally been argued that rapidly changing social structures can produce crime through anomie, a state of normlessness (e.g., see Merton, 1938, 1968; Messner and Rosenfeld, 2001), or social disorganization (e.g., Shaw and McKay, 1942).

Durkheim's view of punishment was, not surprisingly, the same as his view of crime. A society had a normal or average level of punishment, and this could be ascertained. Likewise, the punishment of the criminal helped maintain the moral boundaries of society. But, like crime, there could be too much (or too little) punishment, and rapid changes in punishment also signaled rapid social change and trouble in other segments of social organization.

Interestingly, Durkheim argued that the primary function of punishment was to help demarcate social boundaries, that punishment was a reaction to crime, and that punishment could not be used for other purposes, such as deterrence, although it could be said to play a role in social defense. As a social defense mechanism, punishment defended secular order, but not as a repressive mechanism as it is used in the United States; rather, its defense of secular order was ideological, or operated to reinforce agreed upon norms and values. As an outcome of crime, punishment did not, in this view, determine crime, and efforts to manipulate crime by increasing penalty were sure to fail. It is easy to understand why Durkheim believed that this was true—normal societies had a given level of crime, and either could not repress it through punishment, or, in choosing to attempt to do so, created other social problems.

If Durkheim was correct, his view provides a broad-ranging theoretical critique of the use of imprisonment in the United States. The effort to control crime through punishment is, first, impossible, and, second, indicative of a society with other significant social problems. The growth of the punitive response is not, in reality, a response to crime, but an inappropriate response other social problems, such as widespread economic inequality. The United States, for instance, has the highest level of economic inequality of Westernized nations.

2. If, indeed, the punitive public exists in large number, its existence requires some explanation, especially if theories of punishment or explanations of punishment are going to credit public opinion with influencing penal policy

in America. Many researchers cite public opinion as a basis of public policy, but do not make public opinion into a theoretical issue. The public's opinion is treated as a given or natural object in the social world. The public's opinion, however, is shaped by numerous forces, and understanding how it is shaped, and the factors that shape it, is an essential part of the study of penal policy, especially if researchers are engaged in the kinds of policy research they hope will be implemented. If, for example, a researcher hopes to implement a policy that appears inconsistent with public opinion, the researcher must first engage in change strategies that will increase the success chances of the policy in question.

If a sizeable segment of the population favors punitive responses, an explanation of their desires should become a subject of penological interest. It is plausible, for instance, that the punitive attitudes of the American public is the opposite of the one Foucault (1979) observed in his study of punishment. Foucault argued that the overuse of severe corporal punishments created a legitimacy problem that lead to public indifference and disrespect of this form of punishment. That is, Foucault argued that when a nation employs severe punishments too often, the punishment begins to lose its effect and significance, and may even come to be viewed as an illegitimate reaction. When such a point is reached, punishment will (need to) be reinvented and take on new forms to fulfill its function. As Foucault argued, this exact problem surfaced earlier in the history of "modern" punishments (nineteenth century), which in his view accounts for part of the reason behind the demise of corporal punishment and the invention of imprisonment. English historians have also documented a similar reaction in response to the widespread use of capital punishment in England (see Hay et al., 1976).

In contemporary America, however, the reaction appears to have occurred in reverse: in the 1970s, reacting to what were perceived as mild punishments, the United States extended its most severe form of social control, the prison. But it is also plausible that the punitive preferences of Americans can be explained relative to Rusche and Kirchheimer's (1939) proposition on least eligibility, or the revision of that proposition offered in chapter 5 of this book. In short, Rusche and Kirchheimer's proposition contends that in order to maintain legitimacy, punishment must lower those who are punished to a status below that occupied by the lowest free social class. Thus, as the conditions of the lowest free social class deteriorates, the conditions of punishment should become harsher. Since the 1970s, economic inequality in America has accelerated, producing enhanced relative deprivation and greater interclass disparities. Increasing the number of people punished is one means of expanding the scope of punishment so that a greater number of people can be lowered beneath the lowest free social class. Inequality may also explain why the public perceives punitive responses as legitimate, especially when rates of crime are high. The law-abiding citizen who works hard but makes little economic progress gains status and social separation when a greater number of people in similar economic circumstances who survive through criminal means are punished, since the punished are given a negative status.

3. The relationship between fear, respect, and authority is often central to discussions of punishment and conformity. Because this book is not about what makes people conform, or the content and shape of authority, I will largely sidestep this discussion because it cannot be reasonably pursued here,

and I am not an expert on these matters. Nevertheless, it is useful to make a few observations.

The origins of authority are typically traced to respect and fear, and both may form the basis of authority, either alone or in combination with one another. Authority based purely on respect will tend to have greater importance to individuals, and be less susceptible to disintegration than authority that is based purely on fear. There are several reasons for this assertion. First, fear is an emotional state, and in order to maintain a person in such an emotional state, they must be constantly exposed to fear-inducing stimuli. Over time, it is likely that the stimuli have less effect, or produce less fear, meaning that the strength of the stimuli must be continually enhanced. At some point, the stimuli can no longer be enhanced without threatening the legitimacy of the authority figure. Second, let us take a case where fear is used as the basis of authority in a parent-child relationship between a father and a son. Fear may work very well on small children (though it will also have detrimental effects on the long-term father-son relationship), and the difference in size between a child and father can be the source of some aspect of fear and authority. The child, for example, may fear the father's ability to use strength in applying punishments, such as spankings or other more noxious physical encounters and threats. But, as the child grows, the fear generated by physical differences diminishes. This means that the father must either increase the force used to generate fear and authority, or become increasingly delegitimized (lose authority) by challenges that may emanate from the child. If, by age fourteen or fifteen, the child has obtained the same physical capabilities as the father, then the father no longer possess a legitimate basis for generating fear through physical intimidation, and risks losing his authority *if the authority of the father is based solely on fear.* This is why fear makes a bad basis for authority.

In contrast, if the child has been raised to value respect, and respects his father, and respects the source of the father's authority that is derived from occupying the position of father, then the child will not lose respect, nor the father authority (unless, of course, the father does something to undermine the basis of the parent-child respect relationship).

Social systems have similar issues. Respect for the authority of a social system can be generated through teaching respect or fear. It is much easier, of course, to manipulate behavior, at least in the short term, though fear, and social systems often use fear and punishment in this way. In social systems, the use of punishments has a certain limit, and exceeding the limits of punishment challenge the legitimacy of the system, and undermine authority (for example, see, Foucault's [1979] discussion of the transformation from penal systems based on corporal punishment to those based on incarceration). Furthermore, where fear is the basis of social authority, there is a continual need to reinforce authority by inventing new, harsher, more-feared punishments. At some point, this system of reinforcing authority must break down, because the authority of the system is completely derived from fear, and contains no aspect of respect. In addition, there are diminishing returns associated with the tendency to increase the severity of punishment, so that each time an increase in punishment is exerted to maintain a given level of authority, the amount by which the punishment must be increased is a multiple of the previous level of punishment. Thus, at some point, the punishments themselves come to be viewed as illegitimate, and once this occurs, severe punishments can no longer serve as the basis of authority. This conditions leads to massive challenges to the system itself.

Further, in the modern age, social systems are composed of people who occupy different class positions. Class location itself is an important factor that conditions the extent to which individuals will believe in the authority of a social system, and the level of physical coercion which they fear. The lower a person's social class, the more difficult it will be to generate fear of losing status through punishment because, clearly, the lower your social status, the shorter the fall to the bottom. The middle-class person, who often has the hope of rising into the upper strata, will tend to fear punishment the most, believing that they have a great deal to lose. This is also the segment of the population that is more likely to believe that sever punishments will deter criminals.

CHAPTER 5   EXPLAINING PRISON GROWTH IN THE UNITED STATES

1. Several factors influenced this movement. First, some were concerned that the identifier "radical" was or could be used against those who were so labeled in an attempt to deny them tenure, promotion, and job opportunities. Second, radical theorists were being widely influenced by European scholarship written by a group identified as critical theorists (and later, by postmodernists and deconstructionists). The term "radical" did not fit within the conventions of these views. Third, a growing number of researchers who had been identified as radicals objected to what they saw as this view's single-minded commitment to how economic and social-class issues influenced crime and justice. These researchers rightfully pointed out that forms of inequality inherent in U.S. race and gender relations also had important associations with crime and justice. In some respect, what each of these groups had pointed out was that economic marginalization and social-class concerns were not the only forms of inequality that ought to be associated with the term "radical criminology." In an effort to broaden the appeal of this view and assuage widespread feelings of academic marginalization experienced by a significant cross-section of radical criminologists, criminologists who shared a commitment to examining the impact of inequality on crime and justice renamed themselves "critical" criminologists.

On a personal note, I still refer to myself as a radical criminologist. While my own research includes issues such as racial and gender issues found in the critical approach, I continue to also emphasize class issues that have largely disappeared from critical criminological literature. In addition, the various critical and postmodern views do not, in my view, place the needed emphasis on economic and social change as a remedy to crime and justice problems. Consequently, I prefer the term radical criminologist because it implies a concentration on economic and class issues, as well as the need for solutions to social problems to be based in economic reform.

CHAPTER 6   PRISON EFFECTS

1. In reality, only 0.7 cocaine users are reported as Hispanic. This figure was rounded to simplify the example that is provided here. Rounding this figure to ten causes the number of whites and blacks in the sample of 100 cocaine

users to be slightly underrepresented, and the number of Hispanic users to be slightly over represented. Thus, any race-based or ethnicity-related conclusions drawn here reflect a small bias based on Hispanic overrepresentation.

## CHAPTER 7   THE IMPRISONMENT BINGE AND CRIME

1. The data used in table 7.1 were calculated using changes in the number of crimes and the number of people in prison. This table could also be constructed using changes in the rate of index crimes per 100,000 population and the rate of imprisonment per 100,000 population. Both analyses produce similar results. While the rate-based data results are slightly different and produce a slightly stronger CSE effect, the rate based analysis also failed to support the contentions of deterrence or incapacitative approaches. To illustrate this slightly greater effect, the Pearson R correlation between the percent change in the number of crimes and the percent change in number imprisoned was $-0.129$ ($p = 0.497$), while the Pearson R between the change in the rate of crime and the percent change in imprisonment was $-0.297$ ($p = 0.147$). In neither case is the relationship statistically significant.

## CHAPTER 8   THE END OF OIL AND THE FUTURE OF AMERICAN PRISONS?

1. As a criminologist, I have not been trained as a geologist or as an environmental scientist. My knowledge of these issues is derived from reading literature on these topics. As in other research literatures, there are claims made on both sides of each issue. Some literature (the peak oil literature) suggests that the world oil supply will peak shortly, and that at *current levels of consumption* or expected increases in consumption, and given the lack of a viable alternative energy source, the world oil supply will be depleted as early as 2040. With respect to environmental issues, there is substantial evidence of global warming, and extensive health effects on humans and animals from toxic chemicals (for summary of my views, see Lynch and Stretesky, 2003; Lynch and Michalowski, 2006; Burns and Lynch, 2004).

2. To be sure, there are a number of alternative energy sources. Here, we have referred primarily to solar, wind, and geothermal energy forms as fossil-fuel alternatives. Many continue to see a future energy economy operated on fossil fuels made available through altered technology. These alternatives, however, have severe limitations at the present time (Rifkin, 2002). One alternative is coal fuels. Estimates on the life of the world's coal reserve vary widely from 67 to 300 years. This life span depends on the form in which coal energy is used—solid or liquefied. Liquefied coal could replace oil, but there are dangers to this approach. Liquefied coal, for example, has a much higher concentration of carbon atoms than other fossil fuels, and will accelerate global warming. Natural gas reserve estimates are slightly higher than those for oil. Each of these natural resources, however, is limited, and each contributes to other environmental problems. An alternative fuel that may also be useful for conversion into electricity is biomass, which has lower, more controllable levels of carbon dioxide emission (90 percent lower), and is a sustainable fuel. Biomass farms could supply a significant portion of U.S. energy needs, and it could also promote a revitalized rural economy (Union of Concerned Scientists, http:// www.ucsusa.org/clean_energy/renewable_energy/ page.cfm?pageID=78).

Emerging technologies that make more efficient use of fossil fuels should not be overlooked. These technologies differ from fossil-fuel conversion strategies (e.g., liquefied coal). For example, plug-in electric cars with high-powered lithium–ion batteries (see http://www.calcars.org) are more efficient that the current hybrid technology used in vehicles such as the Toyota Prius. Traditionally, the objection to plug-in vehicles is that they did not solve global warming because the electricity required to charge the batteries came from coal-powered electrical plants. The electricity needed to fuel a plug-in, however, generates less $CO_2$ than gasoline per distance traveled. On average, the burning of 1 gallon of gasoline will yield about 19.6 pounds of carbon dioxide (see information presented by the Carbon Dioxide Information Analysis Center, an office of the U.S. Department of Energy, http://cdiac.esd.ornl.gov/pns/ faq.html). If the average person drives approximately 15,000 miles in a year, this translates into about 680 gallons of gasoline used, or 13,328 pounds of carbon dioxide. For the same distance, a plug-in hybrid operated without the gasoline engine would require the use of 6 pounds of coal to generate the electricity needed to cover 24 miles, or 625 pounds of coal (assuming the electricity is generated using coal, and not some combination of coal and wind or water power, which is becoming more common). The combustion of 1 pound of coal produces approximately 17.16 pounds of carbon dioxide (depending on the type of coal; Hong and Slatick, 1994), yielding 10,725 pounds of carbon dioxide. Compared to the traditional gasoline combustion engine, the electric hybrid reduced the production of carbon dioxide by 2,603 pounds per vehicle (a reduction of 19.5 percent in global warming gases).

One cannot discuss energy concerns without also addressing global warming. Again, there are two sides to the issue. In the United States, for example, the political leaders who have staffed the Bush White House, with their backgrounds in the fossil-fuel industries, have done little to address global warming. As a group, they believe that global warming is not an issue, and have refused to participate in, for example, the Kyoto Protocol on global warming. On the other side stand thousands of scientists who study global warming, its path, and consequences, and who have petitioned White House to change its views and act on global warming (see, e.g., the Union of Concerned Scientists petition, http://www.ucsusa.org).

Before continuing, it is useful to note my position on the end of oil or the peak oil issue, and global warming, because this view obviously affects the discussion that follows. First, peak oil and global warming are intimately connected. Peak oil is good news for global warming to the extent that the end of oil will help reduce global warming *if it promotes the development of alternatives to fossil-fuel energy sources* since the most significant portion of global warming results from burning fossil fuels (Goodstein, 2004). Second, however, the end of oil will occur so far in the future that its effect on global warming will occur much too late to impede the impact on the earth's environment. We need to act now to curb global warming. We also need to act now, as the chairman of Chevron noted, to devise alterative energy sources and economies. These energy alternatives must, because of global warming, be non–fossil fuel in origin. That means that plans to convert the energy infrastructure to natural gas, or increase the use of coal, or the extract coal oils and tars, or oil from shale, are not useful energy strategies; they will exacerbate rather than solve the related problems of global warming and environmental pollution (see Goodstein, 2004).

One difficulty in generating a new energy economy is that the average citizen does not really appreciate the extent of the peak oil or global warming problems, and takes an optimistic view that these problems will be solved by scientists and corporate innovations that occur in ways that will not affect their ordinary lives. For the most part, the public is detached from peak oil and global warming concerns, and have faith that the government is doing its best to solve the problem, or that the free market will rally to solve the problem. The public doesn't read scientific literature, and instead relies on the media—primarily television—as a source of information on energy issues and global warming. But global warming and the end of oil are hardly discussed in the media, and when they are, individuals and groups who demonstrate the greatest concern with peak oil and global warming are depicted as akin to fringe lunatics or as espousing "junk science."

For example, while listening to a CNN talk show, I heard a listener call in to discuss high oil prices in the United States in the wake of the impact of Hurricane Katrina on the U.S. Gulf Coast. Following the lead of discussions on other talk shows, the caller noted that high oil prices are due to a lack of refining capacity in the United States, and that the government should force oil companies to build new refineries. This is a common reaction to the reality that the price of oil is rising—the problem must be a supply deficiency that is artificial or "manmade." If we produced more refined oil, the argument runs, then the price of oil and gas would naturally decline. There are several important deficiencies in this viewpoint. First, oil production data actually indicate that there is excess oil refining capacity in the United States. Second, the problem isn't capacity, but the supply of oil found in the United States. The peak oil curve or the peak in oil discovery and production hit the United States in the early 1970s. Since then, U.S. refining has declined because the supply of oil the United States is able to produce has declined as U.S. oil reserves were depleted. Thus, the problem isn't the capacity to produce oil, but in the shrinking supply of oil found within U.S. borders. What the radio show caller failed to recognize—which represents a common error on this point—is that building new refineries won't solve the peak oil problem (nor will it slow down the related problem of global warming). Peak oil is the result of using up the world's limited supply of oil. It is not a supply-side or production issue; it's an issue of natural limits. Furthermore, what the caller also failed to recognize is that oil companies are not going to build new refineries in the United States because they know about the peak oil problem: adding new refineries makes no economic sense in a world where the energy infrastructure is in need of reform, as the leaders of oil companies themselves admit, and where the supply of oil is continually diminishing.

3. Colin Campbell earned his Ph.D. in geology from Oxford in the late 1950s, and spent much of his career (1958–1985) as oil exploration geologist for major oil companies including Texaco, BP, and Amoco. He is also the founder of the Association for the Study of Peak Oil and Gas, and has published on this issue since 1991.

4. According to U.S. Department of Energy data, U.S. peak-oil production occurred in 1970 when domestic crude product was 9,408,000 barrels. In 2000,

domestic crude oil production had dropped to less than half this amount: 4,761,000 barrels (U.S. Department of Energy, 2004a). At the same time that U.S. oil production was declining, crude-oil consumption was rising, though at lower rates in recent decades than in the 1950s through the 1970s (Duncan, 2005). Declining domestic reserves coupled with rising demand led to an increased reliance on foreign crude oil. In 1960, the United States imported 1,815,000 barrels of foreign crude; by 2002, this total had increased more than sixfold to 11,580,000 barrels (U.S. Department of Energy, 2004a). In short, between 1960 and 2002, U.S. crude oil production fell over 32 percent, while foreign crude oil imports had risen by more than 630 percent. It should be noted that the increased reliance on foreign oil is not simply a result of declining crude-oil production *capacity* in the United States, since production capacity expanded during the period under examination (U.S. Department of Energy, 2004b).

5. Recently (2005) the George W. Bush administration—which is closely connected to the oil industry (e.g., the White House Energy Task Force was headed by Vice President Cheney, former CEO of Halliburton, one of the world's largest suppliers of products and services to the oil and gas industry)—opened the Arctic National Wildlife Refuge (ANWR) to oil exploration in an effort to remedy the peak-oil problem. Historically, the oil found in this region was designated as a military reserve and held for military emergencies. Environmentally, the damage of this policy will be large. But, moreover, the policy will not alleviate the problem it addresses—a diminishing oil supply in the United States. First, it is estimated that it will take up to ten years for ANWR oil to come on line, which includes a point in time that is, in all likelihood, after the world peak in oil production. By that time, dwindling oil supplies will have caused the price of domestic oil to rise dramatically, and is likely to mean that the search for alternative energy sources will be well underway. Second, the amount of oil in the ANWR is estimated to be about 10 billion barrels, or about the amount of oil the United States is estimated to consume in 16–18 months once ANWR oil is available. Thus, opening the ANWR to oil exploration will, at best, add two years of oil supply to domestic markets, while, at the same time, expanding the environmental destructive outcomes (e.g., global warming) of burning oil. In short, these policies are inadequate responses to both the energy problems facing the United States and the issue of global warming.

6. Natural gas reserves are also limited, and currently have a peak of ten to fifteen years beyond the oil peak. Once placed into more widespread use, natural gas availability will decline dramatically. The best alternative is the development of renewable energy sources that would make human populations independent of fossil fuels, and which have lower environmental costs or impacts (Rifkin, 2002).

7. The CIA has been tracking world oil production and reserve levels for the past decade. For example, a paper written by Senator Richard Lugar and former CIA chief James Woolsey that appeared in the January 1999 issue of *Foreign Affairs* predicted the world oil crisis and urged the creation of new U.S. policies to deal with this situation.

8. As fertilizers and pesticides produced from oil become more expensive, the cost of operating farm equipment and shipping food escalates. As prices for pesticides, herbicides, fertilizers, and equipment operations rise, and oil becomes

scare, human labor will be reintroduced to farms to replace the tasks performed by herbicides and farm machinery, which will help maintain the food supply, but will not lower costs. Thus, the simple act of feeding and clothing large populations of prison inmates may become very expensive.

9. Indeed, the Presidential Energy Task Force has recommended energy policies that reinforce fossil-fuel dependence (see the Energy Task Force Report, "Reliable, Affordable, and Environmentally Sound Energy for America's Future," http://www.whitehouse.gov/energy).

# References

Agnew, Robert. 2005. *Why Do Criminals Offend? A General Theory of Crime and Delinquency*. Belmont, CA: Roxbury.

American Iron and Steel Institute. (n.d.). "The New Steel Industry." *AISI FACT SHEETS*. Washington, DC: AISI.

Austin, James, John Clark, Patricia Hardyman, and D. Alan Henry. 1999. "The Impact of 'Three Strikes and You're Out.'" *Punishment & Society* 1,2: 131–162.

Austin, James and John Irwin. 2003. *Its About Time: America's Imprisonment Binge*. Belmont, CA: Wadsworth.

Austin, Roy L. and Mark D. Allen. 2000. "Racial Disparities in Arrest Rates as an Explanation for Racial Disparities in Commitment to Pennsylvania's Prisons." *Journal of Research in Crime and Delinquency* 37,2: 200–220.

Bandura, Alfred. 1986. *Social Foundations of Thought and Action: A Social Cognitive Theory*. Englewood Cliffs, NJ: Prentice Hall.

———. 1977. *Social Learning Theory*. Englewood Cliffs, NY: Prentice Hall.

Barnes, Harry and Negley Teeters. 1945. *New Horizons in Criminology*. New York: Prentice Hall.

Bartlett, Donald L. and James B. Steele. 1996. *America: What Went Wrong?* Riverside, NJ: Andrews McMeel Publishing.

Becker, Gary S. 1968. "Crime and Punishment: An Economic Approach." *The Journal of Political Economy* 76,2: 169–217.

Beckett, Katherine. 1997. *Making Crime Pay: Law and Order in Contemporary American Politics*. Oxford: Oxford University Press.

Beckett, Katherine and Bruce Western. 2001. "Governing Social Marginality: Welfare, Incarceration and the Transformation of State Policy." *Punishment & Society* 3,1: 43–59.

Beirne, Piers and Nigel South (eds). 2006. *Green Criminology*. Hampshire, UK: Ashgate.

Black, William, Kitty Calavita, and Henry N. Pontell. 1995. "The Savings and Loan Debacle of the 1980s: White-Collar Crime or Risky Business?" *Law and Policy* 17,1: 23–55.

Blumstein, Alfred. 1998. "U.S. Criminal Justice Conundrum: Rising Prison Populations and Stable Crime Rates." *Crime and Delinquency* 44,1: 127–135.

Bonczar, Thomas P. 2003. "Prevalent of Imprisonment in the U.S. Population, 1974–2001." Bureau of Justice Statistics, Special Report. NCJ 197976. Washington DC: U.S. Department of Justice.

Bonczar, Thomas P. and Allen. J. Beck. 1997. "Lifetime Likelihood of Going to State or Federal Prison." Bureau of Justice Statistics, NCJ-160092. Washington DC: U.S. Department of Justice.

Brownstein, Henry. 2000. *The Social Reality of Violence and Violent Crime*. Boston: Allyn and Bacon.

Burdon, Roy H. 2004. *The Suffering Gene: Environmental Threats to Our Health*. London: Zed Books.

———. 1999. *Genes and the Environment*. Boca Raton, FL: CRC Press.

Burns, Ronald G. and Michael J. Lynch. 2004. *Environmental Crime: A Sourcebook*. New York: LFB Scholarly Publishers.

Calavita, Kitty and Henry N. Pontell. 1994. "The State and White-Collar Crime: Saving the Savings and Loans." *Law and Society Review* 28,2: 297–324.

Calavita, Kitty, Robert Tillman, and Henry N. Pontell. 1997. "The Savings and Loan Debacle, Financial Crime, and the State." Annual Review of Sociology 23: 19–38.

Campbell, Colin J. 2003. *The Coming Oil Crisis*. Santa Cruz, CA: R.B. Swenson.

———. 2001. "Peak Oil: A Turning Point for Mankind." *M. King Hubbert Newsletter*. 2,1. M. King Hubbert Center, Colorado School of Mines. http://hubbert. mines.edu/news/Campbell_01–2.pdf.

———. 1998. "Running Out of Gas: This Time the Wolf Is Coming." *The National Interest* 51: 47–55.

Campbell, Colon J. and Jean Laherrere. 1998. "The End of Cheap Oil?" *Scientific American* March: 78–83. http://dieoff.org/page140.htm.

Campbell, Donald T. and Julian C. Stanley. 1962. *Experimental and Quasi-Experimental Designs for Research*. Chicago: Rand McNally.

Cantor, David and Kenneth C. Land. 2001. "Unemployment and Crime Rate Fluctuations: A Comment on Greenberg." *Journal of Quantitative Criminology* 17,4: 329–344.

———. 1985. "Unemployment and Crime Rates in the Post-World War II United States: A Theoretical and Empirical Analysis." *American Sociological Review* 50,3: 317–332.

Carlson, Susan M. and Raymond J. Michalowski. 1997. "Crime, Unemployment and Social Structures of Accumulation: An Investigation into Historical Contingency." *Justice Quarterly* 14.2: 209–241.

Carnoy, Martin. 1994. *Faded Dreams: The Politics and Economics of Race in America*. Cambridge, UK: Cambridge University Press.

Chambliss, William J. and Robert B. Seidman. 1982. *Law, Order and Power*. New York: Addison-Wesley.

Christianson, Scott. 1981. "Our Black Prisons." *Journal of Research in Crime and Delinquency* 27,1:364–375.

Christie, Nils. 1994. *Crime Control as Industry, Towards Gulags, Western Style*. New York: Routledge.

Clear, Todd. 2003. "The Problem with 'Addition by Subtraction': The Prison-Crime Relationship in Low Income Communities." In M. Mauer and M. Chesney-Lind (eds), *Invisible Punishment: The Collateral Consequences of Mass Imprisonment*. New York: The New Press.

———. "Science and the Punishment/Control Movement." *Social Pathology* 2,1: 1–22.

———. 1994. *Harm in American Penology: Offenders, Victims and Their Communities*. Albany: State University of New York Press.

Clear, Todd and Dina Rose. 1999. "When Neighbors Go to Jail: Impact on Attitudes About Formal and Informal Social Control." National Institute of Justice, Research Preview. July (FS 0002 43). Washington DC: NIJ.

———. 1998. "Incarceration, Social Capital and Crime: Examining the Unintended Consequences of Incarceration." *Criminology* 36,3: 441–479.

Clear, Todd, Dina Rose, and Judith A. Ryder. 2001. "Incarceration and Community: The Problem of Removing and Returning Offenders." *Crime and Delinquency* 47,3: 335–351.

Clear, Todd, Dina Rose, and Elin Waring. 2003. "Coercive Mobility and Crime: A Preliminary Examination of Concentrated Incarceration and Social Disorganization." *Justice Quarterly* 20,1: 33–64.

Cochran, John K., Mitchell B. Chamlin, and Mark Seth. 1994. "Deterrence or Brutalization? An Assessment of Oklahoma's Return to Capital Punishment." *Criminology* 32:107–134.

Corrections Corporation of America, 2005. Annual Report. http://www.shareholder.com/cxw/.

Cullen, Francis T. 2005. "Twelve People Who Saved Rehabilitation: How the Science of Criminology Made a Difference." *Criminology* 43,1: 1–42.

Cullen, Francis T., Bonnie S. Fisher, and Brandon K. Applegate. 2000. "Public Opinion About Punishment and Corrections." In Michael Tonry (ed), *Crime and Justice: A Review of Research*. Chicago: University of Chicago Press.

Cullen, Francis T. and Paul Gendreau. 2000. "Assessing Correctional Rehabilitation: Policy, Practice, and Prospects." In Julie Horney (ed), *Criminal Justice 2000: Volume 3—Policies, Processes, and Decisions of the Criminal Justice System*. Washington DC: U.S. Department of Justice, National Institute of Justice.

———. 1989. "The Effectiveness of Correctional Rehabilitation: Reconsidering the 'Nothing Works' Debate." In Lynne Goodstein and Doris MacKenzie (eds), *American Prisons: Issues in Research and Policy*. New York: Plenum.

Cullen, Francis T. and Karen E. Gilbert. 1982. *Reaffirming Rehabilitation*. Cincinnati: Anderson.

Cullen, Francis T., William J. Maakestad, and Gray Cavender. 1987. *Corporate Crime Under Attack: The Ford Pinto Case and Beyond*. Cincinnati: Anderson.

Deffeyes, Kenneth S. 2001. *Hubbert's Peak: The Impending World Oil Shortage*. Princeton, NJ: Princeton University Press.

DeFina, R. H. and T. M. Arvanites. 2002. "The Weak Effect of Imprisonment on Crime: 1971–1998." *Social Science Quarterly* 83,3: 635–653.

Devine, Joel A., Joseph F. Shelley, and M. Dwayne Smith. 1988. "Macroeconomic and Social Control Policy Influences on Crime Rate Changes, 1948–1985." *American Sociological Review* 53,3: 407–420.

DiIulio, John. 1994. "Let 'Em Rot." *Wall Street Journal,* January 26: A 14.

Doob, Anthony N. and Cheryl Marie Webster. 2003. "Sentence Severity and Crime: Accepting the Null Hypothesis." *Crime and Justice* 30: 143–195.

DuBoff, Richard B. 2003. "U.S. Hegemony: Continuing Decline, Enduring Danger." *Monthly Review* 55,7. http://www.monthlyreview.org/1203duboff.htm.

Duncan, Richard C. 2005. "The Peak of World Oil Production and the Road to the Olduvai Gorge. Institute on Man and Energy." http://www.hubbertpeak.com/Duncan/olduvai2000.htm.

Durkheim, Emile. 1897 [1977]. *Suicide.* New York: The Free Press.

———. 1895 [1964]. *The Rules of Sociological Method.* New York: The Free Press.

———. 1893 [1968]. *The Division of Labor in Society.* New York: The Free Press.

Durose, Matthew R. and Patrick A. Langan. 2001. "Court Sentencing of Convicted Felons, 1998." NCJ-190637. Washington DC: U.S. Department of Justice. http://www.ojp.usdoj.gov/bjs/pub/pdf/scscf98.pdf.

Economic Policy Institute, *Pulling Apart.* 2006. http://www.epi.org/content.cfm/studies_pulling_apart_2006.

Energy Information Administration (EIA), U.S. Department of Energy. 2003. "2002 Summary Statistics, California." http://www.eia.doe.gov/cneaf/electricity/st_profiles/california.pdf.

Farrington, David P. 2000. "Cross-National Comparative Studies in Criminology." In H. N. Pontell and D. Shichor (eds), *Contemporary Issues in Crime and Criminal Justice: Essays in Honor of Gilbert Geis.* Upper Saddle River, NJ: Prentice Hall.

Farrington, David P., Patrick Langan, and Michael Tonry. 2004. "Cross National Studies in Crime and Justice." Bureau of Justice Statistics. NCJ 200988. Washington DC: U.S. Department of Justice. http://www.ojp.usdoj.gov/bjs/pub/pdf/cnscj.pdf.

Federal Bureau of Investigation. 2002. *Uniform Crime Report, 2002.* http://www.fbi.gov/ucr/02cius.htm.

Federal Reserve. 2003. "Recent Changes in U.S. Family Finances: Evidence from the 1998 and 2001 Survey of Consumer Finances." http://www.federalreserve.gov/pubs/bulletin/2003/0103Lead.pdf.

Feeley, Malcolm. 2004. "Crime, Social Order and the Rise of Neo-Conservative Politics." *Theoretical Criminology* 7,1: 111–130.

Fellner, J. and M. Mauer. 1998. *Losing the Vote: The Impact of Felon Dienfranchisement Laws in the United States.* New York: Human Rights Watch and the Sentencing Project.

Flanagan, Timothy J. 1982. "Risk and the Timing of Recidivism in Three Cohorts of Prison Releasees." *Criminal Justice Review* 7,2: 34–45.

Flanagan Timothy J., Pauline Gasdow Brennan, and Debra Cohen. 1991. "Crime Control Ideology and Policy Positions in a State Legislature (Revisited)." *Criminal Justice Policy Review* 5,3: 183–206.

Flanagan, Timothy J., Deborah Cohen, and Pauline G. Brennan. 1993. "Crime Control Ideology Among New York State Legislators." *Legislative Studies Quarterly* 18,3: 411–422.

Flanagan, Timothy J. and Edmund F. McGarrell. 1986. *Attitudes of New York Legislators Toward Crime and Criminal Justice: A Report of the State Legislator Survey—1985.* Albany: Hindelang Criminal Justice Research Center, State University of New York at Albany.

Flanagan, Timothy J., Edmund F. McGarrell, and Alan J. Lizotte. 1989. "Ideology and Crime Control Policy Positions in a State Legislature." *Journal of Criminal Justice* 17:81–101.

Flanagan, William G. 2003. *Dirty Rotten CEOs: How Business Leaders Are Fleecing America.* New York: Citadel Press.

Foucault, Michel. 1979. *Discipline and Punish: The Birth of the Prison.* New York: Vintage.

Fox, James Alan and Marianne W. Zawitz. 2006. "Homicide Trends in the United States." U.S. Department of Justice, Bureau of Justice Statistics. http://www.ojp. usdoj.gov/bjs/pub/pdf/htius.pdf.

Frank, Nancy and Michael J. Lynch. 1992. *Corporate Crime, Corporate Violence.* Albany, NY: Harrow and Heston.

Frank, Robert H. and Phillip Cook. 1996. *The Winner-Take-All Society: Why the Few at the Top Get So Much More Than the Rest of Us.* New York: Penguin.

Friedrichs, David. 2004. *Trusted Criminals.* Belmont, CA: Wadsworth.

Gainsborough, Jenni and Marc Mauer. 2000. "Diminishing Returns: Crime and Incarcerations in the 1990s." The Sentencing Project. http://www.sentencing-project.org/pdfs/9039.pdf.

Gendreau, Paul, Claire Goggin, and Francis T. Cullen. 1999. *The Effect of Prison Sentences on Recidivism.* Public Works and Government Services of Canada. Cat. No.: J42–87/1999E; ISBN: 0–662–28406–2.

Goldfarb, Ronald, 1969. "Prison: The National Poorhouse." *The New Republic,* December 13.

Goodstein, David. 2004. *Out of Gas: The End of the Age of Oil.* New York: W.W. Norton.

Gordon, Diana. 1994. *The Return of the Dangerous Classes: Prohibition and Policy Politics.* New York: W.W. Norton.

Grasmick, Harold G. and G. J. Bryjack. 1980 "The Deterrent Effects of Perceived Severity of Punishment." Social Forces 59,2: 471–491.

Greenberg, David F. 2001a. "Novus Ordo Saeclorum?: A Commentary on Downes, and on Beckett and Western." *Punishment & Society* 3,1: 81–93.

———. 2001b. "Time Series Analysis of Crime Rates." *Journal of Quantitative Criminology* 17,4: 281–327.

———. 1990. "The Cost-Benefit Analysis of Imprisonment." *Social Justice* 17,4: 49–75.

———. 1989. "Imprisonment and Unemployment: A Comment." *Journal of Quantitative Criminology* 5,2: 187–191.

———. 1977. "The Dynamics of Oscillatory Punishment Processes." *The Journal of Criminal Law and Criminology* 68,4: 643–651.

Greenberg, David F. and Valerie West. 2001. "State Prison Populations and their Growth, 1971–1991." *Criminology* 39,3: 615–654.

Hacker, James. 1995. *Two Nations: Black and White, Separate, Hostile and Unequal.* New York: Ballantine.

Hagan, John. 1997. *Crime and Disrepute.* Thousand Oaks, CA: Pine Forge Press.

Harrison, Paige M. and Allen J. Beck. 2006. "Prison and Jail Inmates at Mid-Year 2005." Washington DC: U.S. Department of Justice. http://www.ojp.usdoj.gov/bjs/pub/pdf/pjim05.pdf.

———. 2003. "Prisoners in 2002." Washington DC: U.S. Department of Justice. http://www.ojp.usdoj.gov/bjs/pub/pdf/p02.pdf.

Hay, Douglas, Peter Linebaugh, John G. Rule, E. P. Thompson, and Cal Winslow. 1976. *Albion's Fatal Tree: Crime and Society in Eighteenth Century England.* New York: Pantheon.

Hayward, Steven and Lance T. Izumi. 1996. *Crime and Punishment in California: Are We Too Tough or Not Tough Enough?* San Francisco: Pacific Research Institute for Public Policy.

Heinberg, Richard. 2003. *The Party's Over: Oil, War and the Fate of Industrial Societies.* Gabriola Island, BC: New World Publishers.

Henry, Jules. 1965. *Culture Against Man.* New York: Random House.

Hong, B. D. and E. R. Slatick. 1994. "Carbon Dioxide Emission Factors for Coal." Quarterly Coal Report. Washington DC: DOE/EIA. http://www.eia.doe.gov/cneaf/coal/quarterly/co2_article/co2.html.

Huffington, Arianna 2003. *Pigs at the Trough: How Corporate Greed and Political Corruption are Undermining America.* New York: Crown.

Irwin, John. 2005. *The Warehouse Prison: Disposal of the New Dangerous Class.* Los Angeles: Roxbury.

Jacobs, David and Jason T. Carmichael. 2001. "The Politics of Punishment Across Time and Space: A Pooled Time Series Analysis of Imprisonment Rates." *Social Forces* 80,1: 61–81.

Jacobson, Michael. 2005. *Downsizing Prisons: How to Reduce Crime and End Mass Incarceration.* New York: New York University Press.

Johnston, C. Wayne. 1999. "Incapacitation and Deterrent Effects of Incarceration: A Pennsylvania Study." *Corrections Compendium* 24,12: 1–11.

Keister, Lisa A. 2000. *Wealth in America: Trends in Wealth Inequality.* Cambridge, UK: Cambridge University Press.

Kessler, Daniel and Steven D. Levitt. 1999. "Using Sentence Enhancements to Distinguish Between Deterrence and Incapacitation." *Journal of Law and Economics* 42,1: 343–363.

Kleeper, Steven and Daniel Nagin. 1989. "The Deterrent Effect of Perceived Certainty and Severity of Punishment Revisited" Criminology 27,4: 721–746.

Kovandzic, Tomislav V.; Thomas B. Marvell, Lynne M. Vieraitis, and Carlisle E. Moody. 2004. "When Prisoners Get Out: The Impact of Prison Releases on Homicide Rates, 1975–1999." *Criminal Justice Policy Review* 15,2: 212–228.

Kristof, Nicholas D. 2006. "100-M.P.G. Cars: It's a Start." *New York Times.* February 5: 4, 13.

Leigh, J. Paul, Steven Markovitz, Marianne Fahs, and Phillip Landigren. 2000. *The Cost of Occupational Injuries and Illnesses.* Ann Arbor: University of Michigan Press.

Lippke, Richard L. 2002. "Crime Reduction and the Length of Prison Sentences." *Law & Policy* 24,1: 17–35.

Lovins, Amory B., E. K. Datta, O. E. Bustnes, J. G. Koomey, and N. J. Glasgow. 2005. *Winning the Oil Endgame: Innovations for Profits, Jobs and Security.* Snowmass, CO: Rocky Mountain Institute.

Lynch, James P. 1988. "A Comparison of Imprisonment in the United States, Canada, England, and West Germany: A Limited Test of the Punitiveness Hypothesis." *Journal of Criminal Law and Criminology* 79: 180–217.

———. 1993. "A Cross-National Comparison of the Length of Custodial Sentences for Serious Crimes." *Justice Quarterly* 10,4: 639–659.

Lynch, Michael J. 2004. "Towards a Radical Ecology of Urban Violence: Integrating Medical, Epidemiological, Environmental and Criminological Research On Class, Race, Lead (Pb) and Crime." In Margaret Zahn, Henry Brownstein, and Shelly Jackson (eds), *Violence: From Theory to Research.* Cincinnati: Anderson.

———. 2002. "Misleading 'Evidence' and the Misguided Attempt to Generate Racial Profiles of Criminals: Correcting Fallacies and Calculations Concerning

Race and Crime in Taylor and Whitney's Analysis of Racial Profiling." *The Mankind Quarterly* 42,3: 313–330.

———. 2000. "J. Philippe Rushton on Crime: An Examination and Critique of the Explanation of Crime in 'Race, Evolution and Behavior.'" *Social Pathology.* 6,3: 228–244.

———. 1999. "Beating a Dead Horse: Is There Any Basic Empirical Evidence for a Deterrent Effect of Imprisonment?" *Crime, Law and Social Change* 31: 347–362.

———. 1996. "Race, Class, Gender and Criminology: Structured Choices and the Life Course." In M. Schwartz and D. Milovanovic (eds), *Gender, Race and Class in Criminology.* Hamden, CT: Garland.

———. 1988. "The Extraction of Surplus Value, Crime and Punishment: A Preliminary Empirical Analysis for the U.S." *Contemporary Crises* 12: 329–344.

———. 1987. "Quantitative Analysis and Marxist Criminology: Old Answers to a Dilemma in Marxist Criminology." *Crime and Social Justice* 29: 110–127.

Lynch, Michael J., W. Byron Groves, and Alan Lizotte. 1994. "The Rate of Surplus Value and Crime: Theoretical and Empirical Examination of Marxian Economic Theory and Criminology." *Crime, Law and Social Change* 21,1: 15–48.

Lynch, Michael J., Michael J. Hogan, and Paul Stretesky. 1999. "A Further Look at Long Cycles, Legislation and Crime." *Justice Quarterly* 16,2: 431–450.

Lynch, Michael J. and Raymond J. Michalowski. 2006. *Primer in Radical Criminology, 4th Edition.* Monsey, NY: Criminal Justice Press.

Lynch, Michael J. Raymond J. Michalowski, and W. Byron Groves. 2000. *The New Primer in Radical Criminology.* Monsey, NY: Criminal Justice Press.

Lynch, Michael J. and E. Britt Patterson (eds). 1996. *Justice with Prejudice.* Albany, NY: Harrow and Heston.

———. 1991. *Race and Criminal Justice.* Albany, NY: Harrow and Heston.

Lynch, Michael J. and Amie Schuck. 2003. "Picasso as Criminologist: The Abstract Art of Racial Profiling." In M. Free (ed), *Racial Issues in Criminal Justice: The Case of African Americans.* Westport, CT: Praeger.

Lynch, Michael J. and Paul B. Stretesky. 2003. "The Meaning of Green: Contrasting Criminological Perspectives." *Theoretical Criminology* 7,2: 217–238.

Lynch, Michael J. and Paul B. Stretesky. 2001. "Toxic Crimes: Examining Corporate Victimization of the General Public Employing Medical and Epidemiological Evidence." *Critical Criminology* 10,3: 153–172.

Lynch, Michael J., Paul B. Stretesky and Ronald G. Burns. 2004a. "Determinants of Environmental Law Violation Fines Against Oil Refineries: Race, Ethnicity, Income and Aggregation Effects." *Society and Natural Resources* 17,4: 333–347.

———. 2004b. "Slippery Business: Race, Class and Legal Determinants of Penalties Against Petroleum Refineries." *Journal of Black Studies* 34,3: 421–440.

Marion, Nancy and Rick Farmer. 2004. "A Preliminary Examination of Presidential Anticrime Promises." *Criminal Justice Review* 29,1: 173–195.

Marvel, Thomas B. and Carlisle E. Moody. 1998. "The Impact of Out-of-State Prison Population on State Homicide Rates: Displacement and Free-Rider Effects." *Criminology* 36,3: 513–535.

———. 1997. "The Impact of Prison Growth on Homicide." *Homicide Studies* 1,3: 205–233.

———. 1995. "The Impact of Enhanced Prison Terms for Felonies Committed with Guns." *Criminology* 33,2: 247–281.

———. 1994. "Prison Population and Crime Reduction." *Journal of Quantitative Criminology* 10: 109–139.

Massey, Douglas Nancy Denton. 1993. *American Apartheid: The Making of the Underclass.* Cambridge, MA: Harvard University Press.

Mauer, Marc. 2003. "Comparative International Rates of Incarceration: An Examination of Causes and Trends." Paper Presented to the U.S. Commission on Civil Rights. http://www.sentencingproject.org/pdfs/pub9036.pdf.

———. 1999. *Race to Incarcerate.* New York: The New Press.

McGarrell, Edmund F. and Timothy J. Flanagan. 1987. "Measuring and Explaining Legislator Crime Control Ideology." *Journal of Research in Crime and Delinquency* 24,2: 102–118.

Meierhoefer, B. S. 1992. "The General Effects of Mandatory Minimum Prison Terms: A Longitudinal Study of Federal Sentences Imposed." Washington DC: Federal Judiciary Center.

Merton, Robert K. 1968. *Social Theory and Social Structure.* New York: The Free Press.

———. 1938. "Social Structure and Anomie." *American Sociological Review* 3,5: 672–682.

Messner, Stephen and Richard Rosenfeld. 2001. *Crime and the American Dream.* Belmont, CA: Wadsworth.

Michalowski, Raymond J. and Susan Carlson. 1999. "Unemployment, Imprisonment, and Social Structures of Accumulation: Historical Contingency in the Rusche-Kirchheimer Hypothesis." *Criminology* 37,2: 217–250.

Miller, Jerome. 1996. *Search and Destroy: African American Males and the Criminal Justice System.* Cambridge, UK: Cambridge University Press.

Mills, C. Wright. 1959. *The Sociological Imagination.* New York: Fordham University Press.

Murray, Charles. 1997. *Does Prison Work?* London, Institute of Economic Affairs: Coronet Books.

Myrdal, Gunnar. 1944. *An American Dilemma: The Negro Problem and Modern Democracy.* New York: Harper.

Nalla, Mahesh, Michael J. Lynch, and Michael J. Leiber. 1997. "Determinants of Police Growth in Phoenix, Arizona, 1950–1988." *Justice Quarterly* 14,1: 115–144.

National Center for Policy Analysis. 1995. *Crime and Punishment in America.* http://www.ncpa.org/studies/s193/s193e.html.

Newman, Graeme R. 1985. *The Punishment Response.* Monsey, NY: Criminal Justice Press.

———. 1980. *Crime and Deviance: A Comparative Perspective.* Beverly Hills: Sage.

O'Connor, James. 1973. *The Fiscal Crisis of the State.* New York: St. Martin's Press.

Oliver, William and David Barlow. 2005. "Following the Leader? Presidential Influence Over Congress in the Passage of Federal Crime Control Policy." *Criminal Justice Policy Review* 16,3: 267–286.

Ouimet, Marc. 2002. "Explaining the American and Canadian Crime 'Drop' in the 1990's." *Canadian Journal of Criminology* 44,1: 33–50.

Paternoster, Raymond and Leeann Iovanni. 1986. "The Deterrent Effect of Perceived Seriousness: A Reexamination." *Social Forces* 64,3: 751–777.

Pettit, Becky and Bruce Western. 2004. "Mass Imprisonment and the Life Course Race and Class Inequality in U.S. Incarceration." *American Sociological Review* 69,2: 151–169.

Pinkney, Alfonso. 1994. *The Myth of Black Progress.* Cambridge, UK: Cambridge University Press.

Reiman, Jeffrey. 2003. *The Rich Get Richer and the Poor Get Prison.* Boston: Allyn and Bacon.

Reynolds, Morgan O. 2000. "Does Punishment Work to Reduce Crime?" Heartland Institute. http://www.heartland.org/Article.cfm?artId=125.

––––––. 1997. *Crime and Punishment in America: 1997 Update.* Dallas: National Center for Policy Analysis.

Ridley, Matt. 2000. *Genome: The Autobiography of a Species in 23 Chapters.* New York: Harper Perennial.

Rifkin, Jeremy. 2002. *The Hydrogen Economy.* New York: Jeremy P. Tarcher/Putnam.

Roberts, Paul. 2004. *The End of Oil: On the Edge of a Perilous New World.* London: Bloomsbury Publishing.

––––––. 1998. "Incarceration, Social Capital and Crime: Examining the Unintended Consequences of Incarceration." *Criminology* 36,3: 441–479.

Rose, Dina and Todd Clear. 1995. "Incarceration, Social Capital and Crime: Examining the Unintended Consequences of Imprisonment." *Criminology* 36,3:441–479.

Ross, Jeffrey Ian. 2000. "Grants R-US: Inside a Federal Grant Making Agency." *American Behavioral Scientist* 43,10: 1704–1723.

Ruddell, Rick. 2005. "Social Disruption, State Priorities, and Minority Threat: A Cross-National Study of Imprisonment." *Punishment & Society* 7,1: 7–28.

Rusche, Georg, and Otto Kirchheimer. 1939[1968]. *Punishment and Social Structure.* New York: Russell and Russell.

Ryan, William. 1982. *Equality.* New York: Vintage.

Sahlins, Marshall. 1972. *Stone Age Economics.* Piscataway, NJ: Aldine Transaction.

Sapp, Stephen G. 2002. "Incomplete Knowledge and Attitude-Behavior Consistency." *Social Behavior and Personality* 30: 37–44.

Savelsberg, Jaochim J., Lara Cleveland, and Ryan D. King. 2004. "Institutional Environments and Scholarly Work: American Criminology, 1951–1993." *Social Forces* 82,4: 1275–1302.

Shaw, Clifford and Henry McKay. 1942. *Juvenile Delinquency and Urban Areas: a Study of Rates of Delinquents in Relation to Differential Characteristics of Local Communities in American Cities.* Chicago: University of Chicago Press.

Sheldon, Randall. 2000. *Controlling the Dangerous Classes.* Boston: Allyn and Bacon.

Simon, David R. and D. S. Eitzen. 2000. *Elite Deviance.* Boston: Allyn and Bacon.

Smith, Kevin B. 2004. "The Politics of Punishment: Evaluating Political Explanations of Incarceration Rates." *The Journal of Politics* 66,3: 925–938.

––––––. 1997. "Explaining Variation in State-Level Homicide Rates: Does Crime Policy Pay?" *Journal of Politics* 59,2: 350–367.

Smith, Paula, Claire Goggin, and Paul Gendreau. 2002. *The Effect of Prison Sentences and Intermediate Sanctions on Recidivism: General effects and Individual Differences.* Public Works and Government Services of Canada. Cat No.: JS42–103/2002. ISBN: 0–662–66475–2.

South, Nigel. 1998. "A Green Field for Criminology? A Proposal for a Perspective." *Theoretical Criminology* 2,2: 211–233.

South, Nigel and Piers Beirne. 1998. "Editors' Introduction." *Theoretical Criminology* 2,2: 147–148.

Stretesky, Paul B. and Michael J. Lynch. 2004. "The Relationship Between Lead and Crime." *Journal of Health and Social Behavior* 45,2: 214–229.

———. 2003. "Environmental Hazards and School Segregation in Hillsborough, 1987–1999." *The Sociological Quarterly* 43,4: 553–573.

———. 2001. "The Relationship Between Lead and Homicide." *Archives of Pediatric and Adolescent Medicine* 155,5: 579–582.

———. 1999a. "Corporate Environmental Violence and Racism." *Crime, Law and Social Change* 30,2: 163–184.

———. 1999b. "Environmental Justice and the Prediction of Distance to Accidental Chemical Releases in Hillsborough County, Florida." *Social Science Quarterly* 80,4: 830–846.

Sutton, John. 2004. "The Political Economy of Imprisonment in Affluent Western Democracies, 1960–1990." *American Sociological Review* 69,22: 170–189.

———. 2000. "Imprisonment and Social Classification in Five Commonlaw Democracies, 1955–1985." *American Journal of Sociology* 106,2: 350–386.

Tillman, Robert and Henry N. Pontell. 1995. "Organizations and Fraud in the Savings and Loan Industry." *Social Forces* 73,4: 1439–1463.

Tillman, Robert, Henry N. Pontell, and Kitty Calavita. 1997. "Criminalizing White-Collar Misconduct: Determinants of Prosecution in Savings and Loan Fraud Cases." *Crime, Law and Social Change* 26,1: 53–76.

Tyler, Tom. 1990. *Why People Obey the Law.* New Haven, CT: Yale University Press.

U.S. Department of Energy. 2004a. Petroleum Overview, 1949–2003. http://www.eia.doe.gov/emeu/aer/txt/ptb0501.html.

U.S. Department of Energy. 2004b. Refinery Capacity and Utilization, 1949–2003. http://www.eia.doe.gov/emeu/aer/txt/ptb0509.html.

Veblen, Thorsten. 1899 [1967]. *Theory of the Leisure Class.* New York: Viking Press.

Visher, Christie A. 1987. "Incapacitation and Crime Control: Does a 'Lock 'em Up' Strategy Reduce Crime?" *Justice Quarterly* 4,4: 513–543.

Vold, George B., Thomas J. Bernard, and Jeffrey B. Snipes. 2002. *Theoretical Criminology.* New York: Oxford University Press.

Vogel, Richard. 2003. "Capitalism and Incarceration Revisited: Factors Affecting Incarceration Rates." *Monthly Review* 55,4: 38–55. http://www.monthlyreview.org/0903vogel.htm.

Weinrath, Michael and John Gartrell. 2001. "Specific Deterrence and Sentence Length: The Case of Drunk Drivers." Journal of Contemporary Criminal Justice 17,2: 105–122.

Weisberg, David, E. Waring, and Ellen Chayet. 1995. "Specific Deterrence in a Sample of Offenders Convicted of White-Collar Crimes." *Criminology* 33,4: 587–605.

Weitzer, Ronald and Charles E. Kubrin. 2004. "Breaking News: How Local TV News and Real-World Conditions Affect Fear of Crime." *Justice Quarterly* 21,3: 497–520.

Welch, Michael. 2004a. *Ironies of Imprisonment.* Thousand Oaks, CA: Sage.

————. 2004b. *Corrections: A Critical Approach. 2nd Edition.* Thousand Oaks, CA: Sage.

Welch, Michael. 1999. *Punishment in America.* Thousand Oaks, CA: Sage.

West, Cornell. 1994. *Race Matters.* New York: Vintage.

Wolff, Edward N. 2002. *Top Heavy: The Increasing Inequality of Wealth in America and What Can Be Done About It.* New York: W. W. Norton.

Yates, Jeff. 1997. "Racial Incarceration Disparity among the States." *Social Science Quarterly* 78,4: 1001–1111.

Yates, Jeff and Richard Fording. 2005. "Politics and State Punitiveness in Black and White." *The Journal of Black Politics* 67,4: 1099–1121.

# Index

253